HOW THE
VICTORIANS
LIVED

For Claudia, who knows how to live.

HOW THE
VICTORIANS
LIVED

SHONA PARKER

AN IMPRINT OF PEN & SWORD BOOKS LTD.
YORKSHIRE – PHILADELPHIA

First published in Great Britain in 2024 by
PEN AND SWORD HISTORY
An imprint of
Pen & Sword Books Ltd
Yorkshire – Philadelphia

Copyright © Shona Parker, 2024

ISBN 978 1 39905 666 3

The right of Shona Parker to be identified as Author of this work has been asserted by her in accordance with the Copyright, Designs and Patents Act 1988.

A CIP catalogue record for this book is available from the British Library.

All rights reserved. No part of this book may be reproduced or transmitted in any form or by any means, electronic or mechanical including photocopying, recording or by any information storage and retrieval system, without permission from the Publisher in writing.

Typeset in Times New Roman 10.5/13 by
SJmagic DESIGN SERVICES, India.
Printed and bound in the UK by CPI Group (UK) Ltd.

Pen & Sword Books Limited incorporates the imprints of Atlas, Archaeology, Aviation, Discovery, Family History, Fiction, History, Maritime, Military, After the Battle, Military Classics, Politics, Select, Transport, True Crime, Air World, Frontline Publishing, Leo Cooper, Remember When, Seaforth Publishing, The Praetorian Press, Wharncliffe Local History, Wharncliffe Transport, Wharncliffe True Crime and White Owl.

For a complete list of Pen & Sword titles please contact
PEN & SWORD BOOKS LIMITED
George House, Units 12 & 13, Beevor Street, Off Pontefract Road,
Barnsley, South Yorkshire, S71 1HN, England
E-mail: enquiries@pen-and-sword.co.uk
Website: www.pen-and-sword.co.uk

or
PEN AND SWORD BOOKS
1950 Lawrence Rd, Havertown, PA 19083, USA
E-mail: uspen-and-sword@casematepublishers.com
Website: www.penandswordbooks.com

Contents

Acknowledgements vi
Introduction vii

Chapter One	A Victorian Way of Life	1
Chapter Two	Who ran the Country?	10
Chapter Three	Gender Roles and Separate Spheres	23
Chapter Four	Home and Hearth	33
Chapter Five	Education	48
Chapter Six	The World of Work	63
Chapter Seven	Money	77
Chapter Eight	Poverty, the Poor Laws and the Workhouse	88
Chapter Nine	The State of the Water	101
Chapter Ten	Fashion and Beauty	110
Chapter Eleven	Food Glorious Food?	120
Chapter Twelve	Communication and Travel	131
Chapter Thirteen	Science	144
Chapter Fourteen	Inventions	156
Chapter Fifteen	Victorian Medicine	163
Chapter Sixteen	Crime and Punishment and the Police Force	179

Endnotes 199

Acknowledgements

I am grateful to many people and places for making this book possible: Reading Library Services for providing me with free access to tens of books for months at a time; The British Library for its amazing online collection of articles and images; The Museum for English Rural Life in Reading for allowing me to stay all day wandering around and drinking tea; the many museums in London for providing the most wonderful displays of information; my family for keeping me company on my many research trips and for giving me the space to write.

Introduction

If you had been born at the beginning of the Victorian era, and not died before your fifth birthday, as one in five children were prone to doing so, you would have lived through arguably the most exciting and invigorating reign of an English monarch ever. You would have worked close to or from home, cooked on an open fire and hauled water from a well. Your toilet would have consisted of a wooden seat over a hole in the ground, you would have walked everywhere or travelled by horse and carriage and candles were your only form of night light. As for education – well, if you were a boy, you would have received some depending on your class. If you were a girl, forget it.

But the Victorian era was one of progress on a massive scale. By the time Queen Victoria died in 1901, England was almost unrecognisable. Railways had replaced stagecoaches; mass manufacturing had replaced hand crafted goods and gas and electricity warmed up the country. Life expectancy had increased and free education for all was firmly in place. Gentlemen no longer duelled with pistols at dawn to settle disputes, as a large police force kept law and order instead. Between 1837 and 1901, the Victorians neatly avoided revolution, built upon what the Georgians started and turned Britain into a political powerhouse which ran the biggest Empire the world had ever seen.

Meanwhile, Victorian writers and journalists were observing, questioning, and recording for prosperity the life and times of what would become known as the Victorian era: a steady, relentless building of the modern world.

There is a lot of history to take in, but *How the Victorians Lived* will help you on your way to exploring one of the most exciting and innovative centuries England has ever seen.

Chapter One

A Victorian Way of Life

'Human history becomes more and more a race
between education and catastrophe.'[1]

Queen Victoria inherited the throne of a country where the Industrial Revolution and empire building was in full swing. England was also agitating for reform.

Three years previously, in 1834, Parliament was in turmoil as three Prime Ministers were appointed and removed with the fourth, Robert Peel, forming a new type of government known as the Conservatives. Six Dorset farm workers, known as the Tolpuddle Martyrs, were sentenced to transportation for forming a workers' union. Slavery was abolished throughout most of the empire, but slave owners were compensated for their monetary loss and the hated Poor Law Amendment Act was finally passed. All of these events led to a widespread debate and protest in both the press and on the streets. Up and down the country, workers went on strike, attended political meetings and protested against low wages, the use of machinery replacing workers and being unable to vote in elections to name just a few of the social issues affecting the people. The Riot Act was read again and again to mobs of angry protestors up and down the country.

Reform was still slow though and for the first two decades of the Victorian era people were still very 'Georgian' in their habits and customs[2]. The Georgians oversaw significant progression in the sciences and arts against a brutal backdrop of starvation, war, domestic violence, alcohol-fuelled crime, public hangings and floggings and industrial accidents[3]. Many older Victorians in particular would be used to this harsh way of life and wonder what the fuss was all about, encompassed in Dickens' character Scrooge who asks if there are no prisons or workhouses to keep the poor in their place[4]. He doesn't seem to want to know or understand the problems the poor are facing, and why he should help.

Victorian Life circa 1837

Despite this industrial and economic progress, England was still predominantly an agricultural country, with folk dependent upon the climate, seasons and soil in order to live. With a population of 11 million people throughout the whole of England, and only five cities home to 100,000 residents each, most people lived in small towns and villages and rarely left them, preferring to marry and settle down locally. The average life expectancy varied around the country and figures are skewed by the high rate of child mortality. Generally, though, if a person survived childhood and avoided disease and accident, they could easily live into their seventies.

At the beginning of the nineteenth century, it was normal for people to work from home or live above their workplace. In town, shopkeepers lived above their shops, as did bakers, tailors, and publicans. Dressmakers, spinners, and weavers had a small workshop out the back of their house or a space inside dedicated to their craft. Doctors' and lawyers' consulting rooms were part of their grander houses. Many urban working-class street sellers stored their barrow or stall and goods at home. Working class women took on laundry or childminding so they could earn some money whilst running the home. Some even set up small schools in their living rooms. Village dwelling working class women grew fruit and vegetables in a small garden, kept chickens and sold the produce at local markets. Middle class women supported their husband's businesses by serving customers, writing letters and keeping the books.

To a certain extent, people were in charge of their own working day, eating when they wanted and completing tasks at their own pace although most people were up at 6am regardless of their work start time, with a hot main meal break at midday.

General Routine

Early Victorian life was routine, with folk working Monday to Saturday and resting on a Sunday as all shops and businesses were closed in respect of the Sabbath. Mondays were a leisurely day at work with lower expectations and sometimes a later starting time. Christmas Day, Easter Sunday and 8 half day holidays a year for employees made up the only holidays. For the spinners and weavers and others who worked for themselves, the 8 half days didn't really exist.

For the upper- and middle-class boys who went to boarding school, they attended all through the summer with time off only at Christmas and Easter. All other children worked either supporting the family business or looking after siblings.

In rural areas, the year was punctuated by traditional celebrations such as May Queen and Guy Fawkes. The end of spring sheep shearing was the time for a shared village meal with music, dancing and copious amounts of ale, as was the end of the harvest in September. There wasn't much time for leisure activities though. After a long day's hard work, men had enough energy for trip to the pub and women undertook clothes mending and embroidery before retiring to bed around half past nine.[5]

Religion

The Victorian middle and upper classes took religion seriously, attending church on Sundays in their best clothes followed by a Sunday dinner back home. The working classes weren't so keen on attending church as Sunday was their only day off and a chance to catch up with household chores and have a rest after a week of 70 odd hours of physical labour. However, nearly all households owned a family bible and a common prayer book, reading (if literate) or reciting from heart the important passages.

The main religion in the Victorian era was Christianity in its various shapes and forms. Queen Victoria was head of the Church of England, as all monarchs are, and defender of the faith. England was a catholic country and followed the Pope's teachings up until Henry VIII set up the Church of England in 1534 and made himself and all future monarchs the supreme governors of England's spirituality. Further Acts repressed Catholics and other nonconformists and it wasn't until the Victorian era that nonconformists were allowed to freely express their opinions and have a say in the running of the country.

Churches

Victorian England was split up into parishes, a unit of local government usually centred on several villages or small towns, or a part of a city. As towns and cities grew bigger, they would be split into several parishes with a church for each. The parish was headed by a local vicar who was responsible for the spiritual health of his congregation. As well as delivering church services and the sacraments, and presiding over baptisms, marriages and funerals, the vicar was there to listen, counsel and administer charity as required.

Like today, in the nineteenth century there were lots of different churches where Christians could worship and the buildings themselves were linked to the type of Christianity followed. Many older church buildings were Church of England or catholic whereas newer chapels were often places of worship for nonconformist Christians such as Baptists, Methodists, and Evangelicals. Chapels were often found where the congregations were smaller such as next to hospitals, prisons, and schools, and on private estates. They were smaller and sparser places of worship but still shared the same features as the bigger churches[6].

The inside layout of Christian churches had not changed since the middle ages and so were still based on the shape of a cross with the Altar at the far end, decorated with a precious gold and jewelled cross and laid out with the bread and wine ready for the Eucharist or Holy Communion, a pulpit for sermons to one side and a lectern to hold the bible for readings either in the pulpit or to the other side. The congregation sat in the Nave on polished wooden pews. All churches had a font for baptisms but not all had a bell tower or stained-glass windows. The Victorians built many new churches in the gothic style, most of which still exist today.

Christianity

All Christians follow the teachings of Jesus Christ and the Bible through worship and prayer. However, the different branches of Christianity interpret the teachings differently and so they have different beliefs and rituals within their sect.

The main nonconformist churches in England in the Victorian era were the Catholics, Baptists, Methodists, the Quakers and the Salvation Army. The *Illustrative London Almanack* for 1879 lists 19,486 religious sects of England who registered places of worship with the Registrar General between 1877 and 1878. The amount is hardly surprising given the Victorian religious fervour, but amongst the Jews, Methodists, Catholics, Baptists and Church of England groups were the 'Believers in the Divine Visitation of Joanna Southcote, Prophetess of Exeter', the 'Hallelujah Band', the 'Peculiar People' and the 'Ranters'[7]

Evangelicalism

The Evangelical Party, although part of the Church of England, considered themselves as an independent church. It flourished between 1789 and 1850 and its extreme protestant beliefs were based upon those of Oliver Cromwell and the puritans of the seventeenth century.[8] Evangelicals believed not only that every word of the bible was true, but that it also held complex symbolism, codes and signals which needed to be interpreted. They also saw this symbolism in art, literature and history.

Although evangelicals followed the usual rituals of a church service, for them the most important aspect was the conversion of ordinary sinner to a follower of Christ. They believed that all human beings were depraved and only an intense conversion experience could show their commitment to God, no matter how often a person prayed or went to church. Victorian Evangelicals placed huge importance on emotions and feelings and felt that imagination and passion were as important as the intellectual understanding of Christianity. In other words, once converted, Evangelicals were encouraged to go out into society and preach the word of God using their emotions, feelings and tales of their own conversion experience to communicate the values of Christianity. Because of the intensity of their passion, Victorian evangelicals believed they would be laughed at, ridiculed and even persecuted. In fact, it was said that the more persecuted the believer, the holier they were and so this encouraged converts to martyr themselves for good causes or political, social and religious opposition. The converted were also expected to demonstrate their holiness by working for others and so many evangelicals devoted themselves to missionary work, bible societies, the anti-slavery movement, education, hospital work and many other good causes. Victorian evangelicals did a lot of social good and brought order, manners, sincerity and kind heartedness to everyday life. Many poor people gladly accepted their help, but others rejected them, finding them bossy and judgemental.

Evangelicalism was very much a religion of the middle and upper classes with the working classes attracted to Baptism, Catholicism and Methodism. Many Victorian men, including Charles Dickens, disliked Evangelicalism because it encouraged women to leave their home and domestic duties and do God's work instead. Due to the passion of evangelical preaching, many husbands were worried about their wives and daughters falling in love with the preachers and blindly following them.

Generally, Christian values were entrenched in Victorian society whether people considered themselves believers or not. Englishness and Christianity went together like bread and butter.[9]

Victorians as Reformers

Evangelicals weren't the only reformers of the Victorian era. Both Non-Conformists and Church of England followers and atheists freely gave their time and energy to help those without a voice in Britain and throughout the empire. These reformers though, caused conflict between the positives of progress and the desire to hold onto the old, Georgian ways in a rapidly changing world.

Throughout the century, educated British Victorians saw themselves as improvers of their country and the world in general. They were very proud of Britain and believed they had a duty to God and country to make it the best it could be and then to pass this enthusiasm and knowledge onto others. The industrious Victorians put in long hours in factories and offices, hospitals and laboratories as they toiled away making breakthrough after breakthrough in science, medicine, engineering, literature, law and order, all underpinned by the numerous charities and trusts set up to help the poor whilst the social reformers consistently petitioned parliament for change.

Victorian Values

British Victorians believed deeply in truthfulness, thriftiness and everything in its place. Wealthy Victorians regarded themselves as the ones chosen to be in charge and liked to adhere to traditional behaviours to keep the status quo. Many of the wealthy land and country estate owners possessed titles passed down to them through the centuries. These ennobled landowners believed in family values and traditions. They were also the only citizens allowed to vote.[10]

Meanwhile, middle class and working-class Victorians upheld the same family values but had to make their own way in the world and create their own wealth. They were happy to start up small businesses, moving from street barrow to market pitch to a shop selling whatever was the latest fancy, toiling for 15-hour days and taking pride in their achievements.

All men, whether rich or poor, were seen as the head of the family and keeper of the family morals. He was expected to be ambitious, assertive and aggressive when called for. Women were viewed as the property of men and second-class citizens and held very few rights. In wealthier households, women were delicate flowers to be protected from the ravages of the real world whilst working class women were expected to get on with earning some money and organising the home. All women, regardless of class, were tasked with raising the children of the family, which all women were expected to want and produce.

Classic British Liberalism

However, all this reform and progress could only happen if the ruling parties and the citizens of the country had the same ideas as to how they should live as a society and believed in the rules which governed them.

Classic British Liberalism was a political ideology which believed in civil liberties, economic freedom and progress but all within the rule of law. The Georgians had already seen to some progress within society with the abolition of slavery, a rise in literacy levels and prison reforms. This social reform needed to continue as it was recognised that a lack of social progress held back the economic growth of a country and could cause political instability leading to revolution, as witnessed in France. The British Liberalists argued that a society needed to change organically and naturally, without any restraints on the exercise of power if it was to continually improve scientific knowledge, technology and the general way of life for its people. This meant that a free trade market was needed without repressive taxes and other silly import and export rules imposed by the government.

British Liberalists wanted a minimal state and minimal interference from a government which should only provide services that the free trade state could not. In other words, the Liberalists felt the government shouldn't fund the new house building schemes for instance, and that these should be paid for by private investors who would then recoup the money plus profit once the houses were rented. The British liberalists did believe that the government should build and maintain public institutions such as libraries, museums and government buildings, and that they should also build and maintain infrastructure such as roads, canals, harbours, railways, communications, and postal services. A stable currency, standard weights and measures, laws to protect citizens from theft, assault and broken contracts, and a national defence against invaders were also deemed the responsibility of the government. Both government parties, the Whigs and the Conservatives, believed in low taxation and minimal state interference too in order to stimulate economic growth. Nowhere was this happening faster than Britain's capital city of London.[11]

London

The founding of London effectively began with the Roman Emperor Claudius in 43AD. He settled his armies in lush marshland on the north side of the river Thames and called the new settlement Londinium. By 200AD, Londinium was surrounded by a high stone wall for defence with six guarded gateways as entry points.

When the Romans pulled out of England, Londinium was abandoned for two centuries before the Saxons arrived and turned it into a major trading centre, renaming it Lundenwic. Later, Edward the Confessor built the original Westminster Abbey to the west of Lundenwic and in the eleventh century, William I established the Tower of London. The Norman kings decided that Westminster was the ideal place from which to run the country, leaving the walled City of London to continue trading.[12]

By the Elizabethan era, London was split into three distinct areas: The walled City of London, which was home to the manufacturers of goods, traders and merchants and shipping; Southwark, south of the river and connected to the City via London Bridge across the Thames, accommodated theatres, gardens and hospitals. Westminster, to the west of the City was home to the Royal Court and aristocracy. Already, it was a chaotic, vibrant and diverse city where the rich and poor rubbed along fairly well together and immigrants were accepted without question, bringing new culture and business to the ever-expanding London.

The plague of 1665 and the Great Fire of 1666 killed a fifth of the population and destroyed most of the buildings and for a while, the hustle and bustle was a little more subdued. But London needed to be rebuilt, and this was where the problems started.

Georgian London

The new building regulations put in place after the Great Fire of London meant there were strict rules for the design of the new, residential buildings. No more shaky, black beamed, bay windowed Tudor buildings were allowed. Instead, large and elegant houses for merchants and the aristocracy fronted the main London roads and then behind them, narrow alleys and courts made up of smaller houses, shops and stables were built for servants, labourers and other lower-class workers. They had to be made of stone rather than wood, with windows recessed into the walls so the wooden frames wouldn't catch fire easily.[13]

There was a building boom. Bricklayers, glaziers, tilers and stone masons all had a go at building houses conforming to the new rules. Unfortunately, the building standards weren't very high as need outstripped availability and amenities such as privies (old fashioned toilets) and wells were shared amongst several families. Drainage was nearly non-existent leading to damp floors and walls. Residents lived next door to farm animals, leading to a noisy, chaotic and stench filled existence.[14]

Unfortunately, due to the quick growth of the City, the wealthy kept changing their mind on where they wanted to live. Many builders purchased plots of land and materials to build houses in places which quickly became unfashionable, leaving half-built houses to be repurposed for poorer people, usually without adequate drainage and privies to save costs. Many finished properties were stuffed with families to make up the rental costs on such a large property. Meanwhile, wealthier families wanted to live further away from the industrious City with its smoke, smells and dirt. They couldn't move eastwards as the dockworkers lived in the East End of London, and besides, the smoke and filth from industry was even worse there, and so they moved west instead towards Westminster. Here, near the home of the monarch, they built new homes in gated squares. They could stroll in Hyde Park or St. James Park and shop on the new thoroughfare of Oxford Street. The new 'West End' became home to lords, ladies, and government officials. Army officers, doctors, lawyers, architects, bankers, and merchants could also afford to rent smaller houses. Tradesmen who lived over their shops, such as dairymen, plumbers, tailors, cabinet makers and butchers, served the wealthy. Regent Street was built as a barrier between the artisans of Soho and the new West End, and Regents Park was for riding on horseback only, thus excluding the working class.

When the writer Charles Dickens moved from Kent to London as a child, in 1822, it was a huge shock. Compared to spacious, leafy, clean Kent, London was cramped, dirty and teeming with people and animals. Costermongers shouted their wares above the din of the horses and carriages clattering through the streets. Small children, filthy and barefoot, played in the backstreets or begged for money and food along the main thoroughfare. Older ones constantly touted for jobs including road sweeping, shoe cleaning and message running. When Oliver Twist entered London at eleven o'clock at night, 'A dirtier or more wretched place he'd never seen. The street was very narrow and muddy, and the air impregnated with filthy odours. ...Covered ways and yards, which here and there diverged from the main street, disclosed little knots of houses where drunken men and women were positively wallowing in filth.'[15]

Victorian London

By 1837, London was in the midst of a phenomenal change and was unrecognisable from even 30 years earlier. It became the biggest and best marketplace in the country. Eventually, it became the world's wealthiest city. 'Put your ear to the door of the Bank (of England), or the Stock Exchange nearby, and you hear the roar of the world,' stated American author Charles Dudley Warner in 1883.[16]

Other cities throughout England grew just as rapidly with Manchester becoming renowned for cotton production, Birmingham and Sheffield for everything that could be made from steel and iron, Nottingham for its beautiful, fine lace and Bristol for its shipbuilding and trade in slaves.

All encountered the same rapid population growth though, and the same social issues which come from a society desperately trying to find its feet in a river of fast-moving change. The issues we see today as synonymous with the Victorian era, such as poverty, soot, fog, violence, huge factories, child labour, starvation, lack of sanitation, education and voting rights, were encountered by folk up and down the country. But these issues sat hand in hand with reform and no-one and nowhere was immune. Today, all around us we can see the legacy the Victorians left us. There is barely a town in England without a Victorian hospital, prison, railway, bridge or terraced housing of some sort. Many of our laws, medical practices, educational establishments and politics are based on hard fought and won Victorian reforms.

Chapter Two

Who ran the Country?

'Lane's views on marriage seem somewhat lax. Really, if the lower orders don't set us a good example, what on earth is the use of them? They seem, as a class, to have absolutely no sense of moral responsibility.'

The Importance of Being Earnest[1]

Queen Victoria, or Alexandrina Victoria of Kent, to give her full name, was born 24 May 1819. It was thought she would never be queen as she was only 5 in line to the throne, but due to the King's fairly early death and a lack of direct descendants available to inherit the throne, it passed to Victoria. On 20 June 1837, at the tender age of 18, she was crowned Queen of Britain and Ireland.

The popular image we have of Queen Victoria is of the short, fat, grumpy looking old woman from the 1890s who apparently said, 'We are not amused!' This is the image frequently shown to school children through popular history books and programmes. But this image of Queen Victoria is from only a short part of her long 63-year reign. As a young woman, Queen Victoria was pretty, passionate, articulate and very expressive in her opinions and feelings.

Victoria the Linguist

Victoria was brought up in a mainly German speaking household at Kensington Palace, but she mastered English very quickly too. She was intelligent and loved languages, going on to learn French, Italian and Latin.

Her love of language and her forceful, expressive personality led to Queen Victoria keeping copious journals, starting when she was 13 years old. She poured out her feelings on everything, be it fashion, health, the weather or state business. She was a prolific writer, sometimes writing 2500 words a day. When she died in 1901, she left the country an incredible record of nineteenth century Britain including political events, people, meetings, casual conversations, lengthy descriptions, and opinions on everything.[2]

Public Duty

Queen Victoria and Prince Albert of Saxe-Coburg and Gotha married on the 10 February 1840 when she was 21 and he was 20 years old. To an extent, it was an arranged marriage between cousins, which was normal procedure for the aristocracy at the time. Arranged marriages united two families in a mutually beneficial way and fortunately for Queen Victoria, she had some say in who she chose.

Victoria and Albert's relationship was famously passionate. Being two strong, independent characters, they rowed a lot and clashed ideas about everything, from politics to child-rearing. Despite the rowing, their early years of marriage were harmonious. Their nine children had the usual governesses and nurses and so the couple were able to spend plenty of quality time together. It was during this period that the royal couple started to frequently visit Scotland and fall in love with the country. They had a castle built at Balmoral in 1853 especially for their use.

From Victoria's first pregnancy with her daughter Vicky in November 1840, Albert took over the paperwork Victoria was constantly asked to read, comment on or sign. Victoria found paperwork tedious whilst Albert loved it. It suited his meticulous attention to detail. He was happy to read through it all first, explain it to Victoria and then write the replies. Through working together this way, Albert became Victoria's closest confidante, with some influence on her opinions.

Albert also understood how important it was for the monarch to be seen by her subjects and not hidden away in various palaces. Albert thought that being seen out and about would connect the royal family to the people, so they began to undertake excursions with their children on a regular basis.

The royal family visited mines, farms, factories, and industrial towns. The new railway system helped to take the royal family to the people, too. They were able to travel further and more comfortably on a train than in a horse drawn carriage, and so it was easy to take the children too. This endeared the royal family to the people of Britain even more. Suddenly, everyone could see how the Queen dressed her children and how they behaved in public. More importantly though, these visits showed the working class that the monarchy was very much a part of Britain. They were real people, interested in society and wanting to be part of it, not housed away in a posh palace doing nothing except having dinner with visiting dignitaries. Victoria and Albert showed their people they were both welded to running the country properly, setting an example to the Victorian people, supporting the expanding industry and working with parliament for the greater good. In September 1850, the *Globe* newspaper published an account of Queen Victoria and Prince Albert's visit to Edinburgh where they climbed Arthur's seat and then visited Donaldson's hospital. Albert then laid the foundation stone of the new National Gallery, which drew a huge crowd of people to watch. Albert was 'loudly cheered' and treated to several gun salutes. The crowds gathered on top of the bank, around the Scott monument and on the battlements of the castle where they could get a good view. Included in the crowd were several Lords and Ladies, members of the town council and magistrates.[3]

This image was further helped by Victoria's love of writing. She published 'Leaves from a journal of our life in the Highlands'. It was based upon the family visits to Balmoral and included pictures of the family and the area. Never before had a monarch published such intimate details of their life. In doing so, Victoria and Albert made it clear they wanted to connect with everyone, not just the aristocracy.[4]

The Class System

Queen Victoria and the Royal Family were the head of a rigid English class system, a way of placing people into social categories and keeping them there and this was something with which the Victorians were obsessed. The Georgian era had seen the rise of 'the middling sort', with their newly generated wealth through commerce. Previous to the Industrial Revolution, a person's education, occupation, spouse, social and political status and cultural interests all depended upon the 'class' of family they were born into, and there were only two: the upper class and the working class, or as Benjamin Disraeli put it so succinctly in his book 'Sybil or The Two Nations', the rich and the poor.[5]

The Upper Classes

This class was made up of three subcategories with the aristocracy reigning supreme. Aristotle's definition of aristocracy: the rule of the few who are morally and intellectually superior and therefore govern in the interest of all, was closely adhered to and consisted of the Royal Family at the top followed by Dukes, Marquess', Earls, Viscounts and Barons plus their wives and children.[6] Below these sat lower upper-class persons known as the gentry who inherited wealth and land but no titles. All of the upper class inherited their titles, their homes and their wealth from other members of their family. By owning land, the men were eligible to vote and by holding a title, they were eligible to sit in the House of Lords.

The Working Classes

Made up of the majority of the people in England, its overall definition was of people who worked in manual labour earning little money as they were paid only for the hours they worked, they didn't own any land and received little education.

These two classes made up the social structure of England for centuries, but the emergence of a middle class during the Industrial Revolution turned the old order on its head.

The Middle Classes

To be middle class in the Victorian era meant that a person had become economically and culturally wealthy through their work rather than through inherited wealth and titles. A good education also helped them on their way. Middle class Victorians were factory owners, merchants, bankers, lawyers, doctors and shop owners. They had money and weren't afraid to spend it on houses and land, which then allowed them to vote.

Even within each class, there was a hierarchy. For instance, a station master was a higher ranked job than a mere station porter, bringing with it not only more money but respect within the community and a nice station house to live in too. A housekeeper was a higher-ranking servant than a maid, again with more money and respect as she had more responsibility.

So each class system was mainly defined by how much money a person had. The more money someone had, the more opportunities were open to them and this allowed for social mobility; the opportunity for members of a lower class to move up and join the ranks of the one above. This movement between subcategories and classes caused a lot of social anxiety and people started to worry about how they should react to these new acquaintances. Should they be friends with this new person or snub them? Should they act superior or with deference? To know where someone came from and what they did with their time was a seemingly straightforward way to place people in their subcategory. It helped that the class system had its own set of values and rules to live by, which helped society to catalogue people accordingly.[7]

Upper Class Work and Values

Landed gentry, or gentry for short, were landowners whose income came from rental properties or the profit from a country estate.

Many of the landed gentry were wealthier than some nobles but were not considered part of the nobility as they did not have a title. However, this could be achieved through marrying a member of the nobility which was allowed. Owning a rural estate gave the man the legal rights of Lord of the Manor or the less formal title of squire. Manorial rights meant that the landowner could occupy the residence or build his own and work on the land. Most landowners rented out cottages to tenant farmers, but others also built mills for timber, paper and cotton. Others established mines and quarries. The main aim though was to acquire profit and then pass it on to his first-born son through primogeniture. Daughters were usually given cash and stocks instead as they couldn't usually inherit and were expected to 'make a good marriage' instead, uniting noble or gentrified families. Younger sons bought commissions in the army, joining as officers straightaway, or studied theology and joined the church which could lead them to a seat in the House of Lords.

As all upper-class boys were expected to undertake a leadership role of some sort or another in society, they needed a first-class education to start off with. Small boys had live-in private tutors to teach them English, Maths, Religion, Latin and French, as well as a nanny to see to their pastoral care. They then went away to a boarding school, the best being Eton and Harrow, and then onto Oxford or Cambridge University to obtain a degree in Classics, theology and the like.

It was thought that upper class girls didn't need an education in order to become wives and mothers and so although they were tutored in English and maths whilst young, attention was soon turned towards artistic pursuits, deportment, dancing and needlework. Some girls were sent away to finishing schools in Switzerland, to give them the much-needed gloss and polish ready for marriage. It wasn't until the end of the Victorian era that any young women were allowed to be awarded university degrees.

Working Class Work and Values

The Victorian working class consisted of a plethora of skilled, semi-skilled and unskilled workers. Unskilled workers were mainly labourers – urban or agricultural- and cleaners such as chimney sweeps, crossing sweepers, dust men and servants. Semi-skilled workers worked as fishermen, on the railways, in factories and skilled men worked as builders, foremen, plumbers, carpenters and typesetters.

Working class children usually went into the same jobs as their parents and started work quite young. They may have attended a local school to learn basic reading and writing but would start work as soon as they were physically capable, to add their wage to the household.

Victorian Parliament

The expectation for upper-class men to be leaders led many into politics. By the end of the Victorian era, a total of fourteen prime ministers had attended Eton and three had attended Harrow.[8] The Victorian aristocracy dominated government because a man needed to be a landowner to vote and to also have a private income as MPs weren't paid a salary.

The Victorian Houses of Parliament consisted of the House of Commons and The House of Lords, just like today. MPs were voted in by their constituents and they belonged to one of the two main parties, the Whigs (later the Liberal party) or the Tories (later the Conservative party). Both stood for different values, and both held equal power throughout Queen Victoria's reign, almost taking turns of who was in charge. Some MPs did become independents, meaning they were not affiliated to any party and the Labour party did not form until 1900.

The parties themselves were formed during the Restoration of King Charles II to the throne of England and Wales in 1660 following on from the Commonwealth government created by Oliver Cromwell. An event which became to be known as the Exclusion Crisis split parliament in half. Charles II named his brother James, Duke of York as his heir to the throne. James was a Catholic and seeing as England was still trying to stabilise itself as a Protestant country with the Church of England, having a Catholic heir to the throne was seen as damaging.[9]

The Whigs, taken from the longer Scottish word Wiggamaire, were protestants who supported parliament during and following the Exclusion Crisis, but they believed that the political set-up in the country should change to reflect the changes in society. They opposed the idea of James, Duke of York as heir to the throne as he was Catholic. The term Tory came into use around 1680 to describe the opposing MPs who supported King Charles II and his Catholic heir. It originally meant Irish brigand or outlaw and was used to describe the Irish Catholics who supported James Duke of York as heir to the throne. It was later applied to the English supporters too.[10]

Tory MPs were Royalist loyalists who wanted to hold onto the old way of doing things including the chain of succession to the throne remaining intact rather than Parliament choosing the best candidate. They supported the families of 'old money' and hereditary titles and the landowning gentry and Squires. They liked the order of the class system along with all its privileges for those who belonged to the upper class, and the exclusion of those who didn't. They wanted everyone to remain in their God-given place. They supported the high church of Anglicanism, with its hierarchy of Arch Deacons and Bishops, wealth and ritual in beautifully decorated buildings with stained glass windows and gold plates and jewelled crosses. They were defenders of Crown, Church and Constitution.[11]

In contrast, a Whig MP was a protestant dissenter and a reformer, someone who wanted both the church and the state to change itself for the better as required by society. The Whig party went onto become the defenders of the new Hanoverian Kings of the Georgian period, whom Parliament chose as the next Royal family when Queen Anne died leaving no heirs. However, they believed that the sovereign was answerable to the people and could only successfully govern with the people's consent, something which Queen Victoria took seriously. Her natural affiliation was with the Whig party who supported financiers and merchants and personal freedom. Eventually they became known as the Liberal party.[12]

Meanwhile, Toryism was an 'upper class stance' against reform. It stood against any divergence from gender, sexual and religious norms. They still supported the system where subordinates were expected to know their place and stay there. The Tories fiercely opposed Catholics having any political or civic rights, Irish Home Rule and any reform to the electoral process. On the other hand, the Whig Party championed equal rights for Catholics and other non-conformists, Irish Home Rule and electoral reform amongst many other causes seen as unnatural by the Tories.[13]

The Tory party became equated with the conservative ideals of inherited tradition, the values of their ancestors, the defence of wealth and property and political power remaining in the hands of the elite. They remained a party of the land and so still appealed more to landowners and rural dwellers rather than those who lived in the cities. In 1838, Prime Minister Robert Peel laid out what conservatism meant to him and his party. He defended the monarchy and peerage system alongside the Houses of Commons and Lords. The party supported the religion of the Protestant church. It believed in the equality of civil rights and privileges and did want reform, but it also wanted a continuation of what it meant to be British: the habits, rituals, manners and institutions of the British people. The conservative party started to attract some more moderate Whig supporters who didn't like the extremism of the Whig party. By the mid-century the Tory party was known as the Conservative Party and the words conservative and tory have been interchangeable in British politics ever since.[14]

How Did Parliament Affect Everyday People?

The Victorian era became the most managed era so far with a vast range of Parliamentary Acts bringing about striking changes to law and order in England and the rest of the UK. It could be said that the era started with the Representation of the People Act, otherwise known as the Great Reform Act of 1832. The newly wealthy middle class still did not have the vote at all in

Parliament as they needed to own land and pay tax on it too. The Tory Prime Minister, Arthur Wellesley opposed the Bill in 1830 as he wanted to restrict them, whereas the Whigs wanted the middle class to be able to vote, thus creating a better relationship between them and parliament.[15] Also, the current boroughs were uneven, with some boroughs having few residents and an MP and other places such as Manchester and Birmingham having no MPs at all. These towns had fast outgrown their old borough boundaries and were home to approximately 400,000 residents each but had no representation in parliament. Meanwhile, in Old Sarum in Wiltshire, one lucky MP represented a farmhouse, a few fields and some sheep[16].

Later in the year of 1830, the Tory government was replaced by Earl Grey and the Whig party who promised to get the bill through parliament. Despite being heavily opposed by Tory landowner MPs, they managed it on the third attempt. Boroughs and constituency boundaries were redrawn to distribute residents more evenly. More importantly, small landowners, tenant farmers, shop keepers and all householders who paid a yearly rental of £10 or more were now allowed to vote for an MP to represent their interests in parliament.[17]

Interestingly, a legal loophole which had actually allowed some women the vote was closed. Whereas previously the restrictive rules had applied to 'persons', now they applied to men only, excluding women from voting altogether.

Despite these changes, most working men were still unable to vote. It was the second Reform Act of 1867 which allowed homeowners, agricultural landowners, tenants with small parcels of land and lodgers who paid £10 a year or more in rent to be able to vote. This doubled the electorate from 1 million to 2 million across England and Wales[18]

The third Reform Act of 1884 made the requirements for enfranchisement equal throughout rural and urban areas in line with the requirements from the 1867 Act. The Redistribution of Seats Act redrew the boundaries of boroughs and constituencies so most but not all had only one MP representing the people. However, approximately 40% of men still didn't have the right to vote and neither did women.[19]

Who Ran the Country – Parliament or the Monarchy?

For the first third of the century, it could be argued that Parliament was run by the wealthy, land owning families and the monarch and so the aristocracy ran the country.

By the time Victoria came to the throne, William IV was regarded as too conservative and standing in the way of progress and freedom. A young monarch was just what the country needed. Queen Victoria took her parliamentary duties very seriously indeed. She was young, with Whig leanings, and determined to learn everything about parliament. Throughout her reign, she wrote endless letters to her Prime Ministers, expressing her opinions on political decisions and offering advice. Despite being so confident in her writing, Queen Victoria was quite introverted and at first, she lacked confidence in her public role and constantly looked to her various Prime Ministers and her husband, Prince Albert, to support her in her public duties.[20] This reinforced the bond between monarch and parliament though, and the Victorian era progressed to be one of peace and political stability, thus allowing the country to concentrate on building the British Empire.[21]

The Victorian Empire

The colonisation of one civilization by another had been an ongoing process around the world for centuries. In Europe, the continuing search for new resources to make goods from, and new markets to sell them to led to France, Spain, Holland, Portugal and Britain opening up trade routes across to America and then to the East as early as the seventeenth century, with the British East India Trading Company leading the way.

After the Napoleonic wars ended in 1815, Britain found itself in a much stronger political position than its trading counterparts and saw itself as the world's policeman or international peacekeeper.[22] Britain now had no real rivals and its Navy was held in high regard and so Britain set about capturing as much territory as possible to acquire new raw materials and then to create a market to sell the products back to. In 1837, the British Empire comprised of 46 territories; by Queen Victoria's death it held 72 territories and had created the biggest ever empire which covered nearly a quarter of the global land mass and a quarter of people were governed by Britain[23] British Victorians didn't consciously set about to do this but were very open about their belief that the world would be a better place if Britain was in charge and so they just kept going, neatly summed up by Pip in Great Expectations:

> 'We Britons had at that time particularly settled that it was treasonable to doubt our having and our being the best of everything...'[24]

Having established a reputation as honest, reliable and efficient in manufacturing and trading, the Victorians took these traits and applied them to the colonies to improve the locals' way of life. They bult roads, bridges, hospitals, schools and churches and preached education, sport and Protestantism as the pillars of a civilised society.[25] The empire also imposed free trade, free markets, the rule of law, free movement of labour, goods and capital.[26] Because the Victorians regarded most provinces they colonised as lacking in discipline and determination to become prosperous, they were heavy handed in their imposition of British values. Almost continual small skirmishes were required to maintain control of colonies and to protect them from other countries trying to take over.[27]

So although Britain was involved in almost continual small skirmishes to colonise parts of the world, mainly India, and to also stop other countries such as Russia doing the same, British Victorians didn't really see themselves as warmongers, more like the distributers of western ideals by teaching other countries and provinces how to self-govern and become civilised through Christianity and the Christian way of living but underpinned by an army presence.[28]

The Army

The army inherited by Queen Victoria was the same structure which defeated Napoleon at the Battle of Waterloo in 1815 and continued to be run by the war hero the Duke of Wellington. Whereas it used to be used to quell civil unrest on the streets, now it was used to defend the country and the empire. It was also an attractive work prospect for a working-class man with little education or an upper-class middle son with little inheritance. But that's where the similarities ended. Once recruited, these men's paths diverged and their roles in the army became completely different. The class structure of Victorian Britain was very much in evidence in the British army.

If a man decided to accept 'the Queen's shilling' then he was given a medical examination to check that he was fit enough to fight. There was a bare minimum of fitness to be reached as these were working class men who were often undernourished. The majority of recruits were also semi- or unskilled, usually casual labourers looking for regular work and pay. If he passed the medical, the solider was enlisted for 21 years which was considered life in the Victorian era given the life expectancy of working class men[29]. Recruits enlisted themselves for general service which meant they could be sent to any regiment throughout the Empire.

But despite high levels of unemployment, the Victorian army still struggled to find enough recruits. On average, there were 745,000 paupers in Britain in any one year and excluding the women and those men too old or ill to join the army, the largest number of recruits in one year was just 40,000.[30] That is a fair chunk of eligible men who preferred to try their luck with the workhouse or scavenging rather than join the army.

Officers

At the same time that foot soldiers were being persuaded to join the army through want of anything better, middle- and upper-class men were paying the army for a place as an officer of a cavalry or infantry regiment, a practice started by Charles II in 1683. This meant that he didn't have to work his way up through the ranks; he went in at whatever he could afford to buy up to the rank of colonel.

For example, the lowest rank possible to buy in 1837 was that of a Cornet in the Infantry at a whopping £450, the equivalent of £45,000 today. The next rank up, Lieutenant cost £700 and so a Cornet would have to find another £250 to move up to it. Commissions which became available due to the death of the officer through disease had to be purchased, as did the ones from officers who resigned their commission or retired honourably, giving them an income to live off in their old age. But sometimes, a free vacancy occurred due to an officer's death in battle, or the movement of an officer from the battlefield to staff, where he gathered information and assisted the commander of the regiment. When a new regiment was set up, several officer places became available, allowing free transfers across.[31]

It can seem today that this was a typical case of those with money buying more privilege, but there were some strong reasons for this practice. It was thought that by buying a commission, an officer wouldn't abuse his position because the Crown could fire him if needed, without paying him back his commission. Also, those with money were less likely to loot or pillage local villages or sell army supplies to the soldiers at a vastly inflated profit.

Generally, officers came from affluent families or inherited wealth, were well educated and expected to lead.

Army Conditions

Many working-class men signed up to the army thinking they would have a better way of life – regular meals, friendship and a sense of purpose. In reality, a soldier's life was a harsh one. Once enlisted, a soldier found that his one shilling a day was reduced significantly after food, replacement clothing and medical services were paid for out of it. Some soldiers effectively ended up serving in the army for food and clothes only. There was very little opportunity to save up and send money home, or to keep some aside for the future when he was discharged from the army.[32]

Many soldiers drank away what little money they earned and then suffered the effects of liver and kidney damage and strict discipline for disorderly behaviour and drunken brawling. All of this took a toll on the soldier's body, leaving him open to disease. On top of this, soldiers were discouraged from marrying and those who did ran the risk of being separated from their wives and children for life if sent overseas. Some wives and children did live abroad at the barracks with the soldiers, but they had very little in the way of home comforts and were expected to perform essential tasks such as laundry and cooking for everyone.

The British army became known for being battle hardened due to the continuing minor skirmishes required to protect the empire. Soldiers became used to fighting in all weathers on all continents[33]

Army Reforms

A few small reforms were made to the Army during the first part of the Victorian era. In 1847, it became law that soldiers kept one penny of their daily wages regardless how many stoppages had been deducted. In 1849, enlistment periods were reduced from 21 years to 12 years. Despite this, many soldiers reenlisted at the end of their tenure as the army only taught them menial skills and so it was hard to get a job if they left. Eventually, 1868 saw William Gladstone's Liberal Party reform the army under the leadership of Edward Cardwell who was the current Secretary of State for War.[34]

The reforms were a long time coming and tackled the major issues of the day. First and foremost, the purchasing of commissions was scrapped. There had been increasing call for this to happen after it was recognised that the person with the most money was in charge, not the best person for the job, which had led to malpractice. Despite the discontinuation of commissions, the officers still had to uphold an expensive lifestyle and so soldiers without a private income, however small, were still excluded from the ranks.

On the plus side, Cardwell created regiments of reserve soldiers who stayed in Britain until they were needed to bolster the ranks of the army should there be a war on the continent. Regular soldiers could move into the reserves after around 8 years in the ordinary army, meaning they were back living in Britain with all the associated positives. They were also allowed to marry, and wives could live with them in their new barracks but were not allowed to follow their husbands to war.

The new gothic style barracks buildings were spacious with improved sanitation. A pay increase to 1 shilling and 2 pence a day as well as free army meals of meat, bread and potatoes helped to increase soldiers' health and stamina. The stoppages for medical care were reduced although soldiers still had to pay to replace their clothing and equipment.

Between 1871 and 1888, new recruits had to undertake a basic education and by the 1890s the army illiteracy rate was nearly zero although only 40% managed to achieve the lowest standard of education required. Most officers had to attend Sandhurst Military Academy but first they had to pass competitive exams to acquire a place. Once accepted, cadets had to pay for this education and equipment, so they still needed to come from a wealthy background. The young officers still had to maintain standards which often cost more than they were paid. It was also more difficult to move between regiments.[35]

Despite these improvements, recruitment shortages remained in place. Although the minimum recruitment age was put up to 18, 'special enlistments' meant that underage boys could be enlisted if they showed potential. By 1898, 50% of the rank-and-file soldiers were under 18 and only 20% of soldiers were over the age of 20. Exceptions didn't stop at age either. The percentage of men under the height of five foot five increased to 35% by 1898 and only 65% of men were over five feet 6 inches, down from 80% in 1861. To summarise, at the end of the nineteenth century, army recruits were younger, smaller and lighter.[36]

The main reasons to enlist in the army remained constant throughout Queen Victoria's reign. Necessity of secure employment and a regular wage was the main reason as most recruits were labourers and semi-skilled workers who were at constant risk of unemployment. Others joined up to outwit the debt collectors they owed money to. Some men joined up to escape their marriages, others joined up to be with family members. Some were bored with their current job, others just wanted to travel, and this was the only opportunity. Many more thought it a glamorous job where they could earn some respect and attract future wives with tales of their bravery and daring exploits whilst protecting Queen and country.

Chapter Three

Gender Roles and Separate Spheres

'I am no bird; and no net ensnares me; I am a free human being with an independent will, which I now exert to leave you.'

Jane Eyre[1]

The Victorians were strict about gender roles, which were sharply defined within each class and fervently followed as the era moved on. It can be hard for us to comprehend the Victorians' desire to conform to gender roles and responsibilities but in a fast paced and rapidly changing world, this conformity gave stability and a chance for the Victorians to catch their collective breath before the next onslaught of change. Traditional gender expectations barely changed throughout the Victorian era.

Although traditionally, women had always been responsible for all aspects of childcare, many women also worked alongside their husbands in their field of work. Whether the husband was a labourer or shop keeper, a solicitor or a blacksmith, the wife's role was to help and support him and the community in which they lived. Before the Industrial Revolution, most men either worked from home as part of a trade, such as a blacksmith, as an artisan such as a weaver or were agricultural labourers. Either way, their wives and daughters knew what was going on in their world of work and were able to offer support alongside their domestic duties. This support came in the way of bookkeeping, helping with customers, making deliveries and clearing up. In the fields, wives and children would help get in the harvests or organise sheep shearing, and on farms they would help look after the animals, tend the vegetable patches and run the dairy. In towns, they ran errands, did stocktaking, and helped with suppliers. Everyone pitched in to support the 'family business' but the husband was the main wage earner for the family.

However, once manufacturing started to move out of the home and into the factories, men and women's work separated. Most men attended a workplace all day earning the family money whilst most married women stayed at home and worked from there alongside looking after the children and any elderly relatives too.

Separate Spheres

The newly emerging middle class needed a defining role of its own. For centuries, England had been led by the aristocracy with the working class carrying out the work. Now, the new middle class needed to find its place and stake out its parameters and it did so by emulating the aristocracy.[2]

Aristocratic men and women had already been living in 'separate spheres' for centuries, with the husband running the estate, looking after the tenants who farmed there, investing his money and frequently staying over in the nearest city for days to do business, leaving his wife behind to run the household and look after the children and continue her own charity work in the community. This was never really seen as separate spheres though; more it was seen as teamwork where both spouses benefitted from the status and income afforded them from their combined efforts. The middle classes started to do the same, with the husband working in the centre of town or city, and the wife staying at home in the newly built suburbs with the family to run the household and organise the servants.

This separation of work and home developed an ideology known as 'separate spheres'. This ideology took what was seen as the natural characteristics of men and women and used them to define their roles even further. Men were seen as the physically stronger sex but also the better decision makers. So, they did either an incredibly physical job such as labouring, where they fought the enemies of wind and rain to build roads, railways, bridges, housing and schools, or a doctor fighting disease or a soldier fighting the enemies of the Empire. Or they went into a job where they had to be emotionally strong, resilient and prepared to take risks. Banking, running businesses, being a magistrate or a doctor, or a member of Parliament all demanded the man to pit his wits and strength of mind against political and economic forces. After a day of clashing opinions with other such men, or saving lives, they all retreated to recover in the safety of their home where they were nourished and nurtured ready to face a new onslaught the following day.[3]

Women had always been deemed physically and emotionally weaker than men; this was definitely not a new ideology of the Victorian era. But the Victorians thought that women possessed superior morals and so they would be shocked and easily upset if they had to do men's work like doctoring or money lending, where the men came into frequent contact with all sorts of nefarious folk. Therefore, they were seen as the better choice for staying at home and leading the family in their education and religion. Many books and articles were written on how to behave, and it was the woman's job to make sure she was well educated on the subject and that her family followed the rules. A man was truly judged by society upon the character of his wife and how well he was supported at home.[4]

The Role of Men in the Victorian Era

The main role of the Victorian man was to be the 'bread winner' for his family. He was the one who worked all day, earning enough money to pay the rent and put food on the table, of which bread was the cheapest, and in the case of the poor, their only food most days.

So whatever class the Victorian man fell into, in all family structures he was important. All women longed for sons to be born first, either to inherit the property and secure a roof over their heads or to help to look after his parents in their old age. In a world where disease was rife and a cut finger could kill you, women longed for healthy sons first to lead the family, protect the women and earn the money. Daughters were also welcomed as the mother would then have someone to help her with the domestic chores and nursing through illness.

Upper Class Men

All upper-class men knew their place in the family and the expectations placed upon them. This wasn't exclusive to the Victorian era; aristocratic families had worked this way for centuries. The first boys born to aristocratic parents immediately inherited the family estate and whatever land came with it. The second son was expected to go into the army or navy with a bought commission and the third son was expected to join the church as a clergyman with a view towards becoming a Bishop. The lucky sons who followed could pretty much do as they liked as the money had usually run out by this point, unless an older brother died and then they all moved up the pecking order.

The sons were also required to look after their sisters and ensure they made good marriages, connecting aristocratic families and keeping the wealth and land within the family.

So, with the hierarchy firmly in place and the eldest son (sometimes the only son with several sisters as in the case of Bramwell Bronte and his three famous sisters Emily, Charlotte and Anne), set to inherit not only the estate but the massive responsibility which went with running such a thing, boys needed to be educated to a high standard. This usually involved a male tutor until the age of 7 or 8 and then the young boy would be sent to a top boarding school such as Eton, Harrow or Rugby followed by University at Oxford or Cambridge. The son then set to inherit would return to the estate to learn how to run it whilst the younger sons followed their pre-determined path.

The Working-Class Man

Although he didn't immediately inherit a family estate, a working-class boy did inherit the same expectations as an upper-class man. He was expected to work and support his father in his role as breadwinner. He also learnt how to lead the family and make decisions should his father suddenly die. This meant that the boy usually received some form of education and where money was tight, his sisters would go without instead.

How long the boy stayed in education for depended upon the money available but there were many young, working-class boys who couldn't wait to start earning a wage and were incredibly proud of their contribution to the family income. In *A Christmas Carol*, Bob Cratchit tells his family how he has his eye on a job vacancy for his young son Peter which will bring in an extra 5s 6d a week. As the mum and daughters dance for joy, Peter remains serious as he proudly contemplates his age and responsibility.[5]

The work opportunities usually came via the father who knew of openings for employment and would recommend their sons. This was especially the case in mining towns, with boys automatically following their fathers down the pits and where, in early Victorian years, whole families worked down the mines together.

Many working-class boys considered it their duty to provide money to buy food and new items for the home. They concentrated on earning money as they knew their mother couldn't earn as much. But for middle class boys, it was a bit of a different situation.

Middle Class Boys

The young, middle-class boy had a more difficult role to play. Aristocratic boys and working-class boys were firmly in their places – they knew their role and where they fitted in in the world. But for middle class boys, they were expected to behave like aristocratic males but without the income or family name to open doors into lucrative jobs.

They received an education via a cheaper public day school rather than Eton or Harrow and didn't necessarily go onto university unless training to become a doctor or lawyer. Once educated, they took jobs in banks or offices or became schoolmasters at Grammar schools. One thing they weren't allowed to do though, was go into 'trade' or manual labour. So, no matter how little money the family had, the son still couldn't lower the family standards by opening a shop or becoming an entrepreneur. It just wasn't respectable.

Although the middle classes knew that their chances of joining the nobility were slim, the men were still expected to behave like gentlemen.

The Gentleman

'I am instructed to communicate to him,' said Mr Jaggers, throwing his finger at me sideways, 'that he will come into a handsome property. Furthermore, that it is the desire of the present possessor of that property, that he be immediately removed from his present sphere of life and from this place and be brought up as a gentleman – in a word, as a young fellow of great expectations.'[6]

The Victorian gentleman is quite a vague role and to an extent defies description. He owes his creation to the knights of the Medieval period who were the first true gentlemen. Knights believed first and foremost in truth and justice. They righted wrongs, looked out for poorer people and protected ladies from unwanted attention. This behaviour was known as chivalry and knights followed a chivalric code. They were polite, well-mannered and well-spoken despite being efficient killing machines on horseback.[7] Knights were awarded land, property and titles for their services to king and country. This secured their family's future and inheritance and helped to build the aristocracy. Henry VIII resurrected the age of chivalry with his jousting tournaments, masked balls and the courting of his many wives.

By the beginning of the Victorian era, a gentleman was defined as someone who served Britain either as a member of the aristocracy, a clergyman, an army or navy officer or a member of Parliament. As the era progressed, a gentleman was someone whose income came from any source other than retail trade and manual labour[8] It was a given that the gentleman would be chivalrous, but as this couldn't and wouldn't always be the case, the definition of a gentleman became blurred as etiquette began to define what a 'true' gentleman was instead.

Victorian gentlemen were educated, worked hard, believed in truth and justice and were gentle, sympathetic and kind. They showed deference towards all women of their class through following the correct etiquette regardless of their feelings for the woman in question. She could have been a snappy, imperious busy body but still the Victorian gentleman stood up when a woman entered the room or left the dinner table. He kissed a woman's hand in greeting and goodbye. He opened doors for women and waited on them at tea parties. A true gentleman danced with the less popular girls at balls and made conversation with all women in the room regardless of whether he was romantically interested or not. A gentleman did not swear, blaspheme or break wind in front of women. He paid for all the outings when courting and sent flowers not only to his intended wife on a regular basis but the mother as well.[9]

By the later part of the century, it was decided that a gentleman was one who had received a traditional liberal education at one of England's public schools. A gentleman also needed to own land or be involved in politics or council issues. Naturally, this was easy enough for the wealthy middle class banker or financier who could easily afford property and land and then had the right to vote. But the expectations of high, moral standards prevailed, and upper middle-class men were able to fulfil their dream of becoming a gentleman by attending a public school and following the correct etiquette.[10]

Whatever job or business gentlemen undertook, once settled and earning a decent wage, they were expected to marry and have plenty of children. This was an easy task as all Victorian women were primed for marriage from an early age.

The Role of Women in the Victorian Era

For the women of the Victorian era, motherhood was the ultimate goal. Society regarded it as the highest achievement alongside a decent husband and home. Victorians believed deeply in the importance of family, and the job of keeping home and family together was down to the woman. Organising the home, keeping it clean, providing tasty meals and bringing up children was seen as providing enough emotional fulfilment for women.

Most women had little opinion on this because they actually didn't have any rights. When a woman married, she became the property and responsibility of her husband. Anything she owned, including property and land, passed over to her husband who then gave her a monthly or weekly allowance to spend. Her children belonged to her husband, and he had the final say in their upbringing and education. Divorce was practically impossible due to the expense and the shame, and if a wife did leave her husband, then she forfeited all rights over her children. Luckily, most marriages were harmonious, and most husbands were supportive of their wives. But overall, women had very little control over their lives except for the running of their house, and so this was taken very seriously by both parties.

Marriage in the Victorian Era

As you can tell by my frequent use of the words 'husband' and 'wife', marriage was a must in decent Victorian society. In fact, to not be married but to have children led to serious repercussions for everyone. The children were called 'illegitimate' or 'bastards' and looked down upon. They were deemed unworthy of education or inheritance. Many young, unmarried mothers were forced to give their children up for adoption. Men and women were expected to get married but if a man never married it wasn't the end of the world. However, if a woman didn't marry, she was looked down upon and pitied. It was thought that she wasn't good enough, had some awful traits or even worse, she thought she was too good for any of her proposers.

The Expectations of Courting

To get married and have children was the expected ultimate ambition of any woman. So, the first step was to meet a suitable husband, and for the middle- and upper-class girls, this was achieved by attending the right social events such as dances and afternoon tea parties. Here, they could meet many young men and have brief conversations whilst under the watchful eye of their chaperone, an older lady or a servant who accompanied the young woman at such events to make sure the young lady wasn't taken advantage of.

Once a young lady had made her choice of the young men who paid her attention, and picked one she thought most suitable, he would ask her permission to 'court' her. Courting meant that he could call at her house and spend time with her (with a chaperone, of course). This was made public. No man courted more than one woman at a time. If the courtship went smoothly, a marriage proposal followed but only after a conversation with the young lady's father where permission was sought and granted.

But even right up until the wedding day, a young lady was not allowed to be left alone with her betrothed or any man as this could harm her reputation. She could be thought of as 'forward' and 'corrupted'. A forward woman indicated a sexual appetite which was worrying in itself. Women weren't supposed to like sex; they were supposed to like marriage and children.[11]

Working class women attracted a husband through their domestic abilities. They also usually married someone they had known quite a while, so either someone they grew up with or someone from work. A working-class man looked for a healthy and strong woman to keep the home and bring up a brood of children. However, the same practices of courting and chaperoning applied where possible, although for many working-class families this was just not feasible. A working-class young lady would be warned of inappropriate behaviour and then expected to cope with an ardent young man. Unfortunately, history is littered with tales of young, working-class girls who had to marry in a hurry due to pregnancy.

Accomplishments

Middle- and upper-class men required a wife with 'accomplishments. These included the ability to sing, play the piano or harp, dance, speak French and produce beautiful embroidery. As well as all this, she was expected to have perfect posture, a nice tone to her voice (elocution lessons helped with this), and the ability to make polite conversation with anybody. Caroline Bingley sums up the high expectations perfectly in Pride and Prejudice:

> 'No one can be really esteemed accomplished who does not greatly surpass what is usually met with. A woman must have a thorough knowledge of music, singing, drawing, dancing, and the modern languages, to deserve the word; and besides all this she must possess a certain something in her air and manner of walking, the tone of her voice, her address and expressions, or the word will be but half deserved.'[12]

These accomplishments, alongside literature and religious instruction, were learned at home with a governess who lived with the family. Young women were expected to be proud of their accomplishments and willing to show them off at dinner parties, soirees and balls. They were also expected to be discreetly competitive as they were out to catch as wealthy a man as possible. Despite these accomplishments, the middle-class lady was not allowed to be too enthusiastic about her education. If she became too intellectual, she was labelled a 'blue stocking'.

Bluestockings

The Blue-stocking Society was a group of conservative and educated ladies in the eighteenth century, who met with men in the evenings to discuss the latest intellectual ideas in science, literature, religion, politics and the arts because higher education or professional work for women was out of the question.

Therefore, at the beginning of the Victorian era, bluestockings were seen as trying to overtake the men's role in the workplace and in the higher orders of society. They thought themselves on an equal footing with men, and in the rigid order of gender roles in the Victorian era, this was not a good thing. So, being called a bluestocking was derogatory name calling. It labelled the woman as masculine and unattractive, and some doctors even suggested that all this education and discussion made women infertile.[13]

Children

To suggest a woman was infertile and therefore not worth marrying was a huge insult as the expected ultimate aim for all women was to become mothers.[14]

This idea was embodied by Queen Victoria, who with her nine children and Albert showed the nation how fulfilling motherhood could be. Middle class and upper-class society strived to emulate them. Victoria and Albert's marriage was seen as the ideal marriage with Victoria all feminine and domesticated despite being Queen, and Albert with his fierce intellectual interest in science, technology and the arts. When Albert died, Victoria was devastated and stopped carrying out public engagements. Instead, she took comfort at home surrounded by her children.

Victorian middle-class women spent more time with their children than previous generations because they weren't helping their husbands in their work. They breast fed their babies for longer, played with them more and helped to teach them language and skills. This emotional bond was expected by both men and women. But it did mean that the pressure was on to enable the girls to make good marriages as they couldn't work and so had to be supported by their husband's income alone.

For working-class women, children were a financial burden as they stopped the woman from working from home or working in a factory. Therefore, the boys were sent out to work as soon as possible and the girls either undertook factory work or took over the household chores so the mother could do laundry, sewing or manufacturing from home.[15]

Any woman who stayed single or childless was pitied. She was deemed by society as inadequate or a failure. If she didn't like or want children, she was labelled abnormal. The unmarried and childless woman was expected to find work as a governess or nursery maid to make up for her failure in fulfilling her gender role given to her by Victorian society. She certainly couldn't undertake work in the man's sphere.

Leisure

Gender roles also extended into leisure pursuits with separate leisure pursuits for both men and women within their classes. Upper class men staged shooting and hunting weekends on their Estates, inviting the local nobility to partake in pitting their wits against nature. The Lady of the house would then arrange a ball or at least a dinner party for the evening's entertainment. When not at their Estate, upper class men could be found in the local city at their Gentleman's club where they drank, played cards or dice and discussed politics, women and culture. In the summer, many attended local cricket matches and horse races, either as part of the team or as an owner of a racehorse.[16]

Upper-class ladies didn't have such clearly defined leisure time as organising balls and dinner parties was regarded as work rather than leisure, and many were organised for diplomatic purposes: to help a daughter meet a future husband or to raise money for one of her charitable concerns. The duration of the ball or dinner party would be spent as hostess with the responsibility of ensuring everyone had enough food, drink and were talking to the right people.[17]

When they did have some downtime, many upper-class ladies read books and poetry and the bible, embroidered tablecloths or cushion covers or altar cloths or invited the local ladies for afternoon tea. Shopping was another popular leisure activity, especially in the big cities, and could take all day. Gardening was another, although gardeners were employed for the heavy work whilst the Lady planned the gardens, decided what plant went where and did some light dead heading.[18]

Middle class men emulated the aristocracy as much as they could, and strived to be accepted to weekend shoots, hunts and balls at country Estates. They also joined Gentlemen's clubs and attended cricket matches, horseracing and the theatre, income permitting of course. Their wives tried to emulate the ladies as much as possible but without the same number of servants to help and so had to balance work with leisure. To work too hard at charitable causes was frowned upon as the wife's foremost priority was to look after husband and home. Middle class women's leisure pursuits also included reading poetry and the bible, embroidery, shopping, gossiping over afternoon tea and the occasional trip to the theatre.

For the working classes, leisure was something which came to them later on in the century as working hours decreased and Saturday afternoons became free. Many men liked to spend some time with other men either in public houses, coffee shops, at boxing and football matches or at the dog races. What leisure time their wives and daughters managed to grab was spent with family, friends and neighbours catching up on local news and gossip and drinking tea. If they had some quiet time to themselves, this was spent knitting or baking and as the century wore on, many upper working-class women read novels and learnt to embroider. But for the most part, working class leisure time was a premium for the women whose responsibility was work, home, children, religion and morals.[19]

Chapter Four

Home and Hearth

'It is a most miserable thing to feel ashamed of home.'

Great Expectations[1]

The Victorians began to separate the world of work and home as efficiently as they separated the gender roles. The industrial revolution completely changed the dynamics of family life and so housing changed accordingly. Separate spheres within the middle-class home called for more rooms so houses became taller and wider with basements and attics. As the middle classes started to employ servants too, they needed to give them proper accommodation, however small; it no longer sufficed to have servants sleeping on the kitchen floor.

All of this was achieved by building on what had been green fields on the outskirts of small towns and cities. Straight wide streets flanked either side by spacious houses with gardens soon became home to hundreds of middle class and upper working-class families who were looking for cleaner air and bluer skies. There was plenty of this land available for sale too, as estate owners sold off chunks of land for redevelopment, no longer having to keep it back as common land. The enclosure of land, where it was hedged or fenced off, had been happening informally since medieval times. This allowed estate owners, farmers and tenant farmers to plough and fertilise the land and improve crop yield. But from the 1750s, landowners could apply for an Act of Parliament – an Enclosure Act – as formal authorisation thus stopping disputes and trespassing. This brought more land into use to produce crops and cattle for meat and dairy, but historians can't agree on whether or not this enclosing of land drove the poorer agricultural workers into the towns, and if it was to the detriment of the workers and the countryside.[2]

Either way, now that the landowners no longer needed to keep large chunks of land for common use, they were able to rent or sell this land to builders for urban development, or to the canal companies, and later the railway companies to build railway lines. The landowner could build docks for shipping if his estate were near a river. Many also built their own businesses such as cotton mills and manufactories whilst others-built coal mines, which was a very lucrative business.

Whilst some rudimentary building regulations existed, the speculative builder could build what he wanted and where he wanted. There wasn't much thought given to the planning of where houses should be built and why. Anyone could build a house if he had the money for the plot of land and materials and labour. Inevitably, some wonderfully solid and beautiful suburban houses were designed and created and at the same time some awful, cramped two-roomed urban houses became home for many of the poor.

The Speculative Developer and the Building Trade

Victorian developers built their houses on speculation and for the private rental market. Rather than having individuals lined up to buy or rent the houses before they were built, the speculative developer asked investors for money and then used it to buy a section of land where he marked out the plots and had building materials delivered. He then employed builders to build the houses, and the developer rented them out when finished.

Developers started to build on every green field site they could, and individual builders built the houses to their own unique style. Sometimes, the developer continued to own the freehold of the plots; sometimes the builder leased the plots from the developer and collected the rents himself. Sometimes private landlords leased the plots from the developer and so collected the rent for the houses. However, that was if the builder managed to finish building the plot of houses. Many streets were left unfinished as the builder ran out of money for materials or to pay the builders, or the wealthier residents nearby decided another area was more fashionable and upped and moved out. These actions left many developers with large, empty houses and service streets behind. The only way to cover the costs was to rent the larger houses out to several families who lived one family to a floor, and over time as more and more people moved to the cities for work, this became one family per room. The service streets and houses behind became home to poorer people who crammed into the small houses and lived cheek by jowl with their neighbours and various animals.

Back-to-Back Housing

This type of terraced house is synonymous with the north of Victorian England. Houses were built sharing the two side walls and also the back chimney wall, so they didn't have a garden and had only a front entrance to the property. We don't know much about the origin of this design of house, but it is thought that builders saw the empty courts as an ideal opportunity to fill with much needed small houses. By building them facing in on each other on three sides, with the backs of the houses up against the outside wall of the court, the filling of courts this way created a natural wave of back-to-back housing.[3] When speculative builders realised, they could fit in more houses this way, back to backs became a popular choice of house building in the centre of major towns and cities of the midlands, north and London, aimed at the working classes who needed to live near their place of work at the local factory, mill, dock or construction site.

Many back-to-back houses were of a reasonable quality and the chimney placed on the back wall ensured stability, sound proofing and warmth. But shared privies outside and general overcrowding led to poor ventilation and sanitation, which easily spread disease, illness and the subsequent poverty. A lack of standardised building regulations meant that many back to backs were shoddily built and having been literally thrown up in a hurry to fulfil the population boom, they slowly fell down again over time.

Slum Housing

Inevitably, the crowding of families into large houses, and the cheap housing built for the lower classes led to poor sanitation, disease and poverty. Many houses quickly built at the beginning of the Victorian era were only supposed to be temporary and so were built without foundations which hold the house strong and secure and can prevent it against flooding and shaking. Because slum houses were supposed to be knocked down as quickly as they were put up, building without foundations made both processes quicker. Another shortcut was to make the walls only half a brick thick instead of a whole brick. This meant that the walls did not keep out the damp. In some cases, the bricks weren't even held together with proper mortar; a cheaper mortar and street dirt were combined, and this mixture never dried out properly, causing the walls to sag and window frames to leak, adding to the dampness.

The landlords of this slum housing were supposed to look after it and maintain it to a liveable standard, but many landlords didn't see the point as once the lease on the land was up, the houses were to be knocked down. Unfortunately, this didn't always happen, and so roofs leaked, stairs broke, and windows remained empty of glass whilst people continued to live there.

These living conditions made it impossible for the residents to keep themselves and their homes clean. They had no direct water supply and had to fetch their water from street pumps. If they were short of money for coal then they couldn't heat their water to wash themselves or their clothes, not that they would have money for soap and face cloths either. Besides, gaps in windows and roofs made it difficult to maintain heat long enough to get clothes dry.

Furniture could be scarce with the children sitting on the floor and getting dirty, which may not have been swept if the parents couldn't afford to buy a broom.

'In Jacob's Island, the warehouses are roofless and empty; the walls are crumbling down; the windows are windows no more; the doors are falling into the streets; the chimneys are blackened but they yield no smoke.'[4]

Jacob's Island was a place where only desperate people went, either because they were criminals or so destitute, they had nowhere else to go. It wasn't always the case though. Bermondsey was an up-market area of London before the Great Fire in 1666, but from then on, the boggy marshland upon which it was built led to damp, disease, poor living conditions and the inevitable slums Dickens describes as '… the filthiest, the strangest, the most extraordinary …'[5]

The Metropolitan Board of Works, set up in 1855, was made responsible for London's sewers, drainage and the paving and lighting of the streets[6]. The Board was allowed to improve and widen streets as necessary and even create new ones as they saw fit. This gave the Board good reason to clear many of the areas of slum housing to make way for new and better quality housing. When some slum housing was eventually knocked down, the new, wider streets of larger terraced houses were out of the price range for many poor people and so they were forced into the already overcrowded slums that were left.

Common Lodging Houses

For those people who were mobile and not looking for a permanent place to live and call home, or who were so poor they could only pay for a bed if they had earned enough wages that day, common lodging houses were the answer.

These large houses were rented out by the room on a nightly basis. Larger rooms were partitioned by sheets of wooden boards into dormitories, so several people shared the room but with a modicum of privacy. They were sparsely furnished with a bed, pillow, covers and a chamber pot. Customers cooked for themselves in the shared kitchen and washed themselves under the cold-water pump in the back yard.[7]

Rooms cost around 4d a night. Some customers paid for a week's worth of lodging in advance, securing themselves the Sunday for free. Some people even became long term residents, securing themselves the best room in the house, but it still meant living with some salubrious people. Most customers were usually criminals evading arrest or prostitutes, although anyone could end up in a common lodging house depending upon their circumstances. Artisans in between jobs, navvies and labourers who'd moved to the area for their work, street sellers and orphaned children working on the streets. Any single person whose usual place of lodging had disappeared turned to common lodging houses as a temporary solution.[8] For those single people who wanted somewhere more permanent to live because they were in secure employment, they could become lodgers in more respectable houses where they had their own room, their clothes were laundered for them, and their meals were included in the rent.

Rural living

It is not just Victorian terraces which survive today, but rows of cosy, thatched cottages still grace most parts of rural England, especially in the south. With double glazing and plumbing, these cottages are now considered dream housing by many who look to escape to the country or buy a holiday home to get away from city life.

In the early nineteenth century, the reverse was true. The cosy cottages were cramped and unsanitary, the thatched roofs took a lot of work to keep rain proof and provided a cosy home for birds and vermin. Water was collected from the village pond or pump, or in a rain barrel set outside the back door. The cottages shared a privy set in the back gardens, and the hard to remove rubbish attracted vermin and disease. Villagers became used to typhoid, cholera and typhus ravaging the population as much as town and city dwellers.

Slum housing wasn't just for the towns and cities either, it existed in the countryside too. Builders bought bits of land and literally threw up buildings without foundations or proper damp courses and only basic drainage. Many used the cheapest bricks available, which were porous and so absorbed the rain, causing the cottage walls to eventually sag and crack with damp. The ground floors were left as earth floors rather than paved with more expensive flagstones or tiles, turning to mud in winter. As country folk lived longer, many elderly people without families were moved into slum housing by the parish or landowner as this was cheaper.[9]

These squalid living conditions added to the reasons for many young people to move to the larger towns and cities to seek a better way of life. But for those who stayed, as the century wore on, living conditions improved and by the mid nineteenth century, slum housing started to be replaced by properly built plain, brick cottages with adequate drainage and plumbing. The wooden houses of Pip's childhood in *Great Expectations* started to be consigned to the past.

Family estate owners recognised that by having better quality housing on their land, they looked more respectable and trustworthy and so enhanced their reputation. This housing in turn attracted a better class of tenant to the farm, who took pride in their environment, leading to cleanliness and sobriety. Many estate owners didn't expect to see a monetary return in rent on their investment of better housing, but they recognised that if their labourers lived properly then they could work harder and longer, thus increasing the profits of the estate.

The cottages were deliberately kept small to deter families taking in a lodger, but they had two floors with separate bedrooms, a pantry – a cool room facing away from the sun in which food was stored and prepared, a separate dry shed to store coal and wood and a copper for hot water and sometimes a range to cook on rather than an open fire.[10]

The Victorian Suburb

Meanwhile, in the suburbs, the newly emergent Victorian middle class were fuelling the urban building boom. Their separation of the world of work and home and their desire for houses away from the grimy, smelly and increasingly overcrowded town centres led to the development of wide streets of newly built, similarly designed terraced houses on the outskirts of town but near the main roads back into town. The middle classes no longer needed to live within walking distance of their place of work because the cheaper house rent meant they could afford to pay to travel back into town to work, thus they were separated from the working classes and the hustle and bustle of the busy streets, the mess, the poverty and the crime. In a rapidly paced and changing world, an oasis of calm and a warm, clean home and hearth to come home to at the end of a long day's work was seen as the epitome of middle-class Victorian living. The hero of The War of The Worlds describes his neighbourhood whilst out for a walk with his wife:

> 'Coming home, a party of excursionists from Chertsey or Isleworth passed us singing and playing music. There were lights in the upper windows of the houses as the people went to bed. From the railway station in the distance came the sound of shunting trains, ringing and rumbling, softened almost into melody by the distance. My wife pointed out to me the brightness of the red, green and yellow signal lights hanging in a framework against the sky. It seemed so safe and tranquil.'[11]

The Victorian Terrace

A terraced house is one which shares both side party walls with a neighbour. Terraced housing in England dates to the medieval period where it was recognised that by sharing walls, people shared warmth, security and the houses were structurally stronger.[12] For the Victorians, terraced housing was smart and uniformed. It quickly became the standard house for everyone from the working classes to the upper classes, with a similar layout but four separate sizes or rates of house existed, aimed at the different classes of family. A first rate house built with the gentry in mind, was three windows wide, taller and deeper with around 12 rooms to accommodate the family. The second-rate house was built with the middle classes in mind and so was two windows across with 6-8 rooms and fourth rate working class houses had four rooms, otherwise known as '2 up, 2 downs'. Whoever it was designed for, the house wasn't more than 4 times deep front to back as it was wide otherwise it was too dark.[13]

'An Englishman's home is his Castle' is a well-used phrase and perfectly describes the mindset of the Victorian middle class, whose terraced houses came to resemble mini fortresses keeping away the undesirables. Set back from the road with a railing topped wall surrounding the front of the house, protecting both the dweller and the house itself from the mud and rubbish from the street, a porch, sometimes pillars and an imposing front door set atop a small flight of steps put off most people from approaching the house and ringing the bell. To the side of the front path would be a set of steps leading down to a door in the basement. This was the servants and tradesmen's entrance and exit.[14]

Some streets of more expensive terraced houses even had just the one entrance to the road, protected by black railings and a gatekeeper to keep out the riff raff. This was where the upper classes tended to keep their town houses, which the men mainly used when on business in the nearby city and the women used to entertain guests during the summer. In London, this was the case for the duration of the London 'season' between April and July and the upper-class town houses lay in Mayfair, Knightsbridge and Belgravia.

The Victorians weren't too bothered about property ownership, and everyone happily rented. Poorer people paid their rent weekly, middle class and wealthier people leased a house for 1-7 years and paid the rent yearly. By renting, it was easier to downsize or upsize as needed. Also, neighbourhoods changed so rapidly in this era of growth and reconstruction that middle classes looked to move away from an area as soon as there was the slightest hint that it was going down market. In *The Sign of Four*, John Watson describes some suburban housing of London as 'interminable lines of new, staring brick buildings – the monster tentacles which the giant city was throwing out into the country.'[15]

The Interior Layout

Whether big or small, the Victorian terraced house followed the same plan inside. The front door opened into a hallway furnished with a coat stand, a small table with a vase of flowers and a rug on the floor to wipe the feet. Leading off the hall, to the side, were two rooms. One was usually designated as the parlour, the most common room in the Victorian home. It was used for breakfast and sometimes dinner if the family weren't entertaining guests. It was also used to receive visitors throughout the day. Behind the parlour was the study or library or study and library combined.[16]

Leading straight up out of the hall was the stairs to the other floors. The first floor housed the reception rooms such as the drawing room and the dining room. The second floor housed the master bedroom alongside the man's dressing room, and a guest bedroom. The third floor housed the children's bedrooms alongside the servants. Down in the basement sat the kitchen, scullery, cold larder or pantry, wine cellar and coal cellar, hence the afore mentioned tradesmen's entrance into the basement.

Victorians liked their rooms separated and for one purpose only, and so the kitchen became just for cooking and if you were wealthy enough to have a cook, this was her domain and the mistress only ventured in there to discuss menus and check on provisions. Dining rooms were for eating, bedrooms were for sleeping, nurseries were where the children slept, played and were educated.

Victorian Decoration

It wasn't just the size of the house which mattered to the Victorian middle and upper classes. The furniture and dressings and overall decoration was just as important, especially in the rooms frequented by visitors. Although the middle class 'home' was a private affair, the house itself was very much public, and was furnished in a way to show off the family's status and wealth. Carpets, mirrors, curtains, sofas, chairs and tables all had to be new and of the latest colours and fashion. Cabinets displayed ornaments and collections and the ubiquitous gleamingly polished piano was on hand for the daughter of the house to provide entertainment to family and visitors. Any worn furniture and decorations were removed to the bedrooms upstairs. Victorian thriftiness meant bedrooms became cluttered with armchairs, small couches, display cabinets, ornaments and small side tables. Carpets and curtains were cut down and repurposed. Once the mistress of the house was really finished with a piece of furniture, it was passed onto a charitable cause.[17]

The upper classes disliked this display of wealth and thought it ostentatious. But the middle classes didn't care and cheerfully stuffed their houses with the latest modern conveniences, fashions and style. Because the middle classes couldn't afford an army of servants, nor could they house one, they were quick to embrace and invest in new household technology such as piped hot water and gas lights, with the aristocracy slower to catch on having their servants to carry hot water cans up and down the stairs and light the candles in the candelabra every night.

Lighting the Home

Early Victorian homes were lit by a mixture of candles and oil lamps. Portable light sources such as single candlesticks, candelabra – a branched candlestick containing three or four candlesticks, oil lamps and the fire produced the main sources of light for everyone and were always within arm's reach. Candlesticks had a place by the side of the bed and by the side of doors in all the rooms, ready to be carried out into unlit corridors as needed. For those with more money and bigger homes, chandeliers containing several candles were suspended from the ceiling and wall sconces held single candles protected by a glass shield, but these were only used for when the family were entertaining or special occasions such as Christmas.[18]

There were different types of candles to choose from, depending on what the family could afford. The cheapest tallow candles were made of animal fat, so they stank and produced a smoky flame which deposited soot around the room. Superior spermaceti candles were made from whale oil which smelt a little better and produced a clearer flame, as did beeswax candles which smelt the nicest of them all and so were expensive.[19] Very simple oil lamps also made good, portable lights, made from a small, glass container holding whale oil and a plaited wick which burned to produce a clean flame.

Poorer, rural families made their own rushlights for free as opposed to buying candles. Long, green rushes, found growing in marshy land and alongside rivers in the summer, were collected in great bundles. The outer shell was stripped back leaving a core of white pith. These were hung in bunches to dry out and strengthen over several weeks whilst cooking fat was collected and stored. When it was time to make the rushlights, the fat was put into a long, shallow iron dish and melted by the fire. The bunches of died rushes were drawn through the melted fat, giving them a thorough coating, and then were laid to dry and stored ready for use in the winter. When needed, rushlights were clamped vertically upright in a holder and lit from the fire. A whole rushlight burned for up to an hour at most. Although they provided much needed light, rushlight smelled of the fat they burned and left soot stains behind.[20] The use of rushlights was a clear indication of poverty but by 1847, cheap tallow candles cost only 6d a bundle so even poorer people could start to swap rushlights for the odd candle or two.[21]

Gas Lighting

In the early nineteenth century, gas was used for lighting only and mainly for industrial use, enabling factories and mills to work for longer hours rather than just daylight hours. By the time Queen Victoria took the throne, nearly every city in England had a gas works of some sort or another to supply, at minimum, adequate street lighting in all the courts, alleys, parks, bridges, wharfs and quays. Soon, shops adopted gas as it lit up their displays of goods in the front windows and also enabled them to remain open past daylight hours. Theatres embraced gas lighting too as it was far more convenient than the constant replacing of candles and oil in lamps throughout a performance.[22]

In 1859, the Houses of Parliament introduced gas lighting and the popularity of it helped spread gas lighting into the wealthier homes. (Building conservation. com) Newly built homes from 1860 onwards were built with a central gas burner in the ceiling of every room so each room had access to gas lighting.

Gas lighting had its drawbacks though. The stream of gas into homes was controlled by the local gas works, who mainly released it for use during dark mornings and evenings in autumn and winter.[23] It was smelly, and needed a lot of oxygen to burn but Victorian homes were generally poorly ventilated, leaving occupants with headaches and nausea if the gas was on for too long. The gas was also dirty and damaged books, paintings, furniture and clothes.[24] The iron pipes which carried the gas frequently rusted up and the burners themselves silted up causing a need to clean them all out on a regular basis. Gas light could be weak, depending on the pressure, giving a flickering light rather than a constant stream, and could sputter and even fail. Although it enhanced the brightness of silver, glass and jewellery at dinner parties, it made the skin look yellow and tired and enhanced wrinkles. So for dinner parties, expensive candles were generally favoured.[25] By 1901, urban dwellers used a mixture of piped gas, candles and the newly discovered, cleaner paraffin oil to light their homes whilst rural people still relied upon candles and oil.

As it was not available all day, gas was not used for cooking until the end of Queen Victoria's reign, despite the development of gas cookers. For cooking and heating hot water, coal was still the solid fuel of choice for everyone.

The Kitchen

'A dirty house produces dishonest people'[26]

Usually in the basement, the kitchen was the engine room of the middle-class house. It was dominated by a stove or range for cooking, a large wooden table and a terracotta tiled floor. A system of cranks, pulleys and bells across the house allowed the servants to carry out their work here but be on hand to answer a call from their employer when needed.

Keeping the kitchen clean was of utmost importance not only for hygiene reasons but also for moral reasons. The stove was swept out daily and the range was blackened with polish to both protect it and to make it look smart. The stove made the kitchen one of the warmest rooms in the house and so washing was frequently dried here too. It was usual for hedgehogs to be kept in basement kitchens too, in their own little box. At night, they'd run around the kitchen eating the beetles and bugs which ventured into the kitchen. In *The Sign of Four*, Mr. Sherman keeps a slow worm for exactly the same reason. 'It hain't got no fangs so I gives it the run o' the room, for it keeps the beetles down.'[27]. Traps were also set for cockroaches, and these would be emptied every morning. The kitchen was frequently whitewashed to freshen up the walls and keep them clean as the stove produced a lot of soot.

As well as the stove, a large wooden table dominated Victorian basement kitchens. The table was used as a holding area for utensils and prepared food and cleared for the servants to sit at and have their meals once the household had finished theirs. A large, wooden dresser held a store of crockery for everyday use and a sink stood in the corner with a pump for cold water. The water would be heated on the stove and used for cooking, washing up and cleaning the kitchen. In early Victorian houses, a bucket sat under the sink plughole to collect the dirty water which was then slung down a drain outside the kitchen door. In later years when houses were connected to drains by pipes, the servants had the luxury of pulling the plug and seeing the water swirl away.

The Scullery or Wash House

Situated next door to the kitchen, the scullery was used for washing clothes although in some households it was also used for washing up. A scullery held a sink and a water pump, a wooden tub to wash sheets in and a three legged wooden 'dolly stick' to twist them in the soapy water, a scrub board and a mangle for wringing the clothes dry. The best sculleries had a stone 'copper' in which to heat the water and wash the clothes. A copper was a stone structure with a stone bowl sat on top and space inside for a fire to be lit, which heated the cold water placed in the bowl. Once up to temperature, soap flakes and clothes were added to the hot water and scrubbed on the scrub board to get clean. The water was then removed by a jug into a bucket and clean water was added to the bowl to rinse the clothes. Once clean the clothes were rung through the mangle, hung outside to dry or hoisted up to the ceiling on a wooden rack to dry in the scullery, and then ironed, folded and stored with dried herbs to keep them fresh.

Once a year, coppers were cleaned out and Christmas puddings were boiled in them, as is the case in *A Christmas Carol*, '…the two young Cratchits hustled Tiny Tim, and bore him off into the washhouse, that he might hear the pudding singing in the copper.'[28]

Larger houses made and boiled several Christmas puddings at once and then stored them ready to use for celebrations later on in the year. Sometimes, the extras were given to the poor or to servants for their Christmas dinners. For the smaller houses which didn't have room for a scullery or a copper, they used the copper in the nearby washhouse where their washing was taken to be laundered.

Coppers also had other uses such as boiling water for baths and in *Oliver Twist*, an old copper is used to cook the gruel dished out at every meal to the inmates of the workhouse.

The Prep Room

Where room permitted, a small prep room or still room sat next to the kitchen. With a sink in the corner and a small, wooden table, this room was used for making bread and pastry and for drying herbs from the garden. Either the mistress of the house or one of the servants would use this room to make up medicines and tinctures for the household medicine cabinet. It was also used as an extra storage space for tablecloths, napkins and best crockery and cutlery ready for guests.

The Dining Room

The dining room could be situated anywhere on the ground floor or first floor depending upon how many floors there were in the house. Either way, it was used by the family for every meal and for elaborate dinner parties; the latter being the perfect opportunity to show off some wealth. Dining rooms were usually decorated in lighter colours but with the usual mahogany furniture and glass cabinets displaying ornaments and other curiosities. No dining room was complete without a sideboard adorned with decanters of whisky, brandy, port and wine and crystal tumblers and glasses. The mahogany table was laid with a snow-white tablecloth, napkins in silver holders and polished silver cutlery, all glittering in the light of the beeswax candles set in the silver candelabra.

The food was laid out in bowls and platters for the diners to help themselves, although in wealthier households, the servants served the food.

Once the meal was finished, the diners could retire to the Drawing Room.

The Drawing Room

Usually decorated in a more feminine way, the drawing room was used for receiving and entertaining visitors and so demonstrated the resident's wealth. A soft, patterned carpet on the floor, upholstered chairs and sofas to match, patterned wallpaper and heavy draped curtains all came together to make a sumptuous but elegant room. A piano in the corner would be used by the daughter of the house to provide some entertainment, and small tables with lamps next to chairs provided some cosy spots for reading.

The Morning Room

This was the room usually used by the lady of the house when on her own; a little sanctuary in which to do some embroidery, reading, letter writing, play with the children or attend to the household accounts.

The Study

Usually decorated in masculine colours such as dark green or red or navy blue, the study was the refuge for the man of the house. Consisting of a desk, chair and bookcases, all in mahogany, this was somewhere he could go to work or read in peace. Not all households had a study, it was mainly those where the head of the household needed a space to concentrate on writing or business matters.

Bedrooms

On the top floor, the bedrooms again were more feminine in decoration, with lighter coloured wallpaper and carpets. The master bedroom for the husband and wife contained a four-post bed with canopies and drapes. Pillows were long in length and filled the width of the bed. A washstand with a bowl, jug, soap and a cloth stood to one side of the bed. The wife had a mirrored dressing table for her toiletries and cosmetics, and wardrobes housed her clothes. If there was room, the husband had a small dressing room next door where he kept his clothes and washstand. Chamber pots were kept under the bed. Some houses had an inside privy, those that didn't required the residents to use commodes either in a separate room or in the bedroom.

All rooms in Victorian houses had a fireplace and so the bedroom was the ideal place to have a bath. A zinc or porcelain bath was kept in the room, sometimes with a screen to go round it to ensure some privacy, a fire was lit in the fireplace and pails of hot water brought up from the kitchen. Later on, separate bathrooms became popular, but this was only possible in houses which had a spare room to turn into a bathroom or newer houses which were built with a separate bathroom.

The children's room or rooms were known as the nursery and this was where they slept, played and also had some lessons. A typical nursey consisted of beds, a commode chair, a bath, a washstand, wardrobes and toys.

Domesticity

As well as the home viewed as an island in the turbulent sea of Victorian clamour and gaiety, Victorian houses were a status symbol, and the middle classes kept themselves apart from the working classes through their carefully built suburbs only wealthier people could afford. Gardens demonstrated the owners' affordance of time and money to cultivate flowerbeds, fruit and vegetables whilst hothouses showed off delicate and exotic plants from around the Empire. Gardens also provided opportunities for afternoon tea outside, croquet on the lawn and even archery. All of this was overseen by the Victorian wife who did not go out to work but stayed at home instead and dedicated herself to running the household with the help of one or two servants. If she was lucky, her husband could afford to employ a housekeeper to manage the household, but if not, she managed the cook and maid herself. This was a more usual situation in middleclass homes but striving to be better was always the goal and so middleclass Victorians sought to have the very best of everything in their houses, just like the aristocracy. Although the landed gentry owned houses which were more like a small village, with dozens of servants showing off the owner's wealth and superiority, the middle classes still wished to emulate them as much as possible. Dinner parties, afternoon tea and balls were immensely popular with the upper classes and although the middle classes couldn't quite fit a ballroom into their homes, they could certainly host dinner parties and evenings of music, singing and entertainment for their friends, families and influential people they needed to impress. Again, no expense was spared as expensive clothes and horses and carriages became a ubiquitous part of the middle-class social scene, not to mention the endless courses of finest food and the European wines served alongside. The organisation of such soirees was the domain of the wife, and the smoothness with which they were organised and held enhanced the husband's reputation and standing in the local community and at work. The middle-class wife learned these skills as a child so she would be ready for marriage as soon as she was eighteen. This domestic education superseded any other education for middle and upper-class girls.

Chapter Five

Education

> 'The whole theory of modern education is radically unsound. Fortunately in England, at any rate, education produces no effect whatsoever.'
>
> *The Importance of Being Earnest*[1]

At the beginning of the nineteenth century, England was seen as educationally backwards compared to the rest of Europe. It is estimated that only 25% of children were receiving any education at all, and they would have been mostly boys from the upper classes. Half the adult population signed the marriage register with an X rather than their own name, due to a lack of literacy skills.[2]

Unlike today, the cost of educating children was borne by the parent and not the government. Education was seen as a status symbol by the upper classes and a nuisance by the working classes. All classes agreed on one thing though: education was for boys only.

By 1837, the English schooling system was a patchwork of different establishments, where supply met demand. Fee paying local grammar schools provided middle class teenage boys with a decent grounding in English, maths, science and languages including Latin. These boys were preparing for jobs as clerks, bankers, teachers, army and navy officers or clergymen. The upper classes were served by the elite boarding schools such as Eton, Rugby and Harrow where the boys were prepared for life in the civil service as MPs or even prime minister or to run their inherited estates after attending Oxford or Cambridge University of course.

Meanwhile, working class boys attended whatever school was available until they reached the age where they could be employed in factories, mills or as agricultural labourers, then they left to earn money to support their families instead. This meant they were often unable to reach their full academic potential and move on to higher paid jobs with better working conditions.

'Another gentleman of the same class was examining some country lads and asked one of them if he knew what vowels were. 'Fowls, Sir?' answered the boy. 'Why fowls be chickens!'[3]

At the other end of the scale, after an extensive and expensive education, middle- and upper-class boys were not expected or allowed even, to work in a factory or mill or shop, even if they became manager of a department, because trade and labouring was seen as inferior work. So, a skills gap emerged with business owners requiring educated workers to run sections of a factory on their own, but with no one to fill the roles.

Education in the Early Years of the Victorian Era

Between 1838 and 1848, the Chartist Movement helped to further the argument for increased education for the working classes. Chartism campaigned for political rights and influence for the working class. The members published a people's charter stating the six main requirements of the movement. These included all men aged over 21 to be given the vote, a secret ballot system to be installed for voting, members of parliament to be paid a wage by the government, electoral districts to be equal in size and annual elections for parliament to take place.[4]

The Chartists strengthened their argument for educational reform by insisting that a decent education for all would ensure everyone used their vote wisely and that educated individuals made for a prosperous economy. At the same time, factory and large business owners realised that their workers needed to be educated in order to help them keep up with the economic competition found in the rest of the world. They argued that they needed young adults who could read, write and do arithmetic to a high standard. In order to achieve this, *all* children needed to attend school and be allowed the time off of work to do so.

1844 Act – Half-Time Introduced

On the back of the Chartist movement, and the realisation that Britain was beginning to lose its global position as an industrial leader due to an undereducated workforce, the government introduced 3 hours a day compulsory schooling for eight- to thirteen-year-old factory workers. The Half-Time system was born.[5]

As children could only work 6 and a half hours a day, the government decided they could tend school for three hours either in the morning before work or the afternoon after work. For these half-timers though, combining school and work was incredibly tiring and teachers complained of bad manners, surliness, foul language and an unwillingness to learn. School inspectors expected half timers to achieve as much as full-time members, putting the pressure on teachers to keep them up to speed. The only way to do this was to teach the full timers the same lesson twice! Whilst this meant that the full timers learned the subjects in depth and had more chance of passing the standard test at the end of the year, it meant that the half timers were blamed for holding the full-timers back, thus perpetuating the system of everyone in their place.

Critics pointed out that children were still being made to work long hours outside of school which negated their ability to concentrate in school and learn skills which would get them out of poverty. They also complained that the types of jobs on offer to children such as newspaper sellers, rag collecting and matchbox makers taught them how to drink, gamble and swear, traits which they took back into the schoolroom.

The Different Types of Schooling for Working Class Children

From 1840, it was decided that schools not associated with either the British Society or the National Society could receive government grants towards the building of a new venue or the extension of an existing one.[6] This meant that these schools were independent of religious authorities and so weren't run by a specific church. The schools did have to provide daily religious education though and also allow government inspections. Once up and running, the schools then relied upon charitable donations, voluntary donations from local and wealthy philanthropists and any other source of funding to keep paying the teachers, coal on the fires and slates on the desk. This was a precarious existence though. Schools were only really answerable to their local communities and the local people supported it financially and morally. Anyone who opposed the school could withdraw their patronage and effectively close it down.

In the 1840s, the school curriculum was very limited and based upon government guidelines for delivery. This made the lessons tedious and wouldn't have done much to help a child's work chances later on. However, it was a start and built upon the very basic literacy and numeracy children were able to achieve at the first infant schools: Dame Schools.

Dame Schools

From as far back as Shakespeare's time, nearly every village had a dame school, which was open to everyone and very popular. Originally, they were reputable places, run by educated, genteel ladies in return for a small fee, but by the Victorian era they were usually run by elderly men and women who could no longer work in physical labour but had some skills they could pass along. Dame schools provided parents with reliable childcare alongside basic literacy and maths tuition. Practical skills such as plaiting, weaving, knitting and lace making were offered depending upon the teacher's past employment. Most Dame schools steered clear of religion, which meant everyone could apply to attend.[7]

Dame schools tended to teach what the parents wanted, and this varied depending upon the area in which the school was set up. If craft and homemaking skills were required by the parents, that's what was on offer. The teachers were also sympathetic and responsive to the parent's need to remove the children from school for short periods of time, such as harvest time in the countryside. Even the smallest child had a role to play in the gathering of crops ready for the winter. It was also usual for a child to stop attending school if a member of their family was sick and the child was needed to help at home, or if a family member lost their job and so could not continue to pay the penny a week for a place. As at this point, there was no requirement for pupils to undertake tests and there was no government regulation anyway, prolonged absence did not matter.

Both working class boys and girls attended dame schools until they were aged seven or eight and then they were old enough to go to work. Exactly how much learning took place at Dame schools is hard to judge, but it was better than nothing and kept the attending child safe off the streets – mostly. There are accounts of some terribly run dame schools where children had little education and worked for the teacher instead, churning out lace or baskets to sell for profit.

However, parents still had to pay, even if it was a penny a week. For some though, this was a penny too much. Many parents found it difficult to invest in their child's future when the child needed to eat that night.

Ragged Schools

For the very poor, Ragged Schools were championed by Lord Ashley, a factory reformer who became president of the Ragged Schools Union in the 1850s.[8] The Ragged School movement had the aim of preventing children from turning to crime. These free schools often ran during the afternoon and evening so children could go to work first. The schools also offered hot meals and free second-hand clothing which no doubt enticed many a pupil through the doors.

Charles Dickens was a supporter of the Ragged School movement and visited the Field Lane Ragged School in 1843, afterwards writing extensively of his experience in The Daily News.

'The name implies the purpose. They who are too ragged, wretched, filthy and forlorn to enter any other place; who could gain admission into no charity school, and who would be driven from any church door; are invited to come in here, and find some people not depraved, willing to teach them something, and show them some sympathy, and stretch a handout, which is not the iron hand of law, for their correction.[9]'

A very basic curriculum including the ubiquitous reading, writing and arithmetic was offered alongside scripture study and then practical skills such as tailoring, shoemaking, sewing and laundry work, all with the intention of helping these children to get steady jobs, look after themselves properly and become useful members of society rather than criminals clogging up the prisons.

Industrial Schools or Schools of Industry

It was recognised that in certain urban areas in London, Manchester and other major cities, incredibly poor and homeless children were at risk of turning to crime to feed themselves. Industrial schools were set up to both educate these neglected children and to help them into a trade. Alongside reading, writing and arithmetic, pupils learned 'workable' skills such as knitting, spinning, obedience and domestic servitude, carpentry and gardening (space permitting).[10]

Daily life in industrial schools was strict, starting at 6am and finishing at 7pm. Children were expected to have schooling, take part in worship at the local church or within the school and then carry out the necessary household tasks. Girls did the housework, laundry, cooking and sewing whilst the boys learned to tailor, garden and mend shoes. Homeless children were able to sleep over at the school if there were enough beds available.

This education was provided free of charge by teachers. Food, clothes and buildings were paid for by wealthy donors. Parents were supposed to help with the cost of educating their children but as most were homeless or living in slums, this was nigh on impossible and so industrial schools relied upon charity instead.

Historians think that a whopping 300,000 poor children received an education of sorts from Ragged and Industrial schools before the Elementary Education Act of 1870 finally introduced compulsory education for the masses.[11]

Reasons for Children Not to Attend School

Despite the persistent clamour from campaigners for free education for the working classes, and an increase in government support and funding, a Royal Commission on Education conducted in 1858 found that only one in eight children of all ages and classes attended school.[12]

Education

It seemed that there was still a reluctance amongst parents to commit their children to an educational system where the types of lessons offered in the 1840s wouldn't have done much to help a child's work chances later on. There were many parents who felt that children shouldn't receive too much education as it would upset the status quo and give their child ideas above their station in life. Many farmers didn't support the education of agricultural labourer's children, as they thought the youngsters wouldn't want to stay on and work in the countryside after being educated about the big wide world. Farmers blamed education for the mass migration of young people to the towns and cities or into the army and navy. Exciting jobs on the railways, in warm factories or as postmen or policemen beckoned, enticing educated youngsters away from the fields, where farmers worked young boys hard, believing this to be the only way to make them good labourers as men. Meanwhile, mill owners preached how early work for young children helped to sharpen their wits and nerves to make them solid adult workers, whilst sending their own children to Eton, Rugby or Harrow and then onto Oxford or Cambridge University.

The children themselves had many things stacked against them, preventing them from fully immersing themselves in education. In the countryside, seasonal jobs such as the weeding of crops, lambing, sheep shearing and the reaping of the harvest required all hands-on deck, however small. Then there were the seasonal celebrations such as harvest festival, summer fairs, autumn hiring fairs, circuses and barn dances to entice pupils away from their studying. Not that they needed much enticement to truant as one boy was quick to tell a journalist: 'I like going to school well enough ... but I don't like staying when I get there!'[13]

Not all parents could afford the school fees of 1 or 2 pence per child per week, or their child did not have suitable clothing to wear to school, or sturdy enough shoes to walk to school in. Even the most devoted parents couldn't always afford books, paper, pens and ink or slates and chalk for their studious child to practice their reading and writing.

On top of this, in village and town schools alike, disease could sweep through the school like wildfire, causing mass absenteeism as the pupils were either ill themselves, needed at home to help with other poorly members of the family or needed to work in place of a poorly family member. A lack of adequate sanitation and cleaning in cramped conditions alongside a poor diet caused repeated outbreaks of diphtheria, whooping cough, scarlet fever and consumption (now known as tuberculosis).[14] It seemed that educating the masses was an uphill struggle and the government really needed to step in and take control.

The 1870 Education Act

By 1870, England's education system consisted of an amalgamation of British Society schools, National Society schools and Voluntary Aided schools.[15] Luckily, Britain's Prime Minister William Gladstone pushed a Bill through Parliament, the first piece of legislation put together to sort out Britain's education system and was only brought about by the National Education League. Set up in 1869, the National Education League campaigned for free schools for everyone, which were also non-religious and required compulsory attendance. Their aim was to stop child labour altogether. The result was the 1870 Education Act which showed a commitment by Parliament to actively do something about the inequality in education.

Gladstone's Bill doubled the money paid to British and National schools. It also allowed for new schools to be set up and paid for out of local taxes. The plan was for these schools to be run by local people elected to Boards. Those elected were chosen by local rate payers, ensuring a sense of community ownership of the school. As these Board Schools were required to fill the gaps, those on the school board then had to work out how many school places were needed to cover the district. As Board Schools were non-religious, they attracted non-conformist parents such as Methodists and Catholics who didn't want their children following Church of England rituals at school. Although Religious Education was offered, parents could opt their children out of it.

The Board Schools' basic finances continued to be topped up by school pence, where the parents could afford it, but more importantly, extra government grants were on offer if the school maintained high attendance levels, kept the school in good working order and could prove a strong record of attainment in the Standard Tests at the end of the year.[16]

Standard Tests

Once a Board School was established, classes were arranged into Standards from I to VII. Each child had to pass the end of year test before moving up to the next Standard. Some moved up every year whilst others were held back to repeat the year as required. When the children left school aged 11, they received a school leaver's certificate and an education roughly the same as a current 8-year-old.

The Standard Tests put pressure on both teacher and School Board to deliver results. If the test score was too low, then the school's grant was cut. The teacher's salary was dependent upon how much money the school received and so a reduction in grant led to a reduction in salary. The quickest way to ensure the pupils learnt the curriculum was through the Monitorial System of teaching.

The Monitorial System

This was also known as the Madras System and was pioneered by Dr Andrew Bell.[17] Older pupils, who were successfully passing their standards, taught the younger pupils what they had learned in their lessons. The original role of the school monitor was to assist the teacher with making ink, preparing pens, drawing lines in books and cleaning chalk off the slates before handing them out to the class. They moved onto tracking down truants and administering discipline before it was realised that the quickest way to get a lot of information across to a lot of mostly uninterested children was by using the Monitors more efficiently.

Unfortunately for the pupils, the teaching was as mechanised as the factories they would eventually go to work in. The teacher taught the Monitor; the Monitor taught the children via large wooden boards of information hung on the wall and pointed to with a wooden stick. The pupils recited historical dates and the names of capes and bays in Africa. This way of teaching ensured eighty to a hundred pupils could be taught at once, in a large hall separated into Standards by curtains. Children sat on wooden benches at shared wooden desks. The cramped, hot, noisy conditions made it difficult to stay awake and concentrate. It was boring, uncreative rote learning and of little use in the real world. Many children went to work afterwards, facing the same conditions and monotonous, uninspiring work.[18]

Victorian elementary schooling worked on the premise that children needed to be taught social and work discipline to enable them to operate machinery safely in the factories, mills or on the railways or to be an obedient and quick servant. They had to learn to watch the clock and work within time constraints and so corporal punishment became the normal way of ensuring children kept to their allotted work at the allotted pace.

The most common form of punishment was several whacks with a cane on the hand or buttocks, closely followed by the humiliation by wearing the Dunce's cap or standing in a corner facing the wall.

There was no recognition of learning impairment, low ability or mental deficiency. Those who ran the Victorian education system believed all children could do the work and pass the exams if they tried hard enough and so many children were unduly punished for not trying hard enough when they had an unrecognised learning impairment such as dyslexia or were perhaps just exhausted from working a factory shift the night before or even from a distinct lack of food and drink.

What Was a School Day Like?

Under the new Act, a typical school day was only 6 hours long but was split into two parts. It started at 9am and finished at 12 for lunch, allowing the pupils to walk home and get something to eat and possibly help their parents with a chore or two. It started again at 2pm and finished at 5pm.[19]

Lessons were around 30 minutes in length for each subject and included spelling, punctuation, arithmetic, religious instruction and Physical Education. Children practised their handwriting in copy books by copying lines from the board using a pen dipped in ink. They had to make sure their letters were all the same size and unsullied by blots, stains or finger-marks. Geography involved memorising lists of countries, seas, capes and bays and pointing to them on a map. For most children who'd never left their hometown or village, they may have well been identifying landmarks on the moon.

As the century wore on, schools could apply for grants to teach other subjects such as geography, science, Latin, French, English grammar, mathematics and domestic economy. These subjects were known as class subjects and schools only received money depending upon how well the whole class learned the subject and so although the children may have enjoyed these more, the pressure was on both staff and children to keep up attendance, fighting against the usual culprits of poverty, disinterest and the need to earn money.

Despite both teachers and pupils' best efforts, many working class school leavers still found it difficult to rise through the class ranks to secure higher paid employment. Many middle- and upper-class people felt that the working classes needed to stay in their prescribed roles of factory worker, servant or labourer. Forty years on from the 1870 Education Act, the 1911 census recorded that nearly one third of girls aged 14-15 were domestic servants whilst another third worked in the clothing or textile industry. Nearly a quarter of all 14-year-old boys worked as messengers and errand boys.[20]

Towards the end of the century, school improvers recognised that vocational teaching needed to be included in the curriculum, educating the pupils to fit into their future careers. So, boys learned woodwork and girls learned needlework, as well as general home making skills, thus limiting the girls' academic lessons as there was only 6 hours in a school day. Fractions and percentages were put to one side in order to squeeze in instruction on laying fires, laying tables and cooking, preparing the girls, of course, for domestic service.

However, some Board Schools were started up for older and more studious pupils to continue their education beyond the age of eleven, mainly in the North of England where millowners required educated men to become engineers, technicians and clerks. A wider and more difficult curriculum was offered alongside literacy and arithmetic. French, German, geometry, algebra,

Latin, shorthand, bookkeeping and science were all on offer. But it was only the working-class families with a bit more money who could afford to lose the wage whilst their child stayed on at school past eleven.

Scholarships were available for clever working-class children to move onto grammar school, thus ensuring some social mobility, but many parents still couldn't afford the school uniform, books, stationery and school trip fees so their children weren't able to take advantage of this opportunity.

The Teachers

At the beginning of Queen Victoria's reign, elementary teachers were educated people who were unable to do any other job or the only jobs available to them was that of domestic servant, seamstress or factory worker. As teacher training was non-existent, teachers weren't paid very much either and earned less than an able-bodied labourer.

In 1846, the government drew up plans for teacher training. Children at school aged thirteen and over could be apprenticed for 5 years to become pupil-teachers. This meant that young people interested in education could pass on what they had learned to the younger pupils, but they had more status than the pupil monitors mentioned previously. Pupil-teachers received extra-curricular tutoring from the headmaster or mistress and were also granted extra time to study. They had to pass an exam set by Her Majesty's school Inspectors at the end of every year. As well as having a decent education, teachers were expected to be of the Anglican faith and hold exemplary morals. This was reflected in the expected dress code of plain dress, simple hair styles and sensible shoes.

At the very end of their apprenticeship, pupil-teachers could sit the Queen's scholarship exam and progress to teacher training college where they could study to become qualified teachers. Alternatively, they didn't go onto teacher training college and instead accepted the job of unqualified assistant teacher, of course earning less money.

Not all pupil-teachers received the quality tuition from their headteachers that they should have and in fact, many were self-taught through their own private study. Many critics of the system voiced their concern that pupil-teachers didn't read enough or have enough cultural interests to make inspiring and efficient teachers. The government tried to recruit teachers from the middle classes, but this didn't catch on, possibly because middle class women were encouraged to stay at home and run the house. Also, as there wasn't an equal pay Act, women were paid substantially less than men. In 1870, a certificated female teacher could earn £58 a year whereas her male counterpart could earn £94 a year, nearly double the wage.[21]

Teacher training did gradually improve, with the setting up of teacher training centres to replace the private tuition offered by schools. This meant that trainee teachers could dedicate themselves to the profession. But alongside their training at the college, trainee teachers were still expected to help with cleaning and laundry, sweeping the floors and fetching coal and water.

Things didn't improve once the teachers were qualified. They soon found that their profession made constant demands on their time. They were expected to help out with church on Sundays by playing the organ, training the choir, assisting with Sunday School, arranging and running trips and much, much more. It was only when the National Union for Teachers gained traction in 1903 that the extra-curricular workload decreased.

Trainee teachers found their social status improved, although the training colleges tried to keep this under control as many trainees had been apprenticed as pupil-teachers first and therefore from a working-class background.

Although educated men could certainly earn more money in other jobs, for the educated working-class woman, teaching was perfect. It was a far more rewarding job than servitude, shop work or factory work and it brought with it an air of respectability and independence.

Many educated middle-class women, who for some reason didn't have a source of income, chose to become governesses instead.

The Governess

The governess was not a new job in the Victorian era as the aristocracy had been using them since the Middle Ages, but it was the middle classes, who by emulating the upper classes, set the precedence for anyone with money to hire a governess.[22]

It was normal for upper- and middle-class boys to receive academic tutoring from a young man until it was time for them to go to grammar or boarding school. As there was a lack of formal schooling for girls, the governess fulfilled the role of home tutor for them instead. The difference between a tutor for the boys and a governess for the girls was that whilst boys were taught science, geography and economics, girls had to be prepared for marriage. But instead of being taught how to cook, clean and housekeep, they were expected to marry men who could afford to pay servants to do this for them. Instead, the governess's primary concern was to ensure the girls in her charge acquired enough skills to attract as affluent a husband as possible by teaching the accomplishments a man would look for in a wife. This included piano playing and singing (ready to entertain at gatherings), dancing (ready for the balls of the season), sewing and embroidery (ready to decorate the home) and drawing and painting (to show a calm and artistic temperament). Alongside this, a governess taught her charges how to speak the Queen's English and walk, curtsey and sit gracefully. Manners, morals and the bible were rigorously taught from a young age, moulding the young girl into the ideal Victorian woman.

As education expanded and boys were expected to know more than reading, writing and arithmetic before they went to school, the wealthier households provided governesses with schoolrooms equipped with blackboards, slates and chalk, books, maps and globes. Textbooks became available for governesses to follow, and many were written especially for the teaching of young girls, so the subjects covered were the ones suitable for becoming a feminine genteel wife and mother. John Grieg's 1816 work 'The Young Ladies' New Guide to Arithmetic' shows how maths problems were adapted for the potential running of a household:

> 'My household expenses stand me in 203 Guineas per annum, how much is that per week and per day? Answer: 4l. 4s. per week and 12s per day.'[23]

A distinct lack of teacher training and a curriculum to follow meant the governess used her own educational experience to decide herself what and how to teach her pupils. Instructing the accomplishments was less hassle and many governesses stuck with these alongside some reading, writing and arithmetic. But others who had been lucky enough to receive a more academic education themselves worked at expanding the minds of their young charges with natural history, etymology, grammar, French, German and Latin, linking together subjects such as botany, science and gardening to give her pupils a more rounded insight.

S. F Ridout agreed. In her book *Letters to a Young Governess on the Principles of Education*, she advised that girls should learn Latin to increase their knowledge of grammar and the meaning of words in science. Anthony F. Thompson disagreed, opining in his book *The English Schoolroom* that Greek was the best language for a lady to study as she could then read the Gospels in their original language, thus keeping the young lady's ambitions firmly in the place of wife and mother-to-be.[24]

As well as attempting to teach an intellectually stimulating curriculum to young girls and boys, the governess was required to supervise her charges at games, horse riding and gardening. Up until the age of 13, girls were encouraged to run in the garden, trundle hoops, play catch and hide and seek, but the onset of puberty was when governess used this time to instruct her girls on deportment, elocution and dancing.

Why Become a Governess?

Middle class ladies did not *choose* to become governesses. If, for some reason, a well-educated and unmarried lady found herself without a family income to support her (maybe her father gambled away the money or maybe she was an orphan brought up by an unwilling Aunt, as in the case of Jane Eyre), she turned to governessing as a respectable way of earning an income. This happened frequently in an era where fortunes fluctuated dramatically.

Economic expansion of Britain in the nineteenth century meant that more and more men were willing to borrow money to put into their businesses or invest in other building projects or business ventures. These didn't always make a profit leaving many men in debt and unable to support the family. Others suffered from gambling and alcohol addictions, spending all their extra income and even putting their houses up as collateral. At the same time, the general health of the public was still poor, the diet was quite unhealthy, pipe and cigar smoking were common and modern medicine was in its infancy, meaning many men died early of strokes and heart disease, leaving their wives and children to fend for themselves.[25]

Middle class women weren't allowed to undertake hard work, but they were allowed to sew and teach as these were seen as respectable and genteel jobs. The role of the governess commanded a higher salary than the role of the seamstress. Despite this, for daughters of civil servants, army and navy officers and clergymen, the role of the governess was still seen as a step down on the social scale.

The governess was frequently viewed with pity as the undertaking of the role clearly showed she came from an educated background but had no means of supporting herself. She was seen as too proud to accept help from her distant family and friends as a paid companion. Crucially, she hadn't managed to snare a wealthy husband to support her and her family, meaning she was failing in her duty as a Victorian woman. To become a governess was seen as the last option, especially in a society which only advocated education for women on a surface level. Despite this, many young women swallowed their pride, lifted their chins and set about finding work.

How the Governess Secured a Job

There was no conventional procedure for finding work as a governess. Some women had family and friends who could introduce them to someone they knew who needed a governess. Others had to advertise their services in newspapers, at the same time advertising their own dire situation. Occasionally, they could respond to newspaper advertisements or apply via agencies. Either way, they had to endure intrusive questioning about their past, either in a face-to-face interview or more often than not through written correspondence.[26] Once a position was secure, she had to leave her home, move in with a new household many miles away, fit in with their way of life, and sort out the education of the children of different ages, ability and sex, all on her own. She needed an abundance of energy and enthusiasm, a thick skin and a huge smile. Bearing in mind she probably wasn't the first governess through the doors, she had to first test the ability of the children to know where to start from. Unfortunately, it wasn't unusual for the mistress of the household to undermine the governess in her teaching methods and discipline and so the governess had to carefully negotiate her way through the child's prior education as discretely as possible.

She was an isolated figure, too, with only her charges or servants for company. In other female professions, such as nursing, teaching or charity work, the women all worked together and supported each other with advice and words of encouragement. They also benefited from the latest government reforms in the workplace. As a lone employee who was not quite family and not quite a servant, the governess had to make her own decisions and then bear out the consequences. The parents of her charges generally expected her to cope on her own.

There was fierce competition for decent governess roles in wealthy households and so many governesses accepted employment from middle income households such as farmers, merchants, shop owners, industrialists and army officers.[27] These employers certainly got their money's worth. Although the governess was still required to instruct the children in the afore mentioned way, after lessons she was expected to entertain the children, supervise their mealtimes and put the children to bed, thus blurring the line between governess and nurse or nanny. A governess could also be expected to chaperone the older girls whilst shopping and at social functions as well as support her girls in piano playing and singing at such gatherings. Here, she endured the scrutiny of high society. It wasn't just her clothes and deportment which were analysed and gossiped about, but her expertise as a teacher too.

Another particular bugbear of governesses was the expectation she would mend the children's clothes merely because she held good embroidery skills and was teaching the girls how to sew, knit and embroider. This undertaking of menial tasks undermined the role of the governess as the work of a seamstress was seen by society as a lower, more pitied role which no governess wanted to be cast into. It also lowered her status in the eyes of the servants who could use this to avoid serving her. Governesses rightly felt they had worked hard for their education and deserved due respect. But the governess was usually the last employee to be added to a middle-class household and many a mistress expected to get her money's worth. At the end of the day, the lady of the house had the final say in what the governess did or didn't do outside of lesson time and sometimes within. In all households, the governess's time was never really her own.

The Governess in Victorian Literature

The fascinating figure of the governess has populated English Literature for nearly two hundred years, from Jane Eyre through Becky Sharpe to Maria Von Trapp. The enticing story of an educated and accomplished lady fallen on hard times and forced to undertake paid work in a household where she is not quite a servant but not quite a member of the family is as enduring as ever and still entertains modern romance readers today.

Friendless and unprotected, the governess of literature has to fend for herself whilst fending off amorous employers. Snobbish, local ladies belittle her whilst jealously guarding their own precarious social position. She's employed to look after other people's children but is childless herself. She's genteel and needs to dress appropriately and elegantly but doesn't quite earn the money to do so. She is a status symbol of the family she works for but is still poor herself.

Alongside this, the governess is accused of not being academically rigorous or enthusiastic in the role. This is ironic given that women's education was basic and if a woman wanted to know more, she was deemed 'unnatural'. In Oscar Wilde's *The Importance of Being Earnest*, Lady Bracknell sums up the governess Miss Prism as 'a female of repellent aspect, remotely connected with education.'[28]

Unfortunately, for many Victorian governesses there was no fictionised happy ending. Very few were able to declare 'Reader, I married him.'[29] Once her male charges had left for school and her female charges were married, the governess's role became obsolete, and she was rarely kept on. If she was unlucky enough not to find a spouse during her tenure, it was time to advertise her services, move into another household and take charge of a new set of young minds once again.

Chapter Six

The World of Work

> 'A person who has not done one-half his day's work by
> ten o'clock runs a chance of leaving the other half undone.'
>
> *Wuthering Heights*[1]

Work Realities for the Lower Classes

In a harsh, urban world, the working class sought to create their own communities. Urban cities afforded anonymity, which was great for the criminal classes, but could seem bleak and lonely for those used to village community life and social contact. Friendships were formed on the basis of shared interests, family and God being two of the most important and fellow church or chapel goers, pub dwellers and work colleagues forged relationships over tea or beer, shared sorrow and joy and celebrated and commiserated together.

In the Victorian era, it seems on one hand that the working classes were looked down upon and excluded from public life; they couldn't vote and had very little say in public and societal matters, but on the other hand, many working class Victorians knew their position in society and were happy to keep it that way.[2] The working classes resisted the separation of work and family life where possible. To them, work was their life and always had been. Many parents discouraged their children's education for that reason; they felt it would lead to their child having ideas above their station and that they would become dissatisfied with their allocated position.

It seems that the working-class people accepted what happened to them and that existence was a depressing struggle for everyone, but this is not necessarily true. A belief in God meant that there was a certain acceptance of death, and happiness was there in the next life whilst this life was to be endured. Most went about their business uncomplaining about their poverty although many were bewildered as by what they were expected to do about it. The majority of the lower classes just wanted to keep free from sin and debt.[3] But without a social security system other than the dreaded workhouse, keeping free from debt could only happen with constant employment.

Victorian Work

The Victorians held an intense work ethic. With an Empire to run and peace to sustain, Victorians worked almost around the clock. But just like knowing their place within their class, Victorians continued to know their place within their jobs too.

Whatever the job or career, nearly all Victorian work involved heavy labour or extensive exercise of some sort[4], even if it was just walking several miles to work. Whether in a factory or field, working class men and women worked on average a 10-hour day plus the time it took to walk to work and back, and at the beginning of the era, this was six days a week. Even on Sundays, folk were expected to walk to church, and the women still had the cooking, cleaning and washing to do. The women who remained at home certainly had their weeks filled with intense physical labour as they kneaded bread, hand washed clothes, scrubbed floors, fetched water, milked, dug the garden, walked to market and so forth.

Men's Work

Generally, men fitted into one of five classifications for work. Manual work, where the hands were used and education wasn't required, made up most of the jobs of the working class for both men and women. Unskilled manual workers were the lowest paid and these included all labourers who were needed everywhere. Urban labouring involved digging, carrying and pushing trucks as they laid new roads and railway tracks. They were needed to dig out the foundations for houses, the tunnels for the new sewer pipes and later on, the London underground. Dock labourers unloaded and loaded ships of all the merchant goods pouring in and out of the country. Agricultural labourers ploughed the fields, sowed the seeds, weeded the soils and later dug up the crops. They also dug ditches for drainage and roads for ease of access. Some labourers specialised in brick laying, tiling and plumbing, essentially moving them up to lower skilled manual workers.

Lower skilled manual workers referred to those who needed to learn a few skills in order to do their job in a factory, a workshop or a mine. Jobs in manufacturing included making soap and tallow for candles, making rope, making leather in the tanneries, making boots and shoes, making brushes and making metal objects, paints and other chemicals. The working-class men who were able to receive a decent education and undertake an apprenticeship with a good master who trained him properly, was able to earn more money and join the ranks of the higher skilled manual workers. These included blacksmiths, fishermen, plasters, farmers and stone masons.[5]

In *Great Expectations*, Joe the blacksmith, who is a higher skilled manual worker, is very proud to take on Pip as his apprentice. Pip is someone Joe can teach all his skills to, and this is seen as an ambitious job for Pip who is an orphan and mostly uneducated. Pip wants to continue his reading and writing studies though and hates the manual labour of the forge.

'Well then, understand once for all that I never shall or can be comfortable – or anything but miserable – there, Biddy! – unless I can lead a very different sort of life from the one I lead now.'[6]

When Pip learns he has a benefactor, enabling him to finish his education and have a source of unearned income instead, Pip leaves the forge without a backward glance.

Men moved into more non manual work as the century progressed and mechanisation took over. This was particularly the case with the agricultural labourers who moved into lower skilled factory work instead, where they found better paid, regular work indoors in the warm. Either way, manual work was sweaty, dirty and wearing on the skin, muscles and joints. It was easy to spot a manual worker by the scars, red marks and wrinkles to their faces and bodies, and the ingrained dirt in their skin and nails.

For those who aspired to belong to the middle class, then a move into non manual work was required. Clerks, salesmen, bankers, architects, accountants, insurance brokers, chemists and authors were classed as lower skilled non manual workers whilst lawyers, doctors and higher managers made up the professional class of highly skilled and educated non manual workers.[7]

Middle Class Men's Work

One of the biggest sectors of work for middle class men was in trade, that is those who traded in goods for sale. According to the writer Daniel Defoe,[8] a tradesman held different meanings during the eighteenth century, depending upon where he lived in Britain. In northern Britain and Ireland, tradesman meant a mechanic such as a blacksmith, a carpenter, a shoemaker and so forth. In the South of England and London in particular, he stated that a tradesman was a shopkeeper who did not make the goods he sold, including tobacconists, haberdashers, milliners, booksellers, drapers and grocers. Alongside tradesmen, merchants were people who imported the foreign goods from the Empire and then sold them to wholesalers who sold them onto shop and market traders. Warehouse keepers stocked British goods made by artists and manufactories which were then sold to merchants who exported them abroad and back to the Empire. There was a lot of money to be made in trade and as the upper classes deemed it beneath them to deal in the buying and selling of goods, it left the business wide open for the newly educated middle class, leading to 'self-made' wealthy businessmen who accumulated their wealth themselves through their hard work and speculations rather than inheriting it or they may have inherited a small amount of money which they invested wisely leading to more wealth.

Middle class men could also vote and so many took an interest in local politics and became town councillors or poor law guardians.[9] There were those who sat on the School Boards or joined societies such as the society for the for the suppression of vice, which worked to ban dances such as the 'can-can'. Here, they were able to wield some power and have some say in public life, just like the nobility.

An ideal first job for a young, lower middle-class man was that of a clerk. Numerous clerks were needed in every business to write up important documents such as contracts and invoices, and to then make several copies of these. The clerk needed to have beautiful handwriting, an eye for detail, patience and good levels of literacy and numeracy. Different clerks were asked to carry out other duties depending upon the type of business, but their main job was to write.[10]

Although being a clerk may seem an easier job than one involving manual labour, he still had to walk to work and home again, and in the Victorian era, around three miles was seen as reasonable as clerks did not earn enough money to pay for a cab or the later horse drawn buses and trams. A clerk was at work from eight o'clock in the morning until 7 o'clock at night, working by candlelight or gas light, sat on high wooden stools at wooden benches. These eventually caused back pain and curvature of the spine. The large rooms which housed clerks usually only had one fireplace so how warm a clerk kept depended upon how far away from the fire he sat, and it was very difficult to write with cold hands.

Gentlemen's Work

For a noble or landed gentleman, work involved running his estate and looking after his tenants. Whilst there were definitely some lazy estate owners who caused misery for their tenants, there were also the Gentlemen who worked tirelessly to provide an estate which made a profit, housed and fed the employees adequately and shored up against future famine and disaster.

A gentleman's day could be more varied than that of an employee and could start and end when it suited him. His tasks involved riding out on horseback to check on the land and the tenants and organising repairs to houses, fences and so forth and working with his Estate Manager to ensure the smooth running of the farms and fields. He could also be required to help out in times of need such as during the lambing season.

A large chunk of time was spent in his study instructing his clerk or secretary, balancing the books and checking and signing letters. Often, he would travel to the nearest city or town to meet with his bank manager and check on his investments. Whilst in town, it was then usual to meet up with his peers at a Gentleman's Club for drinks and dinner and games of cards. Although this was a chance to relax, it was also an opportunity to network and find out the latest gossip about companies, business investments, and societal events. In later years, the music hall and the theatre were favoured by gentlemen who were in town without their wives. The unmarried gentleman was expected to attend balls, dinners and garden parties as a way of meeting a future wife. All gentlemen were expected to socialise one way or another with their neighbours as eventually they would be looking to marry off sons and daughters and what better match than with a family who owned the adjacent land, thus insuring the wealth and status for another generation.

Many landed gentry acted as Justices of the Peace (JPs) where they helped to maintain law and order on their land and in their local village or town. Others sat on charity boards or school or hospital boards and spent time in meetings for these or visiting institutions or attending fundraising events. However, most of this work was left to the lady of the household who had some very specific duties to fulfil.

Upper-class Women's Work

Newly married aristocratic ladies were very busy. Not only did they have to get to know the servants and check the household was being run effectively but they were also required to call upon their neighbours and hold social events so they could all get to know one another. She was also under pressure to provide a first child.

Once a mother, a lady's life did not change much. She had her servants to cook, clean and do the laundry and a nanny, nurse and governess to look after the children. She was left to make sure everyone was doing their allotted task to the correct standard, leaving her plenty of social time which was where the lady of the house's work really began.

Between them, upper class ladies arranged the social lives of their husbands and children and each other. They controlled who was called upon, who was invited to balls and parties and who was to be acknowledged in town. In the world of shopping, afternoon tea, parks and calling, these ladies set the rules for behaviour, fashion and topics of conversation. They were the upholders of etiquette, a code of conduct families engaged with if they wanted to be part of polite society, and they also set an example to the lower classes through their manners, speech and dress.[11]

No more was this apparent than in the attendance to church every Sunday. It was the lady's responsibility to get the family to church on time and in appropriate clothing denoting their rank but also their respect for the church and God. The family sat in the pew at the front of the church, not only to denote their rank but also so they could set an example to the rest of the congregation on how to sit, pay attention and not fidget during the hymns and sermons.

Once a week attendance to church was enough for etiquette's sake but the lady then involved herself with the church on a social scale. She would involve herself and the children in church fundraising events such as fetes and afternoon teas, and also Christmas carol services, Easter celebrations, harvest home. She may also have made it her business to attend the weddings, christenings and funerals of the tenants on the estate. Visiting the tenants with gifts of food and clothing either in times of need or in times of celebration was also part of her role. A new baby called for extra blankets and clothing, and the lady often passed on items her own children had no need of anymore. A tenant recovering from an accident needed extra bread, fuel and medicine which the lady would provide. Ideally, it was her job to know what was happening, where it was happening and to whom, so she could act accordingly.

Charity work provided an extension of this nurturing role a woman had to undertake but it was normally in a supervisory capacity. She would be a Board member of a hospital or school or advise a charity on how they should spend their hard won money. She may have inspected school rooms, workhouses and hospitals. Her connections in polite society led to fundraising dinners or garden parties. Charity work gave many ladies a chance to escape the house and use their intelligence, wit and organisational skills. It showcased their personalities as individuals as many chose charities, they felt a connection with. They had a chance to exercise some power and make some careful decisions that actually had an effect on other's lives, giving a sense of achievement and even fulfilment. And what better way to woo other members of polite society onto the side of a charitable cause than by holding high class social events at home, where the food, drink and entertainment were all top notch. The house itself had to reflect the wealth and status of the husband but it was the lady's job to get it all in place.

Although not conventionally employed, the lady of the house still had a lot of work to do and she held a lot of responsibility. Her payment was a nice house, lovely clothes, quality food and if she was lucky, a decent, morally upright husband.

Working Class Women

It was unusual for a working-class woman to not have to work to maintain a decent standard of living and so nearly all working-class women worked at some job or another. Common jobs included labouring in factories, working as a domestic servant in richer households or working in the family business. Women who needed to work from home took in 'piece work' where they hand finished garments or shoes for local factories, or they took in laundry for others or if the husband or children were street sellers, they helped with the preparation of goods to sell on the streets.

Women were always paid lower wages than men despite working the same long hours and shift pattern. In factories, men carried out the higher skilled jobs of cleaning and tuning the machines and supervising the workers whereas the women only worked at the machines, so women's wages merely supplemented the male wage and stopped the family from falling into poverty. It is very difficult for historians to determine exactly what women did when working from home because the early Victorian census returns often have a blank space next to the woman's name under the occupation column because working from home didn't count.[12]

Whether in a factory or a field, the working day for women was a long one and there was very little part time work available. In 1844, further Factory Acts were passed, limiting female factory and mill workers to a 12-hour day if over the age of 13. For those under 13, they were allowed to work for only six and a half hours a day and were encouraged to go to school for three hours a day.[13] The 1847 Factory Act limited all female factory and mill workers over the age of 13 to a ten-hour day.[14]

Taking in work at home was the preferred option for many women who had children to look after too but in society's eyes, factory work or domestic service was seen as the modern way to work. Clara Collet, in her 1891 essay 'Women's Work in Leeds' is thankful that 'Leeds has not yet, like East London, become a sink for the deposit of unskilled and good-for-nothing husbands and inefficient women compelled to support themselves and their families; and the factory system has such immense advantages over the domestic system that there is good ground for hoping that East London will either lose its clothing trade entirely, or save it by adopting the much more economical factory system.'[15]

As factory work could be better paid, it made more economical sense for the mother to stay at home tending the house and younger children, and not taking in piece work or laundry, and for the older children to work in a factory or as domestic servants. In both jobs, they earned just as much money, and it was regular work and pay the family could count on.

Children's Work

At the end of the eighteenth century, there were two differing philosophies in regards to childhood. The most popular one equated idleness with sin and it was thought that children needed to be kept busy learning and absorbing the right attitudes and beliefs otherwise they would be led into temptation. The upper classes kept their children busy with dreary education involving memory work, repetition and rote learning. For the lower classes, it involved employment from as early age as possible whether paid or unpaid.[16]

The majority of early working-class Victorian children were employed in agriculture where there were plenty of jobs for small people. Children were perfect for pea picking, digging potatoes, hop picking and flax pulling. They scared crows away from crops, they minded the sheep, they chopped wood and collected willow twigs for basket weaving. They helped with milking the cows and feeding the chickens and pigs.

At home, both boys and girls were expected to gather and chop wood for fuel, fetch water from the well or pump, pick berries from hedgerows and work in the garden or allotment weeding and growing vegetables. Older boys and girls looked after their siblings and helped with the housework.[17]

Young boys and girls were also employed in mines where their father worked. Because a miner was paid for how much coal he managed to mine out of the rock and take up to the surface, it made sense for his wife and children to carry the coal back up to the surface for him whilst he carried on with the physical labour. Children also sat in the dark, opening and closing trap doors for ventilation and to let through those pushing the carts of coal. It was very dirty and hot work, but many young boys were happy to go on a and be miners, following in their father's footsteps.[18]

In the urban factories, children were especially useful for crawling under factory machines to pick up fallen pieces of cotton or untangle threads or sweep the floors and so were employed to do these specific jobs which then led onto better jobs when the child grew older. Small and extremely poor boys were sold to chimney sweeps by poor law guardians or desperate parents. Old Georgian and early Victorian houses had twisting, winding chimney flues which used to get clogged up with soot due to their design. Despite the invention of chimney sweeping machines, people did not trust that they cleaned the chimney properly and also knew that a clogged chimney could lead to fires so small children continued to be used to clean them out.[19]

When Victorian children reached 13 years of age, both boys and girls were ready for adult work. If they were lucky, boys could become an apprentice to a master of a trade. These included butchers, bakers, carpenters, tailors, cobblers and apothecaries amongst others. For 5 years they would learn the profession and were then free to practice it as a qualified person. An apprenticeship cost money upfront though and the parents or a relative would have to pay. Sometimes the parish would pay as it was a way of getting someone off the streets or out of a workhouse and into meaningful work.

The only available apprenticeship for a girl was as a milliner. She would learn some basic sewing skills and make shoes and clothes for as long as her eyesight and health held out. It was not continual work as the need for clothes and shoes fluctuated. A young milliner may have worked all day and all night providing gowns in the run up to a wedding or a new season, but then work could be lax for the next month, making it difficult to budget and manage money.

Girls could earn money in other small jobs, but these were usually insecure professions which depended too much upon the seasons. Many girls became street sellers, selling flowers, food or condiments. But the majority went into service as maids in a large household or straight into factories. Unfortunately, boys could earn more than their sisters and mothers because women were only ever paid half to two-thirds of a male wage. Therefore, it made more sense for the boys to work as soon as possible and in some households, the eldest or only daughter stayed at home to help her mother look after her brothers.

The 1833 Factory Act saw the restriction of working hours for children. Those aged between 9 and 13 years were only allowed to work for 8 hours in any 24-hour period. Those aged 13 to 18 years were restricted to working for 12 hours only.[20] The 1842 Mines Act stopped children under the age of 10 from working down mines. In 1844, another restriction of working hours was introduced where those aged between 9 and 13 could only work for 6 and a half hours a day.[21] In 1864, boys under the age of 10 were banned from being chimney sweeps.[22]

Whilst all this campaigning for shorter working hours made children's lives a little easier, factory and large business owners wanted children educated instead. They argued that they needed young adults who could read, write and do arithmetic to a high standard in order to help businesses keep up with the competition in the rest of the world.

Children who had already been educated at private schools, paid for by their parents, were expected to become clerks, bankers, government workers, Members of Parliament, or go into the military. They weren't encouraged to become the foremen or overseers of factories and mines. So, a skills gap emerged. Business owners required educated men who could be left to run sections of a factory on their own but the only boys who were educated weren't allowed to work in such places. The shortening of working hours coincided with the extension to the state education provision in England and gradually business owners were able to employ the educated men they needed.

By 1851, most children worked in the textile industry, domestic service and farming but the census shows us that 98% of children under the age of 10 years didn't work regularly for wages and 72% of those aged 10-14 years went to school regularly[23] These figures don't include those who did not declare their part time work to the census officials or those who worked at home on domestic chores, and these figures are averages. Across the country, the employment of children varied widely, and the 1851 census shows us that Bedfordshire had the largest proportion of child workers with 50.1% of 10-14 year olds in paid employment whilst at the same time Bedfordshire had one of the highest rates of illiteracy as measured by how many brides and grooms could sign the marriage register with a name or a cross at the time. It seems that the factory owners were right to demand educated skilled adult workers rather than uneducated child workers. Other employers disagreed though. Farmers were very keen for children to start working in agriculture as young as 6 or 7 as they argued it built up the young person's muscles and stamina ready for labouring later on. Very young children were also employed in the lace making and straw plaiting industries as it was light work but required quick, skilled and nimble fingers which needed training from a young age.[24]

Household Management

The life and work of a middle-class married woman was completely different. Her job was to keep her family and home together and to provide the moral compass for her family. A middle-class lifestyle was a remarkably busy one and for the woman, this involved multitasking on a grand scale.

A Refuge

At the beginning of the Victorian era, the Evangelical church including the Methodists, championed the home as the place for a family to be, rather than the gentlemen's clubs, gambling dens and taverns in town which all beckoned to the man of business. A true Christian would embrace the home and family, and religion continued to drive home the message and idealised picture of the wife at the centre of the home providing a calm and loving space where her hard-working husband could unwind after work by reading the paper, having a brandy and a two-course meal then briefly seeing his children before they were removed for bed and he could have his wife all to himself.

On hand to help the mistress of the house was a legion of magazines, books and newspaper articles and it was one such series of twenty-four newspaper columns which led to the well-known Mrs Beeton's Book of Household

Management. Isabella Beeton started writing these aged just 23years old before they were gathered together and published in book form in 1861. The opening paragraph sets out the mission of the middle class married woman:

> 'As with the Commander of an army, or the leader of any enterprise, so is it with the mistress of the house.'[25]

Isabella threw down the gauntlet and challenged anyone to disagree with her view that the mistress of the house was not only in charge, but the home was something to be conquered and made to behave in an orderly manner. The home and hearth were the mistress's domain, and it was her duty to not only provide a haven for her husband but also the best accomplished and behaved children, the most positively talked about dinner parties and social events, and the most up to date and decorated Victorian home you ever saw. And this could only be achieved if the wife viewed the running of the house as her most important life's work. She goes on: 'The modest virgin, the prudent wife, and the careful matron, are much more serviceable in life than petticoated philosophers, blustering heroines or virago queens. She who makes her husband and her children happy, who reclaims the one from vice and trains up the other to virtue, is a much greater character than ladies described in romances, whose whole occupation is to murder mankind with shafts from their quiver, or their eyes.'[26]

Isabella Beeton's book goes on to advise on money management – 'In marketing, that the best articles are the cheapest, may be laid down as a rule'– ladies friendships 'Friendships should not be hastily formed, nor the heart given, at once, to every newcomer', and how a lady may spend her time 'It is right she should give some time to the pleasures of literature, the innocent delights of the garden, and to the improvement of any special abilities for music, painting, and other elegant arts, which she may, happily, posses,'. She also details the roles of the servants and then shares many chapters on meal recipes and different types of food peppered with nuggets of wisdom on how and why foods are preserved and the nutritional differences between white and brown bread. She even lists what to take on a picnic for forty people which is very amusing as it so obviously emulates the gentry's picnics and will require a dozen servants to set it up. But Victorian middleclass housewives loved these types of books, with Isabella Beeton selling 60,000 copies of hers in the first year of publication alone.[27]

Servitude

For the many young girls whose families could not afford to keep them at home, or who did not have the room for them, becoming a domestic servant in a wealthier household was a popular choice of job. The mid-Victorian period saw the biggest increase in servants employed, possibly because the middle classes started taking on as many as they could afford.[28] This meant that the middle-class servant's job description varied depending upon the household which employed them. Aristocratic families employed at a minimum a housekeeper, cook, butler, valet, footmen and maids; how many of the latter depended upon the size of the household and the income.

Maids

Maids of one description or another made up most of the domestic servants throughout the Victorian era. Maids were generally very young as it was a job they did before getting married. There was a definite hierarchy of maids, and it was usual for a thirteen-year-old girl to start at the bottom as a scullery or kitchen maid and then work her way up towards parlour maid or even Housekeeper.

Kitchen and scullery maids kept the kitchen clean, did the washing and drying up, swept the floor and kept the fire going for the cook. Housemaids dusted and swept the rooms, made the beds, carried hot water to where it was required, cleaned the fire grates and made up fires, emptied the chamber pots and slop buckets and cleaned them ready for use again. Laundry maids, employed by wealthier households, washed and dried all the household clothes and linens.

A Parlour maid was employed to wait on the family in the reception rooms, answering the door and showing in visitors, serving meals and afternoon tea, laying and clearing tables, keeping the reception rooms clean and tidy throughout the day. Nursemaids were a little like playmates for the young children and were usually young themselves with experience of looking after siblings. They dressed and undressed the children, bathed them, put them to bed, read them stories, played with them took them and took them on walks. Nursemaids were usually employed by middleclass tradesmen whilst wealthier families employed both a nanny and a nurse.

Only in very wealthy households did the mistress have her own personal maid. An income of £2000 a year necessitated for this. A lady's maid's job was to help her mistress dress and undress, wash and bathe, do her hair and makeup and clean the bedroom. She also repaired and altered her lady's clothes, washed delicate items, prepared beauty lotions and potions and embroidered handkerchiefs and underwear.

The 'maid of all work', the minimum servant a middle class household would employ was the most pitied as she had such a breadth and depth of work to do, from baking pies to scrubbing floors, plucking and roasting chickens to emptying chamber pots, blacking the outside railings, cleaning boots, laying tables, accompanying the daughters on shopping trips, acting as chaperones and so forth. For maids of all work in the countryside, tasks also included feeding the animals and assisting in the dairy.

Male Servants

Only the very wealthy employed male servants as they commanded higher wages and only waited upon the men of the house. The Butler, the highest ranking male servant, announced visitors, served the meals, took charge of the wine cellar and ensured the silver was cleaned properly. He dished out jobs to the footmen below him who dressed in livery after midday and accompanied the household members on shopping trips and to events, standing on the back of the coach as guards, and running errands and delivering messages where needed. Footmen were employed for their height and good looks as they were frequently seen when out and about and when they answered the door to visitors.

A valet was the equivalent of a lady's maid. He dressed, undressed and bathed and shaved his master. He cleaned his clothes and prepared them for wearing. He cleaned shoes, sorted out his ties and accessories, and cut his hair. He took pride in his master's appearance and was faithful and loyal and polite.

For those with less money, a general man servant was a must. This servant could be asked to any number of jobs, but they were usually the dirtier ones such as cleaning the chandeliers and wooden furniture or involved heavy lifting or jobs in the cellar such as drawing beer and moving the casks around or taking in the coal delivery. A man servant could also act as valet to the master and butler when the household was entertaining.

Whilst the use of indoor male servants declined as the century progressed, the use of outdoor male servants rose.[29] The most popular one was the gardener, an accomplished creative who assisted the mistress with the design and planning of the gardens. He was in charge of the greenhouses, conservatories, orangeries and hothouses in which he grew luxurious fruit and vegetables such as cucumbers, melons, pineapples, strawberries and rhubarb and exotic flowers for displays around the house. The under-gardener or odd job man would help with the digging, weeding, clearing of leaves and debris and planting of shrubs. At the very least, households with a garden would have an odd job man to do these jobs and any cleaning of paving and outhouses.

For those households with a carriage and horses, the coachman was the head male servant. He was required to get the horses ready first thing in the morning, and then prepare the carriage for use by airing it and making sure it was clean. He drove the carriage for the household and afterwards he washed and polished it, cleaned the inside and the leather harnesses used on the horses. The grooms looked after the horses. They lived above the stables and fed, watered and groomed the horses, exercised them if they needed it and cleaned out the stalls. In less wealthy households, the groom also did the job of the coachman.

By the end of the century, in affluent areas it became more difficult to recruit servants as due to the different Factory Acts through the century, and an increase in education, young girls in particular were drawn to jobs in shops, offices and factories where the hours were regular and established, Saturday afternoons and all day Sunday were free from work and they had more chance of meeting someone to marry and set up home with. Technological advances such as piped hot water, electric light, carpet sweepers and the telephone reduced the need for so many servants, but servitude still remained the biggest employer of women until after the First World War.[30]

Chapter Seven

Money

> "'And we mean to treat you all,' added Lydia,
> 'but you must lend us the money, for we have
> just spent ours at the shop out there.'"[1]
>
> *Pride and Prejudice*

Pounds, Shillings and Pence

Victorian money came in the denominations of pounds, shillings and pence and mostly in coin form. One shilling (1s) equalled 12d and there were 20 shillings in a pound and so each £1 contained 240 pence or d.

The pound symbol - £ - had developed over the years from the L for the Latin word Libra meaning pound of money. Shilling -S - comes from the Latin for solid coin and penny (d) comes from the Latin word denarius meaning containing ten. The Normans standardised 20 shillings to the pound and 12 denarii to 1 shilling. 240 silver pennies literally weighed 1 pound.[2]

So, if an item cost 3 pounds, 6 shillings and four pence it would be spoken as three pound six and four and written as £3 6s 4d or in shorthand 3/6/4.

Amounts in Coins

£1 was available as a note and as a coin known as a sovereign. A shilling was also known as a bob. A 2s coin was known as a florin, or a 2-bob bit. A half a crown coin was worth 2s and 6d (1/8 of a £) whilst a crown was worth 5 shillings (1/4 of a £). Half a sovereign equalled 10 shillings or 120d. A sovereign (£1) equalled 240d or 80 thrupenny bits or 40 sixpences or 20 shillings or 10 florins or 8 half-crowns or 4 crowns!

Pennies could be split into quarters called farthings and this was the smallest amount of coin. So, 4 farthings equalled a penny. A 2-farthing coin was known as a half penny bit. A three-penny coin was known as a thrupenny bit and a four-penny coin was known as a groat, joey or a four-penny bit. Six pence were available in a coin called a tanner or a half shilling.

How Did People Carry These Coins?

Both working- and middle-class men and women carried coin purses as they were unlikely to receive notes in any shape or form. Poorer people didn't carry bank notes because they didn't earn enough for this to happen, so if a poorer person was shown to have a bank note or a larger coin such as a sovereign in their pocket, it would be presumed it was stolen. Most people only ever carried a few shillings about their person, but for the men who did carry notes, bill fold leather wallets were used, and these were larger than the ones we have nowadays to accommodate the larger banknotes. For those who couldn't afford coin purses, their money went straight in their pockets.

Once paid a weekly wage, the money was given to the wife to pay the rent, buy food and fuel and anything else that was needed. If there were any coins left over, a thrifty housewife would pop them in a tin on the shelf in the kitchen to keep for emergencies. In households where extra money was likely to go missing (maybe the husband had a drink or gambling problem), then any extra coins were kept under the bed mattress or about the housewife's person.

Banks

Working class people generally didn't use banks because as soon as the money was earned it was spent and there was very little to save. A middle-class man could not marry unless he had a substantial amount of savings in the bank as he would not be accepted by the girl of his choice and her family and so he needed to save what he could by living frugally. The 1860s started the age of savings and investments for those who had the spare cash. By 1861, 645 banks had sprung up over Great Britain, helped along by the Savings Bank Movement, penny banks, friendly societies and Trustee Savings banks. An Act of Parliament in 1863 set up regulation for these banks, ensuring they were trustworthy.[3] Wealthy people used banks to store their assets such as wills, money, jewellery, artwork and so forth.

Building Societies were set up to lend middle class people the money to buy their own properties and so they could own a house with a mortgage. Once the mortgage was paid off, they then owned a property to give to their eldest child or arrange for it to be sold and the money split between several siblings.

How much did people earn at work and what did this money go on?

It is very difficult to suggest in today's money what Victorian money was worth due to the growth and slump of the economy throughout the 60-year Victorian period.

It is better to understand the quality of life and what constituted a good standard of living in the Victorian era, rather than just looking at jobs and income. Looking at whether a family rented a whole house or just a room, had access to piped water or a pump in the street; if they had access to a drain or threw the water down into the street gutter; if a privy was shared with other families or if they had their own, if there was room to cook or did they have to buy in their hot food from the bakehouse or did the landlady cook for them; were there open spaces nearby and did they have access to fresh air; were the streets paved or muddy; what were the conditions of their workplace; did they have room to do their own washing or did they have to send it to a laundress; how many changes of clothing and bedding did they have; how many possessions did they own? All these considerations help to paint a picture of how well a family was living at any point in time.[4]

Historian Jerry White suggests in his book *Mansions of Misery*, published in 2012 that in the early nineteenth century, £1 in old money was the equivalent of £350 in 2012 whereas in the eighteenth century, £1 in old money was equivalent to £440 in 2012[5] showing that when Charles Dickens published *A Christmas Carol* in 1843, Victorians were receiving less goods for the same money than they did forty years previously.

What did the working class spend their money on?

The most important expenditure was rent followed by food. If there was enough money left over then fuel for a fire was purchased and beer for the breadwinner. If there was anything left over after that, then clothes, boots and medicine were usually the next requirement. For most lower working-class people, this was all they could afford, especially when the children were young and not yet working. As Benjamin Seebohm Rowntree stated in his book on York in 1902, 'the wages paid for unskilled labour in York are insufficient to provide food, shelter, and clothing adequate to maintain a family of moderate size in a state of bare physical efficiency.'[6] He goes on to state that the diet of said labourer and family will be less than that received in the workhouse and eloquently describes what it is like to live this way:

'A family living upon the scale allowed for in this estimate must never spend a penny on railway fare or omnibus. They must never go into the country unless they walk. They must never purchase a halfpenny newspaper or spend a penny to buy a ticket for a popular concert. They must write no letters to absent children, for they cannot afford to pay the postage. They must never contribute anything to their church or chapel or give any help to a neighbour which costs them money. They cannot save, nor can they join sick club or Trade Union, because they cannot pay the necessary subscriptions. The children must have no pocket money for dolls, marbles, or sweets. The father must smoke no tobacco and must drink no beer. The mother must never buy any pretty clothes for herself or for her children, the character of the family wardrobe as for the family diet being governed by the regulation, 'Nothing must be bought but that which is absolutely necessary for the maintenance of physical health, and what is bought must be of the plainest and most economical description.' Should a child fall ill, it must be attended by the parish doctor; should it die, it must be buried by the parish. Finally, the wage-earner must never be absent from his work for a single day.

If any of these conditions are broken, the extra expenditure involved is met, and can only be met by limiting the diet; or, in other words, by sacrificing physical efficiency.'[7]

In 1844, the earnings for a senior clerk were around £150 a year, or 58 shillings per week.[8]. This wage was taxed, and the rest was spent on rent, coal, food and clothes as above. However, this senior clerk could afford to keep a maid and a washing woman, donate to church and charity, go out occasionally, keep some money aside for the doctor and put some in the savings bank too.

In *A Christmas Carol*, Bob Cratchit is paid 15 shillings a week despite being Scrooge's only clerk. His wages clearly only stretch to rent, food and fuel. Bob himself does not even own a greatcoat but wears a long white scarf instead over his threadbare clothes. His crippled son, Tiny Tim, will die in the future if his family cannot get him the medicine and nutrition he needs. Bob Cratchit is a typical example of a working-class man in the 1840s, keeping his family upon one wage, and coping with the consequences of not having enough money.[9]

What Did Middle Classes Spend their Money On?

In contrast to Seebohm Rowntree's lower working-class family man who's earnings and station in life are always limited, a professional man of the early

1900s with a £700 a year income could afford to rent a larger house, keep two maids, pay to have the washing done outside the home, light the home with the newly invented electric light, have a cellar stocked with wine, pay life insurance to protect the family should he die and pay to travel by train to work. Once at work, he ate his lunches in local taverns and restaurants, as most businessmen did as this was a way to network and make more business deals with other professionals[10]. So, an amount of income was reinvested into the middle-class lifestyle which the professional man had to uphold. In *Great Expectations*, Pip bemoans his procurement of a boy in boots, effectively a young footman, which Pip feels he has to employ to keep up appearances. 'I had to find him a little to do and a great deal to eat and with both of those horrible requirements he haunted my existence'[11]

Middle class families were also able to save money every month, pay for a private doctor and the medicine he prescribed, and eat a better quality of food leading to better overall health. What was also useful for middle class families was the fact that they could buy goods on credit and pay in a month or two's time. This was handy if more money than budgeted was suddenly needed elsewhere: by the time the bill was due to be paid, the money would have been found.

Credit in Shops and Accounts for Middle- and Upper-Class People

Shop accounts took hold in the Georgian era when coins in small denominations were in short supply and so wealthy people would buy whatever they needed on account and then settle a bill at the end of the month using gold, silver or bank notes. This worked for almost everything needed in life. Accounts would be run up at tailors, milliners, shoemakers and modistes for clothing; a meat account at the local butcher, a grocery account with the local miller or grocer and an account with the local farmer for milk, cheese and eggs took care of food; an account with the local wine merchant or brewer ensured a well-stocked cellar whilst an account with a coal merchant ensured a steady supply of fuel for heating and cooking. Accounts could also be set up at local pubs and gambling dens, making it easy to spend money this way too.[12]

As nearly everything was made bespoke, including furniture, furnishings and carriages, the end of month bills could be large. These accounts were settled monthly, three monthly or yearly by the family accountant. Coins were kept for paying employees such as servants and to purchase the odd item at market or for paying cab or coach drivers for journeys or for overnight stays at inns.

Only people known to be wealthy were allowed credit in shops or accounts with merchants. There were no specific rules for money lending, it was a personal agreement between the seller (creditor) and the consumer (debtor). The consumer would agree to the terms of their repayments and the interest rate and how much debt they could be offered before repayment was due. The seller could offer different terms to different customers depending upon their status. This was negotiated face to face which meant that debtors knew their creditors well and where they lived. It also meant that if a debtor was overdue in his payments to all his creditors, then he had a lot of shops and establishments to avoid.[13]

For the working classes and the desperate who couldn't get credit in shops, the only opportunity left to them was to sell their goods or at least pawn them until such a time when they could take them back.

Pawn Shops

The pawn shop was where people took an item they owned and used it to borrow money from the pawn shop owner against the item. Once the person had the money and the interest, they could go back to the pawn broker and pay back the money, thus retrieving their item.

The person who pawned the item was known as a pledger. They would lay their item on the counter in front of the pawn broker who would examine it and make a pledge of money, considering what the item was worth and whether they thought the loan would be repaid.

Once the pledger had negotiated the loan of money with the pawn broker against their item, two printed tickets were issued with the name of the pawn shop, the date, a description of the item, the amount of the loan and the interest charged. The pawn broker kept one and the pledger kept the other. The pledger's name and address were also kept in a register under the counter alongside the details of the item, loan amount interest amount and date. The item was then put in storage and the pledger had fifteen months to redeem the ticket. If they never returned, the item was put for sale in the pawn shop if it was worth less than ten shillings or put up for public auction if it was worth more.[14]

Many Victorian pawn brokers, second hand goods dealers and money lenders were Jewish as non-conformists were barred from many professions, but money lending was one profession where they were allowed to flourish, mainly because Christians looked down on money lending as immoral. Hence, in *Oliver Twist*, Fagin is repeatedly referred to as the Jew and has a front as a second-hand clothes seller, a typical cultural prejudice from the times. Although not Jewish, Scrooge doesn't see himself as a Christian either and therefore has no qualms being a money lender or about not celebrating Christmas.

Money lenders or usurers lent money to customers for a short amount of time at an agreed rate including high interest. If the repayment wasn't made in time, then the interest rate increased, and physical threats and force could be used to persuade the person to pay. Debts were also bought and sold by money lenders and a new lender could foreclose on the debtor sooner than planned, effectively bankrupting him.

London Poverty

London was full of low paid workers throughout the nineteenth century. The low pay was the main cause of poverty and unskilled people suffered the worst as did people who held a skill possessed by many so there was less demand. Due to no social security or unemployment benefit, workers would undercut each other for any wage at all, leading to mainly women and children being forced into slave labour. The clothing industry was the worst paid of all and women were paid for each garment they made rather than an hourly rate. Most women worked from home whilst caring for children or a sick husband or elderly relatives, working through the night by candlelight.

It was also common to have fluctuations in business. Tailors and seamstresses could be extremely busy making clothes for their wealthy clients during the London 'Season' between April and July but then may not have much work until Christmas. The importing and exporting of goods were affected by poor weather which also put dockers out of work for days at a time. This made it very difficult for low wage workers to save any money for times of needs: they simply could not earn enough. 'Misery was never far away from those who suffered an unplanned stoppage of work: three months or so for a clerk pawning everything substantial he possessed, 3 weeks or so for a bricklayer, 36 hours for a sempstress.'[15] With no sick pay or pension pots, an outbreak of sickness or an accident of any kind could swiftly send a family from comfortable living to the brink of despair.

The government did not assist people in finding new jobs, nor did it pay them unemployment benefit whilst they searched for something new, nor did it help or pay for retraining. Workers could lose their job at any point as no notice period was required and neither were employers required to pay redundancy money. People then had to rely upon family, friends, the church and trade unions for donations of money. Local shopkeepers may have extended their credit for a little while, or the local school may have waived the fee but that was the best people could hope for. If they did not secure an income again soon, then they could be looking at the workhouse or the debtor's prison.

Debtor's Prison

Nearly everyone was in debt of some kind or another at some point throughout the Victorian era. Widowed working- and middle-class women with children could swiftly find themselves in a lot of debt due to a lack of income. Women who were abandoned by men could find the same. Men with large families, whatever their status, could swiftly find themselves unable to pay the bills too.

Tradesmen owed suppliers, publicans owed breweries, employers owed their employees' wages, tailors owed drapers for the cloth and thread, furniture makers owed their timber suppliers and bakers owed their grain suppliers and so forth. However, for a creditor to present a bill too early was thought to be bad manners and showed the creditor to be demanding and greedy. Unfortunately, this allowed some debtors to run up large debts before the creditor realised they could not pay them off. Merchants did protect themselves by pricing their goods to allow for the non-payment of some of their customers, and landlords demanded rent in advance plus references. Other creditors secured an IOU note signed by someone more trustworthy, such as a family member or close friend, so if the debtor could not pay then the signatory paid instead. It was then up to them to get their money back from the debtor.

But for those creditors whose patience was worn thin with trying to procure money and who also had their debts to pay too, they could turn to the law to help them. Debtors' prisons existed to detain those who owed money as long as the claimant (creditor) was happy to set proceedings in motion. This was easy enough to do: a creditor started proceedings by producing an affidavit, a sworn statement in writing, that the debtor owed them money. This went before a judge who would approve or disapprove the application. Once approved, if the application was for over 40 shillings (£2) of debt then the debtor could be arrested and detained in prison with the cost of all this being added to the debtor's bill.[16]

Bail could be set if two separate householders agreed to pay the debt if the debtor then absconded, but of course not everyone had family or friends with money to do this. If this was the case, the debtor stayed in prison until his trial, which could take months.

In the meantime, the creditor had to pay maintenance money to keep the debtor in prison and then further legal costs towards the trial. Some creditors decided to drop the claim at this point as it wasn't always financially worth it. But in most cases, the threat of prison was enough to make most debtors pay up with family or friends either paying the debt or selling the debtors belongings to raise funds. Some cases were dropped once it was seen that the debtor owed so much money to several claimants that there was no hope of getting any money back and other debtors absconded the country before arrest. Occasionally at trial, it was decided that some debtors owed nothing as they had been tricked into signing contracts they couldn't read and didn't understand. Others though, were found guilty of being in debt and were imprisoned until the debt could be paid off.

The Case of John Dickens

Charles Dickens's father, John Dickens, was arrested for debt and entered the Marshalsea Debtor's Prison in London in February 1824 when Charles was 12 years old. As the son of a butler and a housekeeper for a wealthy family, John Dickens was treated well when growing up and given a very good education, enabling him to join the Navy Pay Office as a wages clerk. He married Elizabeth, who was also well educated and loved books, dancing and socialising. Her father, Charles Barrow, worked at the Navy Pay Office too but unknown to his family, he spent seven years defrauding the Pay Office before he was found out and he escaped abroad, citing that it was difficult to pay for ten children.[17]

John Dickens enjoyed spending the money he earned on domestic comforts, socialising at the theatre and generally keeping up the appearance of being a gentleman. But where he was moved between Portsmouth and London by the Navy, his income fluctuated and his debts began to build up and the family frequently moved house, moving from larger houses to smaller ones and back again depending upon their income and debts. Charles had fifteen homes in 12 years.[18]. The elder sister Fanny was a talented musician and had a place at the Royal College of Music. John's debts continued to grow, and he paid some off when the threat of arrest became imminent but eventually it was all too much for baker James Karr who was owed £40. He swore an affidavit and John Dickens was arrested by bailiffs. Charles ran all over town trying to beg or borrow money from family and friends to pay off the debt or at least secure bail, but to no avail. Having bailed him out this way many times before, this time his family and friends refused, and John was taken to the Marshalsea.

Inside the Marshalsea

'It was an oblong pile of barrack building, partitioned into squalid houses standing back-to-back, so that there were no back rooms; environed by a narrow paved yard, hemmed in by high walls duly spiked at top. Itself a close and confined prison for debtors, it contained within it a much closer and more confined jail for smugglers. Offenders against the revenue laws, and defaulters to excise or customs who had incurred fines which they were unable to pay, were supposed to be incarcerated behind an iron plated door closing up a second prison, consisting of a strong cell or two ...'[19]

As a gentleman debtor, John lived in the master's part of the new building of the Marshalsea prison which was built on the foundations of the old one. It wasn't a prison block with cells in rows but more a large building made up of sixteen 4-storey back-to-back houses giving a total of 56 rooms, each one approximately 10 feet square with one window. The terraced houses were surrounded by an exercise yard with shared privies and a water pump for drawing water. There was also an alehouse and a chapel.

'We are quiet here; we don't get badgered here; there's no knocker here, sir, to be hammered at by creditors and bring a man's heart into his mouth. Nobody comes here to ask if a man's at home, and to say he'll stand on the door mat till he is. Nobody writes threatening letters about money to this place. It's freedom, sir, it's freedom! I have had to-day's practice at home and abroad, on a march, and aboard ship, and I'll tell you this: I don't know that I have ever pursued it under such quiet circumstances as here this day. Elsewhere, people are restless worried, hurried about, anxious respecting one thing, anxious respecting another. Nothing of the kind here sir. We have done all that – we know the worst of it; we have got to the bottom, we can't fall, and what have we found? and what have we found? Peace. That's the word for it. Peace.'[20]

So, John didn't do so badly in the Marshalsea debtors prison. He was fed, fairly warm and he was still paid by the Navy Pay Office who seemed to be unaware of where he was. He was also away from his noisy household; that was until Elizabeth and Charles sold all their worldly goods to help pay the debt and were left living in two cold, empty rooms when they were rescued by James Lambert, the Dickens' previous lodger.[21]

James was a manager of a small warehouse where black polish was made and packaged. He suggested Charles worked there and lodged nearby whilst Elizabeth moved into the Marshalsea along with the younger siblings. Fanny was still at the Royal College of Music. Families weren't always allowed to live at the Marshalsea, this was only negotiated if there was enough room and so John and Elizabeth were lucky. In true middle-class style though, their maid of all work lived nearby and turned up at the Marshalsea gates at 8am every day to help Elizabeth run the household.

Eventually, John Dickens used the Insolvent Debtor's Act to draw up a list of creditors and the amounts he owed them. This was then published in the London Gazette and clarified the debts which were then paid off bit by bit by any income John had. John was only allowed to keep £20 worth of cash, clothes and goods, everything else went towards paying the debts including Charles' earnings from the blacking factory and the fairly large sum of money John inherited from his mother when she passed away around the same time.

John Dickens left the prison on 28th May 1824, but his money problems continued for the rest of his life, with Charles helping him out where he could. Charles never spoke to anyone of his father's time in the Marshalsea and it only came out in his work Little Dorrit and the accurate description of the prison.

There was a Victorian institution which was feared worse than the debtor's prison though. For those who were in such tremendous poverty that they were left with nothing, the only place they could turn to for help was the workhouse.

Chapter Eight

Poverty, the Poor Laws and the Workhouse

'Well! You have come here to be educated, and taught a useful trade,' said the red-faced gentleman in the high chair.

'So, you'll begin to pick oakum tomorrow morning at six o'clock,' added the surly one in the white waistcoat.'

Oliver Twist[1]

Victorian England is synonymous with poverty, the labouring poor and the workhouse. Victorian literature is awash with descriptions and images of the poor, their lives and their desperation. As well as Charles Dickens, Henry Mayhew, Elizabeth Gaskell, Charlotte Bronte, Charles Booth and many other wrote prolifically about the poor and paupers. The Victorian era was overseen by the spectre of the workhouse; a severe institution in both building and regime put in place to support the 'new poor law', passed in Parliament in 1834 and not changed until well into the twentieth century.

Before the industrial revolution, 'labouring poor' referred to anyone who worked for a living through great physical effort on land which they did not own. They had a hand-to-mouth existence and often slipped into poverty. Poverty was seen as the condition in which people lived when they had no savings or time to do some extra work to earn extra wages for extra things needed. They only had what they had and if they stopped working, they would have nothing. Poverty was seen as the normal existence for most of the population and it was recognised that in order for rich landowners to have their wealth, their tenants would live by basic means. Therefore, it was generally accepted that the labouring poor would need some financial help during times of restricted income or food due to matters beyond their control such as illness, bad harvests and harsh winters. Women's wages were never enough to support a family. The labouring poor were unable to move to another parish to find work due to Elizabethan settlement laws stating a person needed a signed document from their Parish over seer in order to travel otherwise they would be arrested for vagrancy. The Enclosure Acts of the previous century made it more difficult

Right: Her Majesty Queen Victoria, Empress of India 1877. Photograph of the Royal painted portrait of Queen Victoria that was sent to India to mark her rule as Empress of India. (Digital image courtesy of Getty's Open Content Programme)

Below: William Powell Frith 'A Private View at The Royal Academy 1881'. (Digital image courtesy of Wikimedia Commons)

The Gables, Newcastle upon Tyne c1870s. Home to the Richardson family who owned Elswick Leather Works. (Digital image courtesy of Tyne and Wear Archives and Museums. No known copyright restrictions.)

Cottages at Braunstone, Leicestershire 1880s photographed by Captain George Bankart. (Digital image courtesy of Getty's Open Content Programme)

Above: Birling, Kent 1854-1856 photographed by Lady Caroline Neville. (Digital image courtesy of Getty's Open Content Programme)

Below: Florence Leslie-Melville and Sophia Leslie-Melville in the garden at Roehampton House, London, 1860-1864 photographed by Ronald Leslie-Melville. (Digital image courtesy of Getty's Open Content Programme)

Above: The Drawing Room at Roehampton House, London. (Digital image courtesy of Getty's Open Content Programme)

Below: The Workhouse, Poland Street, Soho: the interior 1809, Coloured aquatint by T. Sunderland after AC Pugin and T Rowlandson. (Digital image courtesy of The Wellcome Collection. Public Domain Mark.)

Right: The Temperance Sweep, John Thomson 1 May 1877. (Digital image courtesy of Getty's Open Content Programme)

Below: Risby School, Suffolk about 1860-1869. (Digital image courtesy of Getty's Open Content Programme)

'Hookey Alf' John Thomson 1 November 1877. Here a labourer is waiting outside a pub in Whitechapel for promised casual work shifting coal. (Digital image courtesy of Getty's Open Content Programme)

Covent Garden Labourers, John Thomson 2 July 1877. (Digital image courtesy of Getty's Open Content Programme)

Above: A dealer in fancy ware, John Thomson 1 May 1877. (Digital image courtesy of Getty's Open Content Programme)

Right: The Street Locksmith, John Thomson 1 December 1877. (Digital image courtesy of Getty's Open Content Programme)

Above: The Water-Cart, John Thomson 1 October 1877. (Digital image courtesy of Getty's Open Content Programme)

Left: Halfpenny Ices, John Thomson 1 August 1877. (Digital image courtesy of Getty's Open Content Programme)

Above: The Cheap Fish of St. Giles's, John Thomson 1 August 1877. (Digital image courtesy of Getty's Open Content Programme)

Below: After Luncheon on the Circuit 1854-1856 by Henry Pollock. (Digital image courtesy of Getty's Open Content Programme)

The Old Clothes of St. Giles, John Thomson 1 June 1877. (Digital image courtesy of Getty's Open Content Programme)

Miss Dobson, John Thomson 1890. (Digital image courtesy of Getty's Open Content Programme)

Right: A Carte-de-Visite of Mrs Grant Thorold by Thomas Richard Williams about 1862-1866. (Digital image courtesy of Getty's Open Content Programme)

Below: Beard Trimming Chart 1884 by WW Bode. (File:Beard trimming chart 1884.jpg. (2020, July 7). *Wikimedia Commons*. Retrieved 16:19, May 22, 2023)

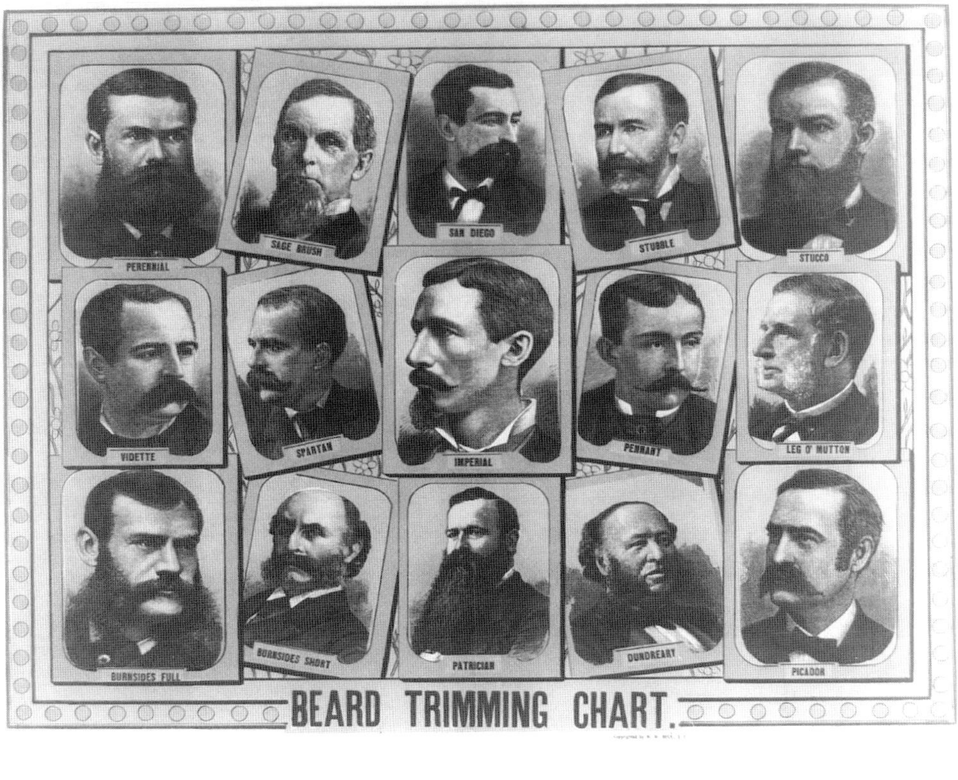

Above: Black Jack, John Thomson 1 August 1877. (Digital image courtesy of Getty's Open Content Programme)

Below: Cockspur Street, London by London Stereoscopic and Photographic Company. Dated between 1860-1880. (Digital image courtesy of Getty's Open Content Programme)

Above: Ballater Station, Aberdeenshire, Scotland. A Model Interior of a Victorian railway saloon carriage. Queen Victoria (left) talks with her daughter, Louise. (© Copyright Nigel Corby and licensed for reuse under creativecommons.org/licenses/by-sa/2.0)

Right: Crystal Palace, Central Knave 1851 by Philip H Delamotte. (Digital image courtesy of Getty's Open Content Programme)

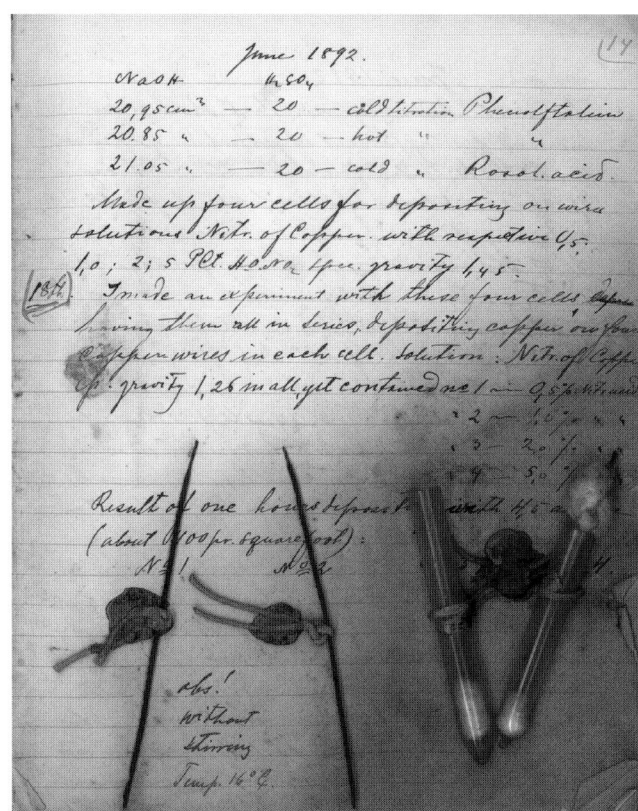

Left: Inventor Joseph Swan's Experiment Journal. (Digital image courtesy of Tyne and Wear Archives and Museums. No known copyright restrictions.)

Below: Inventor Joseph Swan in his Laboratory. (Digital image courtesy of Tyne and Wear Archives and Museums. No known copyright restrictions.)

Above: Clapham Common Industries: Photography on the Common, John Thomson 2 April 1877. (Digital image courtesy of Getty's Open Content Programme)

Right: Street Doctors, John Thomson 2 April 1877. (Digital image courtesy of Getty's Open Content Programme)

Left: Alfred Wilson in Policeman's Uniform from the mid-Victorian period. (Digital image courtesy of East Riding Archives http://www2.eastriding.gov.uk/leisure/archives-family-and-local-history/)

Below: Not Guilty by Abraham Soloman 1859. (Digital image courtesy of Getty's Open Content Programme)

for the rural poor to grow their own food and keep animals for their own use. So, the poor relied upon the landowner and the parish to step in and help them. But it was thought that to give them too much could lead to sin and idleness and so help was provided through bread, fuel, clothing and occasionally help with rent.[2] Every parish also had a poor house of sorts where the elderly and infirm were placed to be looked after by the parish. Workhouses were places where labourers could go to work on public projects and earn wages if they didn't haven't any agricultural work available to them. All of this was funded through rates paid by property owners to parish overseers. Because most parishes had very small populations, the poor house and the workhouse could be one building.

In 1796, all the restrictions on outdoor relief were repealed as parliament feared a revolution like the one France had just been through.[3] In rural England, the tentative introduction of farm machinery showed that labourers could be replaced. The ensuing agricultural riots of machine breaking and rick burning, although tame compared to what was happening in France, were seen as evidence of the labouring poor getting above their station. There was a general consensus in Parliament that farmers were being bankrupted by giving out poor relief as outdoor relief and access to a workhouse was seen as a right by both the labouring poor and their parishes. By the end of the Napoleonic wars in 1815, the high rise in unemployment and the return of disabled and sick soldiers created a burden on a system which was proving to be bitty, expensive and supressing wages. As the threat of revolution had passed along with the agricultural riots, parliament felt it was time to investigate the way poor relief was distributed and to whom.[4]

The 1832 Royal Commission

In 1832, a Royal Commission into the Operation of the Poor Laws was set up by Parliament. Nine commissioners and twenty-six special investigators visited 3,000 of the 15,000 parishes in England and Wales, gathering evidence on what poor relief was offered and how many residents took it up, the poor rates and the amount collected. Questionnaires were also sent to parishes with copious questions on the same concerns. Already, it was apparent that opinion was divided as many were in favour of poor relief as they saw it as Christian charity whilst others thought it should be scrapped altogether and the labouring poor should save money by giving up drinking alcohol and other unthrifty habits.

These thoughts about scrapping poor relief were already common talk amongst the political leaders and the landowners who made up Parliament, helped along by Thomas Malthus's 'First Essay on Population' in 1798. The economist didn't see anything positive in population growth, especially in the labouring class. He predicted that the very poor would bring down the working poor and create an unsustainable labouring poor class of people, reliant upon parishes for unsustainable poor relief.[5]

To avoid this, Malthus believed that population growth should be checked by natural death from war, famine, disease whilst the birth rate should be slowed down by sexual restraint: marriage at a later age and no sex before marriage. He concluded that every individual was responsible for population growth and should restrain themselves in every possible way, so they did not become a burden on the rate payers of the parish. The labouring poor bore the brunt of his displeasure. According to him, they brought all their problems on themselves with their lack of restraint in sex, fun and spending money. They were too idle, careless, drunk and extravagant by far. It seems that Malthus wanted the poor laws abolished altogether and to have the poor left to fend for themselves at the mercy of natural disasters.[6]

It was not only Malthus who seemed to blame the labouring poor for the cost of poor relief. Jeremy Bentham, a political thinker and reformer who died in 1832, helped to make poor law reform more popular with his harsh distinction between the able-bodied pauper who could and should support himself, and the impotent pauper who genuinely needed help. The followers of his ideas were known as Benthamites, of which Edwin Chadwick was one.

Edwin Chadwick, a journalist and administrator, was offered a position as an assistant commissioner and reported his findings in meticulous detail to the commissioners. Assistant commissioners were expected to find two pieces of evidence: that outdoor relief was too expensive and demoralising for the labouring classes and the parish workhouse was ineffective if it was not run properly.

The commission shared his Benthamite beliefs and Chadwick quickly became a commissioner himself. Known for his sharp and tidy mind and his attention to detail, Chadwick had an austere personality which sometimes rendered him to appear inhumane. But he played a very large role in the public health changes throughout the era, and he certainly managed to get backing for his ideas, even if he was didactic in his approach.

A Summary of the 1834 Report

Modern historians tend to agree that the idea for a poor law policy was agreed upon and then the evidence from the commission made to fit the policy rather than the usual case of evidence determining policy.[7] As there was not an official register of births and deaths and the national census was a very basic document compiled to see how many people lived in the country, the government at Whitehall had no idea what local conditions were like up and down the country and relied heavily upon the commissioner's evidence.

The report, written by Nassau Senior and Edwin Chadwick made it clear that the 'natural laws' of family life – where children suffered for the poor conduct of their parents and spouses suffered for the poor conduct of each other – were being interfered with by the parish offering outdoor relief to those in need. The report's main proposal therefore was for all outdoor relief for able-bodied men and their families to be stopped as they were undeserving. No more topping up of the wages with bread or fuel; this was reserved for the deserving old and impotent poor. For the undeserving poor, only help within a workhouse was permittable.

Edwin Chadwick followed Jeremy Bentham's idea of legislation to control whatever was needed to create social harmony. When the commission published its report in 1834, it led to the Poor Law Amendment Act, a radical piece of legislation which was rushed through parliament. The newspapers, which were nearly all against the new poor law, hardly had a chance to protest.[8]

Workhouses pre-1834

Workhouses were originally designed and built to provide a home and workspace for the labouring poor who found it difficult to find regular, paid work due to disability, illness, a mental handicap of some sort or old age. Workhouses were places they got a meal and a bed for the night, and maybe some coins in return for some menial work such as laundry, gardening or stone breaking. The workhouse of Rollesby in Norfolk had its aims on a sign above its door. Dated 1776, it read:

> For the INSTRUCTION of YOUTH
> The ENCOURAGEMENT of INDUSTRY
> The RELIEF of WANT
> The SUPPORT of OLD AGE
> And the COMFORT of
> INFIRMITY and PAIN[9]

Senior and Chadwick's idea for a workhouse was completely different. Firstly, it was to be the sole provider of relief in every union for able-bodied paupers. Secondly, it wasn't to provide a standard of living better than that enjoyed by the lowest class of labourer otherwise no one would want to leave. Thirdly, whole families had to enter the workhouse together or remain homeless.

It was recommended that parishes merged to form Unions so that one big workhouse could be built per union rather than lots of small ones. Every parish was to elect a Guardian to a bord to oversee the running of the workhouse and to check on his parish inmates. The Unions themselves were to be overseen by a committee known as the Central Board of Commissions, or Board for short.

This was an incredibly popular idea, and by 1847, nearly all parishes had joined together to make approximately 646 unions in England and Wales which were to run the contentious poor relief system throughout the whole of the Victorian era.[10]

Inside the Workhouse

The Victorian workhouse came in many shapes and sizes. Many were disused buildings bought by the parish and turned into workhouses, and others were specially built. Despite the different sizes and styles, they were all designed to be forbidding and imposing with high outside walls, windows above head height, locks on the door, gates to keep everyone in, and clocks to keep the monotonous workhouse regime on track. The interiors were all similar with communal dormitories for sleeping in, a communal dining room for eating in, a large kitchen, a bakery, a brewery, an infirmary for the sick, a laundry room, a sewing room, a nursery for the babies, a schoolroom for the children and a garden for growing vegetables or an exercise yard. Some workhouses even kept pigs and chickens. Generally, the workhouses tried to be self-sufficient to keep costs down.

The commissioners of the New Poor Law did want paupers to be fed, clothed and kept warm in a clean building. Afterall, the plan was for them to leave and go back to being self-sufficient members of society. So, the conundrum was how to look after the poor humanely without encouraging entrance into the workhouses and the Board decided upon heavy discipline as the way forward. Afterall, the general consensus was that the poor were in the workhouse due to a lack of self-discipline with money, alcohol, sex and work in the first place and so needed some help to get morally back on track.

Discipline became the focal point of the workhouse system. It was enforced through routine, separation, and work. Men, women and children were all segregated and unable to mix at all, even at mealtimes which were held in silence. The day was split into set times and marked by a tolling bell telling the inmate when it was time to get up, work, eat and sleep. Visitors were rarely allowed, except the local clergyman. Visits and trips outside the workhouse were rarely allowed. To top it off, a complete lack of any material comforts was allowed at all. Not only was tobacco and all alcohol including beer banned, but personal possessions were packed away upon entry too. There was also very little in way of entertainment; no newspapers, books or magazines to read although surprisingly playing cards were allowed.

Inside the workhouse, the décor was deliberately spartan and plain. There was nothing to soften the severe lines of the high empty walls except for notices of rules and regulations and pieces of scripture from the bible. The furniture was plain and basic. Beds, for example, were a plain wooden or metal bedstead with a thin mattress, a pillow and some blankets. Wooden, upright chairs were provided but these were rarely softened by upholstery or cushions, even for the elderly. The dining halls were filled with plain wooden tables with backless benches on which the inmates were squashed together to eat, sometimes with cutlery, sometimes with their fingers, depending on how much the workhouse was looking to keep costs down. Some workhouses provided every inmate with a chamber pot each, in others they had to share. Inmates bathed in a shared bathroom, overseen by the staff.

Sharing was something the inmates had to get used to. They shared sleeping space, they shared eating space, they worked side by side, constantly watched by the guardians. Their loss of privacy and independence was the price the inmate paid for entering the workhouse in the first place.

Entry into the Workhouse

By the time an applicant entered into the workhouse, it's likely they would be extremely poor and possibly malnourished. They usually didn't have any possessions as most people tried selling every item, they owned to keep them out of the workhouse. An interview with a Relieving Officer would determine the applicant's circumstances, and they were usually required to be in dire straits to be considered for a place. The Board of Guardians then reviewed the applicants at their weekly meetings and a place was offered if the family was deemed poor enough.

All inmates (as these unfortunate people were called), were accepted on probation first. If they were sick, they went straight into the Infirmary. If they were healthy, they joined their dormitory straight away. But families were strictly segregated. Husbands and wives, sisters and brothers were all split up into different classifications. Aged or infirm men, aged or infirm women, children under the age of seven, boys aged 7-16, girls aged 7-16, able-bodied women and girls aged 16+ and able-bodied men and boys aged 16+.

Children under the age of 7 stayed with their mother. She could then see her other children once a day or thereabouts depending on the workhouse. Inmates were not allowed to mix unless at allotted times and men and boys all slept together in dormitories, as did the women and girls. Even married couples were split up although the new poor law said the workhouse had to provide provision for married couples to stay together.

All new inmates immediately had to have a bath under the watchful eye of a guardian, and they were treated for lice too. Their clothes were disinfected and packed away with their possessions, ready for when they left. The new inmate then dressed in the regulation workhouse clothing.

Workhouse Clothing

Inmates were issued with identical clothing for purely practical reasons. They were possibly dressed in rags when they entered the workhouse, so they needed to be issued with new clothes which were not only warm but hardwearing too. The clothes were made from a mixture of wool, cotton, linen and calico, all tough fabrics which can withstand physical labour and hot washing temperatures.

Women generally wore a long, shapeless shift dress with an apron over the top. Shawls were worn for warmth and a mop cap to protect the hair. Men wore loose linen shifts and trousers with waistcoats over the top. All inmates wore black, hobnailed boots. The original idea was for inmates to make their own clothes, but it was realised quite early on that many did not possess the skills. Instead, the clothes were made in the local factory.

The Workhouse Routine

In 1835, the Poor Law Commissioners laid out the timings of the workhouse day which all workhouses were expected to follow. Between March and September, inmates rose at 6am, started work at 7am, finished work at 6pm and were in bed by 8pm. In winter, they rose an hour later but still finished work at 6pm.

The inmates were woken in the morning by a tolling bell, and this same bell called the inmates to breakfast, dinner and supper. In between meals, they had to earn their food and bed by working hard at the jobs given to them by the guardians.

Daily Work

Female inmates were expected to run the workhouse, and this consisted of mainly housekeeping duties such as cleaning, cooking, laundry, making and mending clothes. Men had the more arduous tasks of breaking up large stones into rubble which was then sold on for road building; crushing up old animal bones to be made into garden fertiliser; and chopping wood for use as fuel in the workhouse as well as for sale to the general public.

Oakum picking was also a job for both elderly men and women and children and generally hated by everyone. It was where old navy ropes were unwoven and the fibres were teased apart. These fibres were then sold back to the Navy and mixed with tar to make a waterproof sealant for the insides of wooden boats. It was laborious work and caused small paper cuts to the fingers.

Old men worked in the garden tending the vegetable patch. Old women knitted clothes or spun cotton to sell. Able bodied women did the housework, ground barley to feed the pigs and also acted as nurses in the infirmary. As time went on, work within the workhouse began to be designed as a deterrent. The inmates worked long hours in cold and dark rooms stuffing mattresses, breaking stones or walking to turn the millstones to grind flour to make the poor quality workhouse bread.[11]

Food

The daily diet of the workhouse was set by the Board. There were six model diets for the Guardians to choose from which ensured the inmates received adequate nutrition compared to what they would be feeding themselves outside of the workhouse. Afterall, starvation wasn't supposed to be part of the regime in a workhouse, but the food was incredibly basic and unadorned. Breakfast consisted of porridge made with water, or bread and cheese or vegetable broth. Dinner could be beef or mutton stew with bread or suet pudding. Supper was usually bread and cheese. There was water to drink. Small children drank milk. Meat was served two to three times a week and it was always the cheapest cuts. Northern workhouse diets seemed to be based upon potatoes and porridge whereas southern Unions favoured bread and cheese.[12]

Men received around 25% more food than the women and children due to the nature of their work. However, few concessions were made over workhouse food. No allowances were made for decaying teeth, delicate digestion or the fluctuating appetites of the elderly unless a doctor prescribed a certain diet for an inmate. Even then, it was up to the guardians to accept the advice and ensure it was put in place and there was no one to check that this had happened. With the last meagre meal at 6pm, inmates had nothing to eat or drink except water until breakfast the following morning.

How the Workhouse Affected Women

The New Poor Law seemed to affect women disproportionately even though it was mainly concerned about the unemployment status of able-bodied men.

As poor women were inextricably linked to their husbands as dependents and non-wage earners, they had to follow their husband into the workhouse if he chose to apply. At the same time, if the husband refused to go into the workhouse, the wife and children weren't allowed in either, even if it meant homelessness and starvation for them on the outside. For widows or deserted wives, if they applied for help where they lived, settlement laws meant they risked being sent back to the parish of their husband's birth which could be miles away from family and friends. But sometimes it was worth the risk as able-bodied widows could be given outdoor relief so they could continue to work. Unmarried mothers were expected to bear the brunt of the shame and cost of their illegitimate children and there was nothing in place to make the father pay for their children. As it was felt that outdoor relief for unmarried mothers would encourage men to abandon them all the more as they could leave the parish to support their illegitimate children rather than do it themselves, unmarried mothers were also forced into the workhouse whilst the fathers could continue with their lives in the outside. The Poor Law Amendment Act 1844 allowed women to apply to magistrates to sue the father for maintenance, but it was not a straightforward process, and it took a lot of courage for an illiterate woman to start proceedings. The same year, a General Order was issued, finally banning all outdoor relief for able-bodied paupers, whether men, women or children.[13]

Children in the Workhouse

In 1838, nearly half of the workhouse population were children under sixteen.[14] What to do with pauper children and how to treat them in the workhouse proved a headache for the authorities; pauper children couldn't be treated better than their contemporaries on the outside otherwise again, everyone would be looking to offload their starving children to the workhouse. Despite being in the workhouse through no fault of their own, children were treated to the same deterrent scheme as the pauper adults even though they were segregated from their families. Unlike the adults, they also couldn't leave of their own free will and so had to suffer the indignities and injustices of a workhouse regime aimed at adults and designed, above all, for political and economic reasons.

Whilst in the workhouse, the children were expected to be educated. This decision was taken in 1834 when the poor law was designed, but again, some argued that labourers' children on the outside very rarely attended school past the age of five years old as they then started work. Others didn't want labourers' children learning to read and write in case it encouraged them to read pamphlets about political issues and write their own, leading to more agitation and rioting.[15] In the end, these arguments were immaterial because most workhouses economised by having the children taught by other inmates or local teachers who couldn't get work elsewhere. The complete lack of regulation of employment within the workhouse school room and beyond led to immense acts of cruelty, from casual flogging, caning and other beatings to solitary confinement and near starvation diets for insubordinate and usually orphaned children who dared to argue with those in charge and had no one to protect them.

It was this suffering of the children which Charles Dickens had foremost in his mind when he wrote *Oliver Twist* in 1837.

Oliver Twist or 'The Parish Boy's Progress'

'You know you've got no father or mother, and that you were brought up by the parish, don't you?'

'Yes Sir', replied Oliver, weeping bitterly.

'What are you crying for?' inquired the gentleman in the white waistcoat. And to be sure it was very extraordinary. What *could* the boy be crying for?' Oliver Twist[16]

We now know that Dickens lived on Cleveland Street in Fitzrovia, London, on which The Strand Union workhouse also stood. Built in the 1770s and in quite a poor state of disrepair by the time of the new poor law, it's generally agreed it's the workhouse on which Dickens based his one in *Oliver Twist*.[17] Dickens' workhouse symbolises the whole poor law and workhouse system as he saw it: deliberately harsh and deeply unchristian. Oliver Twist himself is starved, beaten, tried for pickpocketing, abducted, shot at and stolen from among other trials during the story.

By the 1860's, the Poor Law Board started to concern itself with what happened to pauper children once they left the workhouse. It was most concerned with girls as it felt they were at risk of becoming unmarried mothers or prostitutes and ending back up in the workhouse or prison. The most obvious training for young girls was as domestic servants and so they were trained in washing clothes and bedding, cleaning, clearing grates, laying fires, mending and altering clothes, peeling and chopping vegetables and washing up. But what they weren't trained in was deportment, speech and manners, leaving them awkward, clumsy, inarticulate and lacking in social graces. Although many workhouse girls did find employment as servants, it was usually as a lower paid one leaving them open to poverty again.

Boys did fare better when they were trained for the Army or semi-skilled manual occupations which required little money to train in such as shoe making and tailoring. Carpentry, window glazing, painting, baking and engineering were also recommended, and boys were frequently found work in factories, stables and as errand boys. The 1834 Poor Law also stopped the apprenticing of young boys, where the workhouse paid up to £10 to have an employer take one of the boys off their hands and train them up in a trade for them. This is the fate of young Oliver who, having dared to ask for more food, '…was ordered into instant confinement; and a bill was next morning pasted on the outside of the gate, offering a reward of five pounds to anybody who would take Oliver Twist off the hands of the parish. In other words, five pounds and Oliver Twist were offered to any man or woman who wanted an apprentice to any trade, business or calling.'[18]

Complaints

Despite the opposition of working class and poor people and their reformers to the workhouse, it survived as an institution because there was no working-class MP in parliament at the time to fight for their cause. John Walter, MP and proprietor of The Times Newspaper did make sure every workhouse scandal was fully covered whilst he was in charge in the early days, and stories were reprinted in local newspapers up and down the country. But generally, complaints from paupers were swept under the carpet despite there being a large pauper voice.[19]

Hundreds of letters, petitions and witness statements all provided evidence of abuse to the central authority on a yearly basis. The main complaints centred around harsh punishments meted out, especially when the inmate was unable to do the hard physical work set by the workhouse. As well as physical punishments such as flogging, the withdrawal of food and solitary confinement in dark cellars, there were threats to keep inmates in the workhouse forever or to have them taken before a magistrate for punishment. Even when Poor Law Guardians visited workhouses for inspection purposes, many inmates were afraid to talk to them in case they were later punished. The Central Board said that inmates were allowed to write to them to complain, but inmates swiftly learnt that complaining to officials marked them out as troublemakers. Their subsequent punishment was never recorded in the punishment books though so difficult to prove. Many brave inmates did continue to complain though, usually by all petitioning together anonymously.

1870 Onwards

Despite the complaints and concerns, the New Poor Law and workhouses continued to be seen as the best way to help the poor. In London, the Metropolitan

Poor Act of 1867 created a common poor fund which all the Unions contributed to and this money was then spent on the building and maintenance of more workhouses. This encouraged parishes to cut their ever-increasing outdoor relief and women who were claiming it were told to send their children to the workhouse whilst they worked and got themselves into a more stable way of life. Single women who needed help were sometimes offered jobs cleaning the workhouse in return for outdoor relief. Where outdoor relief was available, for this had crept back up along with the continuing rise in population, the granting of it was dependent upon the applicant's character and conduct. If they were classed as a moral and upstanding person who had just happened to be unlucky, then help was granted. If, however, they were deemed lazy or unclean, for example, then help was denied. The applicant was judged by a Board with no guidelines, leading to an incredibly unfair system.

In 1871, the Poor Law Policy changed again, and the Poor Law was re-established with cutbacks. The Local Government Board took over the Poor Law Board who had already taken over from the Poor Law Commissioners. Guardians of Unions were reminded that the workhouse was to be the only relief for able bodied single men and women, widows with only one child, unmarried mothers and deserted wives. Deserted women couldn't apply for poor relief for the first few months of their desertion, presumably in case the errant husband or partner returned. Anyone with a child over the age of 13 was told to send them to work and not school.

It was realised that the poor law commissioners had focussed too much on the workhouse as a deterrent rather than a way of helping the poor.[20] The 1834 system was aimed at able bodied men, not the sick, disabled, very young or very old, although Edwin Chadwick's 1832 report did recognise that there were unavoidable reasons for pauperism such as sickness, accident, age, and a lack of suitable housing. He originally recommended that workhouse inmates be housed in separate buildings depending on if they were young, elderly, able bodied or lunatics. This didn't happen for many reasons, not least the haste to get workhouses adapted, built and filled. After 1870, Chadwick's idea was finally put into practice, and workhouse inmates were segregated as he suggested. By this point though, judgements on moral character and the idea of deserving and undeserving poor were fully entrenched in Victorian thinking, and so a scale of comforts were introduced. The most deserving got the most comforts. By this point, the elderly was beginning to be recognised as deserving poor and their rules in the workhouses were relaxed a little. Husbands and wives could now live together and some extra indulgences such as tea and beer were allowed.

From the 1880s politicians and government authorities recognised that unemployment was not voluntary and so work creation schemes were introduced such as lime washing, road cleaning and street building although it was still believed that work was available if only people would go out and seek it. Labour yards were set up within towns and cities to provide work for the unemployed without them entering the workhouse.

In 1900, the food was overhauled and a specially designed cookbook of 50 recipes provided Unions with a choice of provision including fried fish, pasties and Irish Stew and roly poly pudding.[21].

By the end of the century, the workhouse had changed as an institution and residents had access to a better quality of food and entertainment with books, newspapers and the occasional musical concert and outing organised for them and separate accommodation for children was put in place alongside education and training. An improved healthcare system showed that the authorities were beginning to think and act in a more humanitarian way, but it was the overhaul of the water supply and a rethink about the removal of waste which really made a difference to the health of the public towards the end of Queen Victoria's reign.

Chapter Nine

The State of the Water

'Look at the water. Smell it! That's wot we drinks. How do you like it and what do you think of gin, instead?'

Bleak House[1]

The rapid industrialisation of England led to a degree of contamination of the water supply of every town and city across the country. The severity of the contamination depended upon how many people were living in the area and their access to adequate rubbish and waste matter disposal. Whilst the type of waste matter generated during the Victorian era remained relatively unchanged throughout the century, it was the quantities of waste matter and how it was disposed of which caused problems. A lack of connected sewers and infrequent rubbish collections added to the grime pumped out of the chimneys in the industrial towns and cities and eventually it all made its way into the water supply. Although wooden pipes were installed in many towns and cities by the end of the eighteenth century, allowing almost all houses to have a supply of piped water apart from the overcrowded slum areas of the industrial cities, the water itself gradually became more undrinkable as the century progressed.

The Waste Matter Generated by the Victorians

Alongside human waste, horse manure and urine were also the biggest cause of mud. Horses were used for all forms of work and transport throughout the era, and so were constantly on the streets night and day. Other animals such as dairy cattle, chickens and pigs all added to the mud which lined the streets. On market days, when animals were slaughtered in the marketplace ready for sale, blood and offal added to the mud.

No definitive way of clearing rubbish from households existed. Although in the home, servants continued to make as many household products and medicines as possible from scratch, such as blacking for polishing the grates, railings and boots and hair cream using gum arabic, egg whites and a dash of eau de cologne[2], and so there was very little packaging to be disposed of, it was completely normal to hold onto the household waste and then sell it to rubbish collectors who came round with their dust carts, ringing their handbell and calling for rags and bones. This rubbish was taken to local dust yards, private enterprises run for profit.

Once the rubbish was dumped at dust yards, poor women sorted through the waste to categorise it and then sell it on to industry. Pieces of coal were cheaply sold to laundresses or brazier makers, vegetable peelings, animal and fish bones to make fertiliser, broken crockery and oyster shells was used as hardcore for roads, old and worn rags were used in the paper making industry, fat and marrow from meat was sold to soap and glue makers, broken glass was ground down to make emery paper and ash from the fires was used as fertiliser but also mixed with clay to make bricks.[3]

Rural Privies

Before the expansion of the towns and cities, disposing of human waste was quite straight forward. Nearly every house owned some form of outside privy set away from the house. A privy consisted of a small, wooden shed inside which would be a hole dug in the ground. A wooden toilet seat would be raised over it on which a person would sit to go to the toilet. Waste matter fell into the hole in the ground and was left to compost with fibrous material such a straw and leaves. Once the hole was full, it was filled in with soil and left to decompose. The toilet seat and shed were moved over a new hole in a new location.

These privies could be smelly though and so if people kept farm animals such as pigs, the privy was usually put near the animal dwellings, so the smells mingled. For those who didn't have the room to keep moving their privy, they could dig out the hole and move the waste matter onto a nearby compost heap. Either way, the waste matter was broken down and eventually dug back into the ground to fertilise the soil.[4]

Earth Closets

These were common mainly in the countryside as families needed a lot of soil to make an earth closet work. It was similar to a privy, but waste matter landed in a bucket with a layer of soil in the bottom. A lever was then pulled and some soil from a tank above fell down into the bucket, covering the waste. Once the bucket was full, maybe at the end of the day, the bucket of waste and soil was then emptied into a dry area such as a shed where it was turned on a regular basis to break it down and then reused as fertiliser. The tank was refilled with soil ready for the next day. In more built-up areas in

Manchester, pail closets were introduced. Similar to earth closets, the pail of waste matter was put out on a regular basis for the night soil men to collect. Both of these methods were soon discovered to be a cleaner way of disposing of waste matter. Certain areas such as Rochdale near Manchester adopted earth closets as a matter of course, reducing the excess death rate from 27% in 1870 to 21% in 1878.[5]

Toilet Paper

As part of the thrifty mentality, people used whatever paper they could lay their hands on to clean themselves up. Specially made toilet paper only started to be produced towards the end of the century. Until then, old newspapers, envelopes, pamphlets, and advertisements all made useful toilet paper. These were cut neatly into squares, threaded onto string and hung on a hook by the privy, easily pulled off with one hand when needed. Actual readymade toilet paper eventually became widespread in 1880 when the British Perforated Paper Company began trading in medicated toilet paper not unlike very thin tracing paper. The company endeavoured to make their toilet paper an essential household item as knowledge of germs spread throughout the medical society and the press towards the end of the century.

Chamber Pots

At night, because venturing out to the privy in the dark could be cold and unpleasant, everyone had their own chamber pot in their bedroom to use for the toilet instead, and these would be set behind a screen for privacy. Chamber pots were large, round, and squat earthenware pots not unlike a modern casserole dish. Glazed inside and out for easy cleaning, they had one handle to the side and a lid to cover the contents. A chamber pot was a basic household essential which everyone grew up with and everyone used. In the morning, once up and dressed, the women of the house (if they didn't have servants) would have the job of emptying the pots in the privy and then scrubbing them out before replacing them back in the bedrooms.

Cess pools, chamber pots and fairly primitive privies were just something everyone had to put up with. The outdoor privies were initially set away from the house as far as possible, and away from the local water supply of streams and wells and so they were considered safe. It was when the towns and cities started to rapidly expand that privies and the disposal of human waste started to become a public health problem.

Urban Privies

Many of the hastily thrown up houses and slum dwellings did not leave room for a privy per household, especially in the streets of back-to-back dwellings and courts. Communal privies were built instead, with a brick lined cess pool sunk into the ground underneath the toilet seat, into which the waste matter dropped. Cess pools were 'standalone' objects; they were not connected to any type of drain or sewer at first as sewers were used to drain away excess rainwater only. Instead, cess pools were designed so the urine seeped away through the porous bricks and into the ground whilst the faeces and paper stayed put. The cess pools were then emptied out when full, and the waste matter sold to farmers for fertiliser on the outskirts of the town or city. The men who had this enviable task of digging out cess pools were known as night soil men as the cess pools had to be emptied at night due to the disruption and smell.

It took several men to clean out a cess pool. One would be lowered down on a rope alongside some empty buckets. He would then fill these with the night soil, and they'd be hauled back up, taken out to the night soil cart on the street and emptied there before being taken back to the cess pool for refilling. It was a filthy, stinking job and most night soil men had to walk through the house if there wasn't any side or rear access to the backyard. Until 1848, the night soil was taken to local night soil yards to be mixed with used hops bought from the local breweries. This mixture was then spread out to dry until it was ready to use as fertiliser. But gradually, the money night soil men received for selling on the fertiliser became less and less. The more built up the urban areas became, the further they had to ship the fertiliser which added to their costs. Eventually, the night soil men just gave away the fertiliser for free, but they had to make up their deficit somehow and so the cost of having a cess pool cleaned increased, putting this even further out of reach of poorer people.

This was one of the reasons why many people chose not to have their cess pools emptied as often as they should have, as well as the disruption to sleep and the stench. In slum housing in particular, landlords were reluctant to spend this money on cleaning cess pools, leading to an overflow of human waste into the ground and local water courses, and neighbours' cellars. [6]

As builders could design and build internal plumbing as they wished due to a lack of building regulations and so some cess pools were connected to the kitchen sink through a channel or drain to take away dirty washing up water. Sometimes a row of newly built houses was connected to one giant cess pool rather than several smaller ones. Larger houses may have had several small cess pools and privies. The introduction of piped water to houses led to an increase in water usage and wastewater and in wealthier households, flushing toilets were connected to the cess pool too. All of these things contributed to the overloading of an already chaotic and creaky drainage system. Gradually, in the overcrowded cities, the liquid from the leaky cess pools began to make its way into nearby gardens, rivers, streams and wells from where people collected their drinking water or from where street pumps drew the water. Local authorities eventually allowed the connection of sinks and flushing toilets to the sewers instead of cess pools, but all this meant was that the rivers in every town and city soon started to become contaminated by human waste.[7] As the miasma theory of sickness carried in the air still held sway in medical and political circles, burying waste in water was thought to render it harmless.

Drawing Water

Traditionally, country people collected their water from local streams and man-made wells, and urban people collected water from wells sunk through into small streams beneath the streets, public fountains or pumps. Professional water carriers also delivered water into London. Everyone though had to collect their water from somewhere outside their dwelling and carry it back home in a pail of some sort.

As more and more of London's marshland was built on and the small rivers were built over, residents became to rely upon pumps in the street to provide their water. These pumps were installed by various different water companies, and they drew the water from the Thames, or the little rivers which flowed into the Thames. Wealthy households had water piped into a pump in the kitchen and scullery. In better areas, one pump in the street served only a few houses but in the poorer areas, one pump could serve up to twenty houses. This meant queueing at the pump on a regular basis as many water companies only turned the pumps on for a few hours a day. In some areas, the pump was turned on every other day. This intermittent water supply caused poorer people to store their water in large, open cisterns in communal privies which everyone shared, dipping their vessels and hands into it as they collected what they needed. Other households used every tub and bowl they owned to hold the water they needed for up to 48 hours. This rationing of water meant that each household had to carefully work out how much to use for washing, cooking, cleaning, laundry, and drinking and the storing of water caused it to become easily contaminated with dust, soot and flies.

Industrial Fog

The factories, although reusing waste matter, filled the air above towns and cities with thick black smoke and soot. Coupled with the coal fires of every dwelling, it became common for industrial cities to be plagued by fog, no more so than in London. By the 1830s, a 30-mile-wide cloud of smoke hung over the capital city[8]

'It was a September evening and not yet seven o'clock., but the day had been a dreary one and a dense, drizzly fog lay low upon the great city. Mud-coloured clouds drooped sadly over the muddy streets. Down the Strand the lamps were but misty splotches of diffused light which threw a feeble circular glimmer upon the slimy pavement. The yellow glare from the shop-windows streamed out into the steamy, vaporous air and threw a murky, shifting radiance across the crowded thoroughfare.'[9]

The fogs arrived around November and lifted in the spring. They soon became a way of life for city dwellers, despite their blackness and the disruption they caused. The experience of walking through the streets during a fog took on nightmarish proportions as all visibility was severely reduced and the fog stung the eyes. Pedestrians had to rely upon their hearing to get around, listening to coughing and muted conversations as people hurried for the safety of a dwelling. People were frequently robbed during a fog. Others lost their footing on bridges and fell in rivers. Crossing the street was precarious at the best of times due to the amount of traffic, but during a fog, it was dangerous. Carts and carriages could be heard but not seen so it was impossible to judge if a street was clear to cross, resulting in not only pedestrian accidents but traffic collisions too. Those with already weak chests struggled to breathe and incidences of death by pneumonia rose in the winter.

The fogs also cost businesses money, stopping the street sellers from working as no-one could see their goods and they were at risk of being robbed. The boats on the Thames and other rivers were grounded, unable to deliver their goods to the warehouses. The Watermen were unable to ferry their passengers to and fro. The shops had to close early so the workers could get home safely, and besides, women were definitely encouraged to stay indoors during a fog, thus, reducing the potential customer base.

State Intervention

By the 1840s, the government recognised that something needed to be done to clean up the towns and cities across the country. In London, the 1844 Metropolitan Buildings Act established the Metropolitan Buildings Office which held responsibility for the building industry throughout the whole of Metropolitan London. The previous 1774 London Building Act was no longer fit for purpose as London grew at an unprecedented rate with unregulated and unsanitary buildings creating pockets of slums.

The first focus of the Act was to make sure that party walls were thick enough to slow down the spread of fire, a fear still held in all Londoners after the 1666 Great Fire of London. Fire resistant materials were to be used too. But added to the Act was the requirement for all new houses to be built with drains, enclosed privies and a small yard at the rear to allow the circulation of air and light, unless there were windows on all three other sides of the house. Cellars and other small rooms were not to be used for human inhabitation unless they had a fireplace, drain and a window.[10]

At the same time, The Nuisances Removal and Diseases Prevention Acts of 1846 and 1848 were passed. This allowed local authorities to act on anything regarded as a nuisance under the definition of an incredibly filthy and offensive building, ditch, gutter, privy, cesspool or ashpit, and an over-accumulation of manure, dung, offal, filth or refuse.[11] As these nuisances gave off incredibly offensive miasma, they needed to be moved to avoid the spread of disease. If anyone wanted to trade in manure or rubbish, they had to apply for permission to do so.

Local authorities also began to pave streets and walkways so they could be swept clean of debris and filth, but what few drains existed were easily blocked with rubbish, leading to flooding as the rainwater accumulated with nowhere to go.

The Public Health Act 1848

Edwin Chadwick played an important role in the creation of the Public Health Act of 1848. Whilst working as a secretary for the Poor Law Commission and helping to set up the workhouse scheme, he did his own research into sanitary conditions amongst the poor. He found that poor relief was most often claimed by the widows and children of men who had died from an infectious disease. If the health of the poor could be improved, he argued, then the parishes would have less to pay out on poor relief and workhouses. Chadwick identified that by removing all rubbish from houses, streets and the main thoroughfares, supplying clean drinking water for everyone, building adequate drains and sewers and appointing a medical officer for each town, the health of all the people would improve.

The Public Health Act was finally passed after a second outbreak of cholera across the country caused 62,000 deaths as well as economic hardship to the families affected.[12] This Act acknowledged for the first time that the state needed to take responsibility for the welfare of its citizens, especially in a rapidly expanding empire.

Despite Chadwick's best intentions, the Act had its limitations. A lack of funds to support it meant that there was a framework of action but no means of enforcing it. The General Board of Health was set up to oversee the implementation of the Act but again, a lack of funds limited the enforcement. It was step in the right direction though as many towns used the framework to apply for loans to clean up their streets. This was certainly the case in Manchester, the heart of the industrial revolution and the second largest town in Victorian England.

Manchester's growth was due to the cotton industry as whole families moved to the town to work in the new cotton mills. As in London, the town grew but the infrastructure remained basic and soon slum areas grew within the city. Manchester became renowned for its filthy air, water and streets. In 1847, of the 47,000 houses in the town, only a quarter had a piped water supply. Another quarter shared a tap or a pump in the street and the rest drew their water from the nearby wells, streams and rivers.[13]

After the Public Health Act, the Manchester Corporation had to make a start on cleaning up the town. It built reservoirs and aqueducts to collect and flow clean water from the nearby Pennine hills into Manchester. It also put in a series of pipes to carry water around the city. This benefitted the middle-class suburb dwellers but not the factory workers who still had to fetch their water from the street pumps or wells and carry it home through the streets. Plumbed toilets were also allowed in the suburbs but not in the workers houses in the centre of town. They still relied upon communal privies which were emptied into the local rivers. Meanwhile, the factories continued to empty their waste into the rivers.[13]

Victorian Sewer Systems

To build new sewers, a town or city had to apply to parliament for permission. Building sewers took years, even in small towns where everyone agreed with the project. In Sunderland, a town very keen to clean up its streets after its cholera outbreaks, it took from 1851-1860 to get a drainage system and sewer network in place; most of this time was spent waiting for approval from the General Board of Health and for a mortgage to pay for the project.[14]

In London in particular, the Thames eventually became an open sewer where human and animal waste and chemicals rendered it brown and sludgy. Despite the noxious smell emanating from the Thames and the fears over miasma, Parliament still prevaricated over what to do about it. The Metropolitan Board of Works wanted to improve London's sewers but needed the money to do so from Parliament. Eventually, the hottest summer on record in 1858 spurred the Government into action. The above average temperatures lowered the water level of the river, exposing rotting animal carcasses and leaving human and animal excrement and filth from the factories in a stinking tideline on the shore. The politicians in the Houses of Parliament on the bank of the river Thames had to endure the foul stench arising from it and infiltrating their place of work day after day. They soaked the curtains in the houses of parliament in chloride of lime to block the smell, but this had no effect. Unable to concentrate and concerned about the miasma, the Prime Minister was finally convinced to act.[15] A Bill to provide the money needed to build a sewer system was rushed through parliament, taking all of 18 days. Joseph Bazalgette, chief engineer at the Metropolitan Board of Works, was put in charge of the new project.

Bazalgette decided to keep the initial patchwork of drains underneath London but to join them up with an extensive network of sewers, The plan was to flush waste far away from London and dump it in the Thames Estuary to be naturally taken out to sea. To do this, he built 82 miles of new brick lined sewers and 1,100 miles of drains to remove waste immediately from households and the streets. Great pumping stations were built to help with the flow of sewage.[16] Building the brick lined tunnels required thousands of labourers to dig out the tunnels by hand. Their wages rose by 20%, such was the demand for their expertise.

In order for two large intercepting sewer pipes to be built on the north and south banks along the Thames, new stone embankments were built to cover the pipes, effectively narrowing the Thames in certain places and increasing the flow of the river. The embankments also allowed for the metropolitan and district railway to put in a tube line to run across the city.

Although sewage was now collected from London houses, it was still dumped in the Thames. In 1878, the Thames River suffered its biggest ever disaster. A passenger boat, the Princess Alice, carrying day-trippers up and down the Thames collided with a coal carrying ship. 600 passengers were thrown into the Thames and only 130 made it to shore alive. An hour earlier, Bazalgette's sewers had discharged 75 million gallons of raw sewage into the Thames, right where the Princess Alice rapidly sank and many who witnessed the event believed that the victims could not swim in the sludge.[17] Several survivors died soon after, poisoned by the sewage.

This disaster led to the development of sewage treatment plants across Britain, where sewage was collected, chemically treated, processed and reused as fertiliser where possible, with the leftovers loaded onto ships and disposed of in the sea. With the incidences of cholera and typhoid dramatically reduced, by the end of the century the British public had accepted state control over public health and the control of disease.[18]

The improvement in the cleanliness of water was also welcomed to help the Victorians to keep their clothes clean and smart. By the end of the century, it was becoming clearer who could afford to live in a home with clean, hot, piped water and who still fetched theirs cold from a pump in the street.

Chapter Ten

Fashion and Beauty

'I never saw anybody take so long to dress,
and with such little result.'[1]

The Importance of Being Earnest

The beginning of Queen Victoria's reign saw the lavish and colourful styles of Georgian fashions confined to the past along with the wigs, powder and makeup. For women, a more natural style was preferred, with hair parted simply in the middle and drawn back off the face in a chignon and the sort of healthy glow to the skin that can only be achieved by a walk in the countryside. Cosmetics were seen as unsanitary and old-fashioned, and powder was a waste of good rice. The young Queen Victoria was emphatically against make up and instead epitomised the ideal Victorian woman: fresh faced as if in the first flush of love, clear eyed and healthy.[2]

Women's Fashion

Along with hair and makeup styles which were fresh and natural, women's dresses took on a romantic quality with wide necklines, drooping sleeves and bell-shaped skirts which emphasised a small, nipped in waist. This style suited the 20-year-old Queen Victoria, who had her Royal Dressmaker make her a simple ivory silk wedding dress with a short train attached to her waist, a wide scooped neckline and full sleeves. The dress was decorated with orange blossom, and she wore a wreath of artificial orange blossom and a veil made from Honiton lace, emphasising the diminutive Queen's femininity.[3]

Early Victorian clothing helped women to act demurely and to keep them chaste. It must have been very difficult to run around or move with purpose in a corset and several layers of petticoats underneath a large skirt made from yards and yards of fabric gathered into a bodice. These dresses were also expensive garments and so were to be kept as clean and wrinkle free as possible. When Catherine Earnshaw returns to Wuthering Heights after her stay at Thrushcross Grange, she is transformed from the wild savage girl who lost her shoes in the bog on the moor into 'a very dignified person, with brown ringlets falling from the cover of a feathered beaver, and a long cloth habit, which she was obliged to hold up with both hands that she might sail in.'[4]

However, fashion in Victorian England changed swiftly and throughout the 1840s, women were wearing tight fitting dresses with long, pointed sleeves and long bodices in a gothic style. The medieval style chatelaine sporting a bunch of ornaments such as tiny scissors, keys, rings and charms hung from the waist and gloves and leather boots completed the look.[5]. The natural hair and face remained but this style of clothing added to the 'consumptive' pale faced and red cheeked look of tragic heroines from favoured gothic novels such as *Wuthering Heights* and *Frankenstein*.

As the 1840s moved into the 1850s, women's clothing became lighter and brighter due to the new imported Indian cottons and artificial aniline dyes. Skirts grew bigger than ever, the bodices less pointy and round instead with full, pagoda sleeves.[6]. Fashion became fun as evening dresses and ball gowns became very extravagant with skirts ruched up to show off an underskirt in silk and decorated with feathers, bows, flowers, lace and after the Crimean War, Turkish tassels and eastern embroidery in rich oranges, golds, purples and olive green.

The steel wire caged crinoline replaced the layers of petticoats required to create the massive domed shape of the 1850s skirt, affording women more movement and more space in society. There were complaints galore about crinolines: women took up too much room on pavements, in carriages, on omnibuses, at balls and in pews in church, when they weren't being blown over, catching fire or falling off cliffs due to the size of their skirts.

The crinoline remained popular into the 1860s when it then morphed into the crinolette, a smaller wire cage made of half hoops and worn at the back of the dress allowing for large, ruffled trains decorated with tassels, feathers and bows. The bodice became tighter and high necked with detachable collar and cuffs. The trend of wearing shirts with skirts also started up and small jackets were also very fashionable by this point. The 1870s saw lady's gowns become slimmer and simpler in style but with more elaborate adornments in the form of braid, fringe, tassels, buttons and bows. Women's gowns began to match their soft furnishings in the home as the patterned skirt fabric was drawn back and draped in waves over a bustle made of horsehair and straw. The silhouette became narrower and more constrictive but there was more choice than ever of colours, patterns, fabrics and trimmings.[7]

By the 1890s, women could wear dresses with or without trains, bustles, pads or trimmings as long as what they wore was smart and in good taste. However, what they couldn't go without was the corset.

Corset

First adopted in western Europe around the fifteenth century, wearing a corset came to indicate respectability and so going corset less showed an immoral character. Every woman wore one whether she was in prison or the workhouse. A corset supported the wearer's back by preventing stooping, bending and slouching. It was very difficult not to sit or stand upright with perfect posture when wearing a Victorian corset. The stiffer and more upright the wearer, the better were her standards and self-respect. Those who didn't wear a corset would be talked about and presumed to be a prostitute as slouchy posture meant slovenly behaviour and loose morals.

In the early part of the era, corsets were simple structures not unlike the bodice of a dress with only a couple of pieces of boning in the back and a larger piece of boning known as a busk at the front. Wealthier women had their corsets made for them by seamstresses and wore corsets stiffened with whalebone whilst poorer women made their corsets themselves and stiffened them with cane.[8] A corset created a fashionable silhouette and supported the heavy outer garments. A more expensive corset had more panelling and boning so it could be laced tighter at the back, usually by a maid, whilst cheaper corsets had less structure and poorer women wore them laced at the front if they didn't have a maid to help them. In the 1840s, front fastening corsets became widely available for those who were short of money.

A chemise was worn underneath the corset to protect the skin from chafing and to soak up the dirt and sweat from the skin. This light cotton garment with a wide, scooped neck and short sleeves stopped just above the knees and added an extra layer of warmth too. Chemises were easily washed and dried and so could be changed every day to help keep the wearer fresh and the corset clean.

Until the Victorian era, it seems that women didn't wear drawers or knickers at all as there is very little historic evidence for them. Initially, drawers were two tubes of material which covered the top part of the leg and were joined at the waistband but were gusset less between the legs. This allowed easy access for going to the toilet but even so, many women found it an absolute faff and continued to go knicker less. Wearing drawers, which were rather like modern day cotton boxer shorts, was seen as scandalous at first because they looked like men's clothing. But once the crinoline cage became fashionable, women started to wear drawers to protect their modesty should a gust of wind lift their skirts.[9]

British women at the beginning of the nineteenth century had always worn dresses or skirts. It was completely frowned upon for any lady of class to wear men's breeches or trousers and only the very poor girls would do this if they inherited their brother's clothes and worked in a terribly dirty job.

Towards the end of the century, women began to campaign for dress reform and the right to wear trousers, but this didn't really take hold until after the First World War.

So, women had always worn dresses with some sort of corset underneath, undergarments of various styles and stockings (long socks tied with ribbons above the knee), boots and hats if outdoors, cloaks for warmth and to keep out the rain and shawls for extra warmth indoors or outdoors on a dry day. Gloves were always worn outdoors and indoors for formal occasions.

However, the style, fabric and colour of women's clothes determined so much more, and the subtle nuances of fashion determined marital status, wealth and class with the middle and upper classes having a fashionable outfit for every occasion and the poorer working classes having just an outfit.

Ensembles for Every Occasion

Rigid conventions stipulated the 'correct dress' for every occasion. A lot of an upper-class woman's time was taken up with visiting the dress maker to be measured and fitted for new gowns, whereas the middle-class lady's time was taken up with adjusting her gowns herself or instructing her maid on how to do so.

Middle and upper-class men and women were required to change their clothes at least three times a day, from work clothes to dressing for dinner to changing for bed. For men, this was quite straight forward in that they wore a three-piece suit for work, a suit for evening dinner and then night clothes. For horse riding, they had horse riding clothes and for any manual labour they undertook, an old pair of trousers and a simple shirt would do.

For middle- and upper-class women, they had a few more outfits to consider.

Morning Dress

This was the first garment put on when changing out of a nightdress. It was an 'at home' dress – a simple gown with long sleeves, a high neckline and with minimal trimmings. The lady would wear it in the morning to visit the kitchens and chat to the housekeeper and cook, in the garden to collect flowers and herbs, to do light housework and to receive close friends and family members as this was the time for them to call. Sometimes an apron was worn over the top which could then be quickly whisked away should someone call. A morning dress was supposed to be comfortable and easy to move in but they were still structured in the fashion of the time.

Walking Dress

If a lady wished to go for a walk in the morning or afternoon, either with friends or with a gentleman caller, then a walking dress was donned. Again, in the style of the day but slightly shorter at the front so it wasn't stepped on and muddied, and without a train at the back. Walking dresses were fashioned in richer fabrics and colours as they were made to be noticed but they also needed to be warm to cope with the British weather and hats and gloves were made to match.

Afternoon Dress

These were worn to receive visitors at home, or for visiting friends in the afternoon. They had lower necklines than the morning dress and were made from better quality fabrics in richer colours with extra trimmings. The posher the person to be visited, the posher the dress and the jewellery. A short train at the back of the dress signalled that the person had arrived by carriage whereas if a visitor was planning on walking to their destination, a train would get dirty and so a dress without one would be worn instead.

Dinner Dresses

Dinner dresses were more formal than afternoon dresses but not as formal as an evening gown. Dinner dresses touched the floor with a short train, a low neckline to show off jewellery and elbow length sleeves. Made from silk brocade, satin and velvet, they were trimmed with glass and jet beads, lace or flowers and were made to shimmer in the candlelight and flatter the wearer. Dinner dresses were worn for entertaining at home or at dinner parties with friends. Even informal dinner parties amongst family members still called for dinner dresses and expensive jewellery to be worn.

Evening Dresses or Ball Gowns

This would always be the best garment in a lady's wardrobe and always the most fashionable. It wasn't unusual for wealthier ladies to have an array of evening dresses and ball gowns to choose from, all in the latest fashions, depending upon how often they socialised. Evening gowns were worn to theatres and operas and ball gowns for dancing. Matching shoes, gloves and head pieces and bags would be made at the same time as the dress, all in matching or complementary colours and fabrics. A lady's most expensive but appropriate jewellery would be worn too, usually family heirlooms passed down through the generations.

Riding Habits

For those wealthier ladies who kept horses, a smart riding habit was an essential addition to her wardrobe. Fashionable and functional, riding habits, which were essentially a matching dress and jacket, had to withstand dirt, rain, wind and the rigours of horse riding. Therefore, dark colours were more popular as they didn't show the dirt, and fabrics which could be easily cleaned were favoured although the collars and cuffs were always trimmed in velvet. Riding habits were often made by tailors rather than dress makers due to the high level of skill required to construct such a garment.

Underneath the habit, women wore matching trousers and towards the end of the century, these were ditched in favour of knitted tights instead. They wore matching hats but not anything which would protect the head should she take a tumble, leather riding gloves to protect her hands from blisters and flat boots for safety.[10]

Men's Fashion

A man's clothing said just as much about his status as a woman's but the actual garments themselves remained fairly stable in cut and colour throughout the period. Men had always worn breeches or trousers of some sort, shirts, waistcoats, jackets, boots plus hats if outdoors. By the 1830s, Georgian breeches and long boots had already been replaced by the more favourable trousers which were available in all sorts of vivid colours such as yellow ochre, olive green, and fire red and patterns such as checks, plaids and stripes thanks to the new chemical dyes and weaving processes.[11] Neckties, handkerchiefs and braces were all worn in these bright colours and patterns too. Working class men were less able to afford these fashionable clothes and dressed in cotton shirts, waistcoats and trousers in natural browns, creams and greys instead.

As the century wore on, the emphasis was less on a garment's fabric and colour and more on the cut and shape and so middle- and upper-class men's clothing became simplified in style and more sombre in pattern and colour. Sharper and cleaner lines and muted colours became a uniform for the important man of business who had the time and money to spend on this attention to detail.[12]. By the 1860s, the fashionable wealthy man wore trousers, a waistcoat and a frock coat in dark colours set off by a crisp, white shirt. The frock coat, as popularised by Prince Albert, was a knee length coat fitted in at the waist and flaring down to the knees. A single-breasted frock coat was worn for daily business and a double breasted one was donned for formal functions. A top hat and cane topped off the look.[13] Charles Dickens himself dressed very flamboyantly a young man, choosing checked trousers and green coats but by the time he died in 1870, he was wearing the more closely tailored and dark clothing of the wealthier man.

Meanwhile, working class men delighted in wearing brighter coloured clothes as cheaper ready to wear garments became available to buy in shops for the first time.[14] These items weren't cut as cleanly or sharply as tailored clothing but for the working-class man who needed the freedom of movement, it meant he could afford to own several shirts, waistcoats and pairs of trousers rather than just the one suit. Even better, the colours didn't show up the dirt quite so much and the cheaper, lighter weight fabrics were easier to wash and dry. By the end of the century, the checked shirt was the staple of the labourer's wardrobe[15] alongside trousers which reached up to just below the ribcage, keeping the lower back warm whilst bending, stretching and lifting in the fields.

Country fashion allowed for a little more individuality with country squires preferring checks and tweed in shades of brown and grey, but they still wore black or navy for formal occasions. Towards the end of the century, lighter colours came back into fashion for everyone, especially for the summer, with men wearing white, beige and fawn trousers with brightly coloured wool blazers but again, black and navy were worn for formal occasions.

Regardless of income, nearly all men wore underwear for practical reasons. A woollen flannel vest, with or without sleeves, and a pair of long drawers which fastened at the ankles provided a soft, warm base layer which was only ever seen by immediate family so didn't need to be hugely fashionable. This base layer also absorbed sweat and could be easily washed and dried so was frequently changed, keeping the man fresh and clean.

Second Hand Clothing

Despite the advances in spinning and weaving technology, the actual sewing was still done by hand and it was this time and labour which made clothes expensive. Therefore, it made sense to make sure they were made of the best quality fabric, thus adding to the cost and putting new, handmade clothes out of reach of many working-class men and women. This led to a thriving second hand clothing market in every city and large town. Liverpool had Paddy's market, a two-story building packed to the rafters with stalls run by individuals. Here, people could buy individual items or whole outfits although the state of the clothes and how well they'd been laundered varied considerably. Most were clean and ready to wear though. In London, Petticoat Lane served the same purpose, as did Birmingham's Brummagem market and Manchester's Knot Mill Fair. Men in particular happily bought second hand suits for work in town right into the second half of the century[16].

'Then up rose Mrs Cratchit, Cratchit's wife, dressed out but poorly in a twice-turned gown, but brave in ribbons, which are cheap, and make a goodly show for sixpence; and she laid the cloth, assisted by Belinda Cratchit, second of her daughters, also brave in ribbons; while Master Peter Cratchit plunged a fork into the saucepan of potatoes, and getting the corners of his monstrous shirt collar (Bob's private property, conferred upon his son and heir in honour of the day) into his mouth, rejoiced to find himself so gallantly attired, and yearned to show his linen in the fashionable Parks.' *A Christmas Carol*.

Children generally wore hand me down clothes whatever their class with infant boys wearing the same dresses as girls. Children's clothes were expected to be plain and practical so they could withstand the rough and tumble of childhood. As children of wealthier families weren't invited to evening events such as balls and dinner parties, they didn't need many outfits for special occasions either. Older children's clothes were always repurposed for younger siblings, either by the mother, the nanny or even the governess who would make it part of the skills set she taught the daughters. It was only when the children started to be seen out in society that brand new clothes were considered and even then, how many outfits depended upon the affluence of the family. It was still possible for hand me downs to be repurposed effectively.[17]

By the 1870s, the need to buy second hand clothing fell away as the ready to wear market exploded with the invention of the sewing machine. Suddenly, men and women could buy simple, premade clothes in decent fabrics in clean shops with polished wooden counters and mirrors. Town workers started to buy new clothes in darker colours which didn't show up the soot and dirt, especially the clerks who still walked to work and back. The frock coat was gradually replaced by a long, rectangular style coat which could be made ready to wear and clothes for men generally became baggier as it was then easier to make them in a variety of sizes ready to wear. The upper classes however, continued to go to their tailors to be measured and have their clothes handmade to fit, and the very poor continued to buy second hand where possible.[18]

How the Victorians Kept Clean – Washing and Bathing

Having a bath was an expensive and time-consuming business. A tin bath was a costly item to own as it was but filling it with hot water was only for those with the money to spend on fuel and the servants to fetch the water from the pump, heat it in several pans on the range and in the copper and carry it in buckets to the bath upstairs. Once the bath was finished, the water had to be bailed out into buckets, carried back downstairs and disposed of. It was far easier to wash the body all over with small amounts of warm water.

Every middle-class bedroom held a wooden washstand on which sat a bowl, a jug of hot water, a washcloth and a bar of soap. It was normal for a person to begin the day by washing various body parts with the soap and water, emptying the dirty water into the slop pail at the side of the washstand as they went and replacing it with clean water from the jug. A brisk rub dry with a linen towel finished the job. Before bed, Victorians washed their hands and faces and cleaned their teeth, much like we do nowadays.[19]

From the 1870s, indoor plumbing became available for those who could afford it, so it was easier to fetch water and dispose of it, but it still had to be heated on the range or in the copper. As most people rented their houses, the landlord had to foot the bill, and many chose not to until there was a change of tenancy, and he was able to put up the rent to cover the costs.

For the working classes, a quick wash in cold water and a rub with a towel helped to keep them clean. Poorer people who lived in cramp conditions in shared accommodation found washing themselves and their clothes beyond their purses and their energy.

Clothes Maintenance

Despite these basic methods of washing, people remained clean and smelled pleasant as long as they washed their clothes. But if having a bath took effort and energy, even more was needed to complete the weekly wash. Doing the laundry was probably the most loathed of all the chores in the Victorian household as it was hot, smelly, exhausting and inconvenient. It disrupted the normal routine as the range was needed to heat all the hot water and was out of use until the washing was finished.

Monday was the traditional wash day, allowing for the rest of the week to get the clothes dry and ironed. For those families who were able to afford a weekly bath at the weekend, the dirtiest items were put to pre-soak in the used soapy bath water. Once it was time to wash them, the dirty water was bailed out and chucked away and freshly boiled water was added to the tub along with laundry soap. A three-legged dolly, rather like a three legged stool with arms, was used to swish and agitate the clothes in the tub and particularly stubborn stains were scrubbed against a ridged wooden wash board. The dirty water was bailed out and chucked away and fresh boiled water added to the tub to rinse the clothes. This water was bailed out and the clothes put through a wringer or mangle to remove any excess soap or wrung by hand if there wasn't one. The clothes were rinsed again in clean water, and for whites some 'blue' was added to counteract the yellow tinge the laundry soap could leave behind. The clothes were wrung again and then hung to dry.[20]

Some middle-class households could afford for a washer woman to visit the house and do the weekly wash, leaving the mangling, drying and ironing to the servants. For those who did not have room for washing equipment or ready access to water, wash houses were available for women to do the laundry, a bit like a modern-day launderette. Owning a wringer or mangle meant that a woman could hire it out to neighbours, or she could take in their washing and do it for them. This was particularly useful for women who had small children to look after at the same time and they could help too.

Between washes, clothes were brushed down with a clothes brush to remove dust and dirt, particularly men's suits. More complicated garments such as evening gowns and coats were spot cleaned on a regular basis rather than fully washed and dried. As clothes were protected from the body by so many undergarments which were regularly laundered, a full immersion in hot soapy water was not always needed.

It is easy to see how clean, bright white and coloured clothes helped to maintain status between the divisions of classes. Those with less clothes washed them more often, leading to the fading and thinning of fabric. Poor people in shared accommodation who only had the one set of clothes had a dilemma: they either stayed in all day whilst they washed and dried their only set of clothes or they didn't wash them at all and when they were so worn and tatty to be of no use, they bought another second hand set of clothes instead. But, whatever they bought, and however little the clothes cost, Victorians still took pride in their appearance. They still had taste.

Chapter Eleven

Food Glorious Food?

'Please, sir, I want some more.'

Oliver Twist[1]

Nowhere was class more obvious in Victorian England than in the food of the people. The food the Victorians put on their table, if they had one, said everything about their life, from those who indulged in several courses of food per evening to those who could only afford bread and tea once a day. Whilst the poorest survived on potato soup, the wealthiest searched for the best potato peeler. Even those people who could only afford the basics were judged on the quality of what they produced and their ability to make the most of what they could afford. In Victorian novels and Charles Dickens' novels in particular, food is used as a clear indication of wealth or lack of it, and greed or self-abstinence. In a *Christmas Carol*, the generosity of food reflects the generosity of spirit amongst the local people on Christmas Day. The Ghost of Christmas Present resides over '…turkeys, geese, game, poultry, brawn, great joints of meant, sucking pigs, long wreaths of sausages, mince-pies, plum-pudding, barrels of oysters, red-hot chestnuts, cherry-cheeked apples, juicy oranges, luscious pears, immense twelfth-cakes, and seething bowls of punch, that made the chamber dim with their delicious steam.'[2]

Queen Victoria herself advocated for only three courses at evening dinner and the Georgian habit of dining for hours as course after course was served was soon confined to the past. She also preferred her food to be served 'a la Russe', where everything was served onto the plate at once and then the diners settled down to eat.[3] The old French way of piling the table with food in dishes to display wealth had no place in the Royal household as the young queen continued her quest to remodel the Royal Family and the public's perception of it.

Rural Food and Drink

In rural areas in particular, food was seasonal, and all classes based their diets upon what could be grown and made locally, especially before the railways started to move food around the country at a faster rate in the middle of the century. Whether a cottager or an estate owner, there were endless rounds of bread baking, butter churning, cheese making, cow milking, egg collecting, vegetable growing, fruit preservation and beer brewing.[4]

The rural working-class family ate more cheese than meat, brown 'household' bread which was denser and more calorific, vegetable stews and pottage. They ate meat when they could afford it and it was usually bacon or the cheaper cuts of pork such as the shin and cheek which was added to the vegetable stew. Joints of mutton and mutton chops were popular as these were cheaper than lamb. A cheap joint of beef or pork was purchased for Sunday lunch where possible and then eaten cold over the next few days. Chicken, the most popular meat eaten nowadays, was a rarity as chickens were kept for their eggs instead and only eaten when their egg laying days were over. Eggs were an infrequent part of the diet and dependent upon how easily and frequently the hens laid them. Again, those who could afford to buy and keep more chickens ate more eggs. Fish could be bought at market or poached from a nearby estate, as could rabbits. Although poaching was illegal, farmers sometimes turned a blind eye to the poaching of rabbits as it kept the pests from eating their crops.[5] Seasonal fruit was stewed with honey and made into pies if the housewife had enough money to buy the flour and butter or lard to make pastry. If not, apples were stewed to make apple sauce to eat alongside the meat.

All parts of a slaughtered animal were used for food where possible and so offal – the organs of an animal such as the heart, liver and kidneys – was also cheap and readily available from butchers. These would be sliced and fried with onions and served with bread. Poorer people preferred to eat fried liver and onions rather than soup or pottage. The dripping (fat) from roasted meat was drained into a bowl, cooled and then used for frying or spread on bread and eaten as a snack.

The overall variety of rural food was restrictive but getting enough to eat was the main concern of the rural housewife. In leaner times, working class families survived on bread and vegetable soup. In more affluent times they ate more protein and could afford sweet treats. The quantity and variety of food always depended upon income at the time, but fruit and vegetables were organically grown, and the meat was all free range and higher in phytonutrients than our food today.[6]

Wealthier rural people certainly got enough protein to eat. Estate owners bred deer, pheasants and partridges for the late summer shooting season, as was the custom once the London Season had finished. They also reared cows and pigs for slaughter on a regular basis and so their diet was richer in protein and scarce in vegetables. Their bread of choice was a fine, white loaf and eaten with butter and homemade fruit jam. They could then supplement their diets with more expensive, imported food stuffs such as sugar, dried fruits, spices and chocolate, as well as pay for a pastry cook to make the latest desserts and cakes.

Tea and coffee were readily available for those who could afford them although tea was the working classes first choice and coffee was enjoyed more by men accustomed to visiting the town coffee houses of business.

Watered down ale and beer were the most popular drinks in the countryside for most people, even women and older children. It was safer than drinking plain water as the germs from the water were killed off by the brewing process. Estates brewed their own beer and usually paid their workers partly with ale. Small children drank milk where possible and babies were breast fed for as long as possible by working class mothers. Not only was breast milk clean, but it was also free. Unfortunately, it could also be lacking in calories and nutrients if the mother herself wasn't eating properly, and unsatisfying for the baby. If this was the case, the baby was often weaned early, and spoon-fed bread soaked in cow's milk or hot water, or milk thickened with rice or flour.

Urban Food and Drink

Urban working-class Victorians also had to rely upon local, seasonal, fresh food, which was plentiful and cheap, but perhaps a little boring. Twelve onions could be bought for half a penny and so these were eaten with everything. Onions were roasted, fried, cooked in soups and stews and made into onion gravy, a favourite across the working and middle classes. Watercress was also plentiful as the season runs from April round to February. It cost only half a penny for four bunches. Working class people regularly ate it for breakfast along with bread, cheese or cold meat left over from the night before, all washed down with weak beer.

Carrots, cabbage and turnips were also cheap and so were used to fill out stews and soups. Broccoli was readily available throughout the summer, but peas were only available between June and July and runner beans from August to September, so these were a real treat.[7]

There was plenty of local fruit available for most of the year and therefore it was quite cheap. Apples, pears, blackberries and plums were available throughout the autumn and the summer saw gooseberries, greengages, cherries, raspberries and strawberries. Oranges were imported from Spain in the winter but were expensive at the beginning of the era and often given as gifts at Christmas. Towards the end of the era, they were as cheap as apples.

The extremely poor just about survived on bread, tea and potato soup. It was harder for them to purchase quality food ingredients as they started work early in the morning and finished late at night, by which point all the decent food had been sold and only withered vegetables and poor meat would be left. As there was no refrigeration, by the end of the day it would be spoiled.[8] Factory working hours also left little time for the long stewing time required for the cheaper cuts of meat. Also, for those poor people who lived in shared, cramped accommodation in town, cooking a decent evening meal was nigh on impossible as there was hardly any space for cooking equipment or even a fire.

So, the urban working poor would buy street food on the way home from work. Pickled herrings, sheep's trotters, hot eels, pea soup, meat pies and fruit pies, muffins, hot jacket potatoes, tripe, fried cod and haddock, or penny slices of plum pudding, all for sale by street traders and costermongers. Jellied eels were a popular seaside and London dish amongst the working class. Eels were cooked in a broth and then cooled, chopped up and served in the cold broth which had cooled to a jelly-like substance. Cockles, mussels, whelks and oysters were cooked and sold by street vendors too and provided an essential source of protein and zinc. Roasted chestnuts and hazelnuts made a nice snack. Walnuts were readily available too but the more expensive, imported almonds and Brazil nuts were kept as treats for Christmas.

For quite a few workers, it was easier all round to buy a 4-pound weight loaf every day and eat just that for breakfast, lunch and tea instead.[9]

Bread

Victorian bread was completely different to our bread nowadays. The cheapest bread, known variously as labourers' bread, household bread or brown bread, was made up of pease, barley, malt, rye and some wheat. This bread was very nutritious and filling but could be heavy and taste bitter. Wheaten bread was made using flour where most of the bran was removed but not the wheatgerm, leaving some fibre and fat behind but a whiter and lighter loaf. A fine, white loaf was made from flour which had been milled and sieved several times to remove all bran and wheatgerm, enabling an airy and white loaf which was easier to digest but lacking in essential nutrients.[10] The urban poor bought their bread from local bakers if they didn't have the space and resources to make it at home. In the countryside, farmers and labourers' wives made bread every day. Nearly every rural cottage was fitted with a small bread oven in the wall by the main fire and for those who didn't have one, a village baker would run a communal oven, baking everyone's bread in one go for a small charge.[11]

In *Great Expectations*, Charles Dickens makes a big deal about the thick bread and butter Pip and Joe eat for their tea, and how this is rationed by Mrs. Joe, who is a strict housewife.

'First, with her left hand she jammed the loaf hard and fast against her bib – where it sometimes got a pin into it, and sometimes a needle which we afterwards got into our mouths. Then she took some butter (not too much) on a knife and spread it on the loaf, in an apothecary kind of way, as if she was making a plaister – using both sides of the knife with a slapping dexterity and trimming and moulding the butter off round the crust. Then, she gave the knife a final smart wipe on the edge of the plaister, and then sawed a very thick round off the loaf: which she finally, before separating from the loaf, hewed into two halves, of which Joe got one and I got the other.'[12]

Bread made up about 80% of a labourer's diet as it was fairly cheap and filling. However, the corn laws from 1815 through to 1846 blocked the import of grain from America, Canada and Ukraine if it fell below 80 shillings a quarter in price. This kept grain prices artificially high so that British people could only buy British wheat, thus putting money back into the British economy. But it meant that when a harvest failed at home, this expensive imported grain was used to make bread, pushing up the price and making it less affordable leading to widespread hunger. The corn laws also had an effect on meat prices as farmers had to import grain to feed their animals, pushing up the price of the slaughtered animal so they could recoup their increased outlay.[13]

Bakers were also affected as not only did their increased prices cause misery for their customers, but they also had less sales and less people to want to rent their ovens. There were three bad harvests in England from 1839 to 1841[14], alongside the spread of the potato blight fungus which ruined crops in England and Scotland in 1845. The potato blight spread to Ireland and decimated the potato crop there between 1845 and 1849[15] leading to widespread starvation amongst the poorest people in both town and countryside throughout the UK, and the eventual end of the Corn Laws.

Breakfast

Nearly every Victorian ate breakfast but how much was eaten again depended upon what was affordable at that point in time for that particular person. Early on in the era, it was usual to eat leftovers from last night's main meal or leftover bread toasted if the fire was ready alongside tea or weak beer. Fried bacon became an all-round favourite for everyone for breakfast, and sausages were also favoured but often kept for dinner by the working classes. Coddled, poached and fried eggs served alongside bacon for wealthier people. Porridge was another favourite for everyone but how it was made depended upon the money available. Poorer people made it with a mixture of water and milk and ate it unsweetened; others perked it up with more milk, cream, sugar or honey. A saucepan made from cheap thin metal often caused porridge to burn so many poorer people eschewed porridge in favour of bread.[16] Tea and coffee became popular breakfast drinks as a warm pick me up before the day started. So, in a wealthier household at the beginning of the era, the breakfast menu was thus: bacon and eggs followed by porridge, followed by toast and marmalade and washed down with tea or coffee.[17]

The timing of breakfast again depended upon the household's circumstances. A factory worker or labourer was probably breakfasting on bread and tea at 5am before walking to work, or they may have bought some street food such as ham sandwiches and coffee on the way. They may not have had breakfast before work at all if the workers stopped for breakfast later in the morning. In this case, a cold breakfast of bread and anything else spare was taken into work. Agricultural workers usually put in a couple of hours work before stopping for breakfast around eight o'clock. Middle class gentlemen who travelled from the suburbs into the cities were served a hearty breakfast early in the morning before they left. Wealthier families didn't have set breakfast times. Instead, they had breakfast laid out in dishes and kept warm upon spirit burners on a sideboard in the breakfast room and people could wander in and help themselves when up. This was especially the case if guests were staying.

As the century progressed, the breakfast repertoire expanded and began to represent food from the Empire. Cold cuts of English ham, veal and ham pies, game pie, spiced beef, smoked fish, especially kippers, devilled kidneys, Indian kedgeree, muffins and grapes began to appear in various quantities in wealthier households. Black pudding, however, was for the working classes who also sliced and fried cooked potatoes to use up the leftovers from dinner the night before.[18]

The Evening Meal

If a household wasn't entertaining, then a hot evening meal was served when the husband arrived home from work. For most workers, this was usually around seven o'clock. For the suburban husband, he had to travel home first and for the working-class husband, he didn't finish work until around six o'clock. For the wives working in factories, their shifts didn't finish until six o'clock either, leaving little time and energy for them to get home and cook a substantial meal. So, street food such as hot meat pies or jacket potatoes or fried fish were purchased on the way home for dinner. For those women who worked from home, if they had the fuel, space and cooking utensils, they were able to cook up a meat stew and suet dumplings. If they didn't, street food was purchased by them as well.

Lunch

How much lunch a person ate depended entirely upon how much money they had spare. In between a hearty breakfast and a hot evening meal, middle class office workers tended to eat a light snack at midday. Savoury biscuits, which we now call crackers, eaten with cheese, were easily carried into work as were sweet biscuits to have with a cup of tea. Labourers and those who worked outside tried to eat something a little more substantial such as a piece of bread and cheese or cold meat or a piece of cold pie alongside beer or tea if available. Wealthier women who breakfasted late ate lunch late, usually around 4 o'clock. A high tea of bread and butter and cake kept them going until dinner late in the evening.

Dining Out

There were plenty of opportunities to eat out but where again depended upon class and ready money. The lower classes ate in 'ordinaries' which were eating houses which served up a basic fixed menu for a fixed price. Those with more money ate in pubs and coffee houses where again, the food was basic but filling. In *Great Expectations*, Pip dines on chicken with parsley butter, bread and cheese all provided by the local coffee house for him to eat at home.[19]

Towards the middle of the century, the wealthy bachelor male could dine in a Gentleman's Club or Members Only Club. Here, they could be served a hot meal of roasted meat, chops or steak, potatoes and gravy along with wine and brandy. These were good places for aspiring young men to be seen as they made business acquaintances at the same time, and it was an easy place in which to invite another man to dinner in order to discuss a new venture or political idea. For those without the money or credentials to join a private club, cheaper chop houses served chops or steak with mashed potato and gravy and tankards of beer. Scrooge habitually dines in a chop house on his way home from work even though he could easily afford membership to a private club, probably because of the cost but also so he doesn't have to converse with anyone.[20]

The Ordinaries and Chop Houses gave way to the Gentleman's clubs and restaurants and working-class men turned to the public house for somewhere to sit and eat hot food, encouraging Pubs to offer a wider range of fare suitable to the working-class male. Street sellers could also do the rounds of local pubs, offering fried fish, jacket potatoes, oysters, jellied eels and meat pies for men to eat alongside their beer.

Dining In

For the wealthier households, dinner parties formed the basis of social entertaining. A dinner party was perfect for a middleclass household who didn't have the room to hold a ball or even the money to host one. They also allowed for conversation which was perfect for the husband who was looking to impress the local clergyman or magistrate for example. Servants could be hired in from the local workhouses or orphanages, giving young girls a much-needed servitude experience. Dinner parties rivalled each other for the ornate food, décor and guests themselves. Most of a weekly food budget would be spent on a dinner party, with the household dining on leftovers for the rest of the week.

More informal suppers were also popular, if a household had a room in which the furniture could be pushed to the sides. Food such as cold pies, ham and cakes was left out on sideboards for guests to help themselves in between dancing and gossiping.[21]

The Meaning of Abstinence in Women and the Bland Diets of Children

Even though the middle and upper classes enjoyed an abundance of food, women were expected to show restraint. Indulging in food showed loose morals and a lack of discipline. A hunger for food shows a hunger for other experiences which can be damaging to the soul. A woman looking to attract a husband was encouraged to eat little. As women were barred from pubs and clubs, middleclass and upper-class women tended to socialise with each other over lunch or afternoon tea in their own homes. Here, they needed to provide the best sandwiches or thin, white bread and butter and cakes and biscuits on beautiful plates with the finest silver cutlery but weren't allowed to overindulge otherwise they left themselves open to gossip about unhealthy appetites and morals.

In *Great Expectations*, Miss Havisham not only keeps her rotting bridal cake but the whole, vast dining table as laid out for the wedding breakfast as a reminder of her 'failure' to marry. She also starves herself – Pip describes her as skin and bone – as punishment for her desire for her betrothed and her appetite for a future life with him led to her downfall.[22]

During these dinner and tea parties, the taste wasn't as important as the look of the food. The food was there to show status, that the host could afford to buy such vast quantities of food and put on such a display and could afford the servants to prepare it all and serve it.

Girls were thought to do better on a bland, unstimulating diet otherwise they would become overstimulated and then possible 'trouble', a euphemism for opinionated, and start to question their station in life This blandness in food for ladies led to a requirement for bland opinions, deportment, musical instrument playing, language reading material and so forth.[23]. Food was overcooked and overboiled as Victorians felt that undercooked food had the potential to poison the eater and raw vegetables were viewed with a lot of suspicion. Fruit and vegetables were also thought to lack nutrition. They were also thought to be peasant food and only fit for the lower classes who were unable to afford protein.

As the century wore on, the middle classes in particular became more buttoned up and reluctant to show pleasure in anything for a fear of being judged as lower class.[24] Food became more unattractive except at dinner parties and balls where the food was set to impress. In these circumstances, despite being served late after several rounds of dancing, eating the delicious food on offer with any kind of enjoyment or relish was seen as vulgar. Talking with a full mouth or even having a full mouth was regarded as disgusting and unforgivable. This, it was thought, was something the working classes would do, who to many were seen as no better than animals. The publication of Charles Darwin's *On the Origin of Species* in 1859 made many middle class and upper class Victorians uncomfortable to be thought of as descended from apes; Mr Hyde is described as 'apelike' when he tramples and clubs Sir Danvers Carew to death[25] and so, they looked to oppress any bestial behaviour such as greed early on in childhood. They generally used food as a force to keep young people civilised.

In *Jane Eyre*, the Reverend Brocklehurst finds out that Miss Temple has been giving the girls extra bread and cheese.

'You are aware that my plan in bringing up these girls is, not to accustom them to habits of luxury and indulgence, but to render them hardy, patient, self-denying. . . Oh, madam, when you put bread and cheese, instead of burnt porridge, into these children's mouths, you may indeed feed their vile bodies, but you little think how you starve their immortal souls!'[26]

Jane lists the food the girls are given during the course of twenty-four hours: A small bowl of burnt porridge for breakfast, bread and cheese for a snack although this is extra, cheap meat and potatoes for lunch, half a slice of brown bread and a small mug of coffee for tea. A piece of oatcake and water for supper.

Meanwhile, Jane is a growing girl and constantly hungry – for food, for affection but most importantly, for knowledge. She never knows enough. This goes against the Reverend Brocklehurst who believes that by denying the girls a decent, satisfying meal he thought to bring them closer to God, which of course does happen eventually when half of the girls die from Typhus, too weak and malnourished to fight it off.[27]

How Did the Victorians Diet Affect their Health?

The food shortages of the 1840s nutritionally affected the working and middle classes more than the upper classes, shown through the discovery of the marked difference in heights between army recruits to Sandhurst Military School. Those boys whose parents could afford to pay the higher level of entrance fees were found to be between 0.8 and 3.3cm taller than their lower entrance fee paying peers. Poorer boys, enlisted from the slums into the Marine Society as an opportunity to train for the Navy, were on average 22.6cm shorter than the higher fee-paying boys at Sandhurst in 1840, indicating a clear link between nutrition and growth.[28]

After the Hungry Forties, the gradual changes in farming and the importing of new food stuffs from the empire enabled the Victorians to access to an abundance and variety of food never known to their Georgian forebears. If middle era Victorians ate properly, they took in all the calories and nutrients they needed to keep fit and healthy at a time where towns and cities were still unhealthy environments. Despite the lack of medicine and infection control available, the life expectancy in the mid-Victorian era was similar to today: 75 years for men and 73 years for women, putting aside infant mortality rates.[29]

But of course, the amount of food available still relied wholly upon the income available to a family. Inadequate food consumption still had a massive impact on the health of the poorest, helping to keep them trapped in poverty. Slum children suffered from anaemia due to a lack of iron, and rickets (misshapen hips and legs) due to a lack of Vitamin D, both of which are readily available in red meat and animal fat. Vit D absorption is also helped by calcium from dairy products which were also in scarce supply. A lack of vitamin C from fresh fruit and vegetables led to scurvy and a loss of teeth in many. Generally, the poorest fed had lower energy and immune systems leaving them vulnerable to the development of pneumonia in winter and unable to fight off communicable diseases. But rarely did degenerative diseases such as coronary heart disease, diabetes, dementia, stroke and cancer affect older working-class Mid Victorians.[30] Diabetes and strokes affected the middle and upper classes more due to their diets rich in salt, sugar, red meat and alcohol, but was still rare compared to today.

A Change in Diet

From the mid-1870s, cheap imported canned food became more widely available to everyone and has been credited with improving the diet of the working-class Victorians in that there was a wider variety of food to suit all incomes, confining the monotonous, near starvation diets to the past. The Argentinian food firm Fray Bentos began exporting canned corned beef which the working classes in particular liked as it could be sliced and made into sandwiches. Crosse and Blackwell's canned salmon was also popular for the same reason. By the 1880s, canned fruit in syrup was a staple of the middle class store cupboards and cans of sweetened condensed milk was loved by the working classes. Sugar consumption in general increased as sugar became much cheaper, with the working classes developing a taste for bread and jam over bread and dripping. Even bread dropped in price and the more nutritionally deficient white bread became preferred by all.

Towards the end of the century refrigeration was finally perfected after thirty years of experimentation and practice, enabling the import of lamb, beef and pork from New Zealand, Argentina and America. This made unprocessed meat more affordable for the working classes and a roasted joint became a Sunday staple in most houses with the leftovers eaten up over the next few days.

Despite the increase in the variety of food, male life expectancy decreased towards the end of the century, and nutritional defects, an increase in smoking cigarettes and cheaper alcohol can all be attributed to this.[31] Between 1899 and 1900, many working-class men who tried to enlist for the second Boer War were turned down due to malnutrition in infancy leading to discoveries of poor growth, heart problems, poor eyesight and hearing, and decaying teeth.[32] The government became so concerned that in 1904 it set up the Physical Deterioration Committee to explore this further, leading to the introduction of free school meals.[33]

In contrast, by 1900, women's life expectancy had increased, attributed to improvements to family planning and clothing, but also a vastly improved diet. As women no longer needed to go without food to ensure their children and husbands were fed, an increase in calories and therefore nutrients enabled women to fight off infection and recover quicker after childbirth. The establishment of the railway and its distribution of food from the empire helped to widen and consolidate the Victorian diet into a pattern which we still recognise today.

Chapter Twelve

Communication and Travel

'Some persons, when travelling by railway, have a knack of continually thrusting their heads out of the window. Nothing can be more dangerous than this, and numerous are the accidents that have resulted in consequence. The proper place for the head is inside, not outside the carriage, and so long as it is kept there, the chances are that it will remain whole.'[1]

*The Railway Traveller's Handy Book
of Hints, Suggestions and Advice*

Although the Victorian era saw massive leaps forward in every way of life, it was the way people, goods and information travelled from place to place which arguably saw the biggest changes. In 1837, England moved at a much slower pace than later on in the century. For rural people the day started with sunup and ended with sundown. Urban office and factory workers had set hours, but all start and finish times depended upon where a person lived in the country as everyone followed local time set by the sun. Wherever people lived, it was within a reasonable walking distance from work and other destinations important to the family as walking was the only way to get there. The gentry, with money and status to uphold, rode on horseback in the local countryside and ran a private coach and horses out to visit neighbouring estates. Whilst in town, they used their private curricles and horses which were more suitable for shorter, urban journeys. Upper class women were definitely discouraged from travelling anywhere on foot and were taxied around in their family's private carriage. Not only was this for their safety, as well-dressed women tended to attract all sorts of unwanted attention from ne'er-do-wells, but also because this differentiated upper class women from working class women. For the middle classes, a horse and carriage were a must, but the size and frequency of use depended upon the income of the family.

Everyone else walked to where they needed to go, and it was usual for a fit and able young person to walk several miles in one go at a fair pace. In *Pride and Prejudice*, Elizabeth Bennet thinks nothing of striding three miles to Netherfield when her sister Jane is taken ill there. The family carriage is unavailable for reasons unknown, and Lizzie is no horsewoman, so she opts to walk instead.

She arrives 'with weary ankles, dirty stockings, and a face glowing with the warmth of exercise,' causing a small commotion that she should have walked so far so early in the morning and in such dull and damp weather.[2]

Horses and donkeys were man's best friend, not only carrying men, women and children around but also pulling coaches, carts, cabs and barges in all weathers and on all roads. Horses were expensive to keep; they needed regular shoeing by a blacksmith and regular grooming by a competent stableboy. They needed to be rested in a dry stable with plenty of access to fresh water and food which at the beginning of the era could be a challenge due to the fluctuating grain prices. Many an agricultural worker were unable to look after their horse as they would like, even if to replace it was far beyond the pocket of the family. When Tess of the D'Urbervilles falls asleep on her cart on the way to market and the family horse Prince is killed, 'the knacker and tanner would give only a very few shillings for Prince's carcase because of his decrepitude.'[3] Despite facing ruin, Mr Durbeyfield refuses the money and gives Prince a proper burial as 'He've served me well in his lifetime, and I won't part from him now.'[4]

Farmers owned horses and wagons to transport goods and market traders relied upon a pony or donkey and cart to get their wares to market. The animals to be sold at market – sheep, cows, pigs, geese and chickens – were often walked into market by older boys or young men who were skilled in driving the animals before them along the country roads. They would find an area for the night to shelter, usually under a tree, and then carry on the next morning. It was not unusual for journeys to the weekly or monthly market to take 3 or 4 days to walk there and the same to walk back.

Long Distance Travel

For those needing to travel a long distance, a place on a stagecoach could be booked for individuals or a whole family. These stagecoaches stopped at staging inns along the way where the passengers resided overnight, enjoying a basic evening meal, a wash and a bed for the night before getting up early to resume their journey. The horses were stabled overnight, fed and rested and sometimes exchanged if too weary or lame. New passengers were picked up from the Inns in the morning or at the side of the main road by villages as the Stagecoach went past, but the place on the coach still needed to have been booked in advance. Passengers could sit on the outside of the coach, which was cheaper but exposed them to the wind and rain, or on the inside, which was dry but cramped, stuffy and smelly.[5] For these reasons coach journeys were not popular and to add to the rough experience, the coaches themselves had very little suspension so every lump and bump in the road shook the coach and jarred the body. Roads were poorly constructed and often muddy causing the coaches to slip and slide in places and fling the occupants from side to side. Coaching accidents and breakdowns were frequent, adding to the length of time of the journey. It was also an expensive way to travel as tolls were paid on most roads, adding to the cost. It's no wonder that most working-class people only travelled in-between local villages and not further afield[6]

London and Other Cities

Travelling in London was extremely hazardous to say the least. There were no rules of the road; people walked, rode, drove carts and carriages regardless of which side of the road they were on. There were no roundabouts, traffic lights or even road markings to indicate right of way. The travel chaos was made up of private carriages, public transport such as cabs and omnibuses, market trader's carts, costermonger's wheelbarrows and mail coaches to name a few modes of transport. So, if one wanted to get to their destination quickly using public transport, a licensed Hackney Carriage was the best option. The only carriage a passer-by could flag down in the street, just like a taxicab today, they operated a fixed fare system but couldn't be booked in advance so a person had to leave their house and hope they could find one when needed.[7] Hansom cabs were later introduced, and these could only hold two passengers at most with the driver sat on the roof. Pulled by only one horse, hansom cabs were smaller, lighter and quicker to get around in.

Just like today, a cheaper alternative to the Hackney cab was the Omnibus. These large coaches, pulled by two horses could carry around twelve people at once. Passengers could sit inside the coach or on the outside but both seating arrangements required a certain amount of bravery. Inside, the coaches could be dirty, stuffy and smelly and passengers frequently shared their space with baskets of birds, chickens or meat from the butchers. Outside, they were exposed to the weather and the pollution. Omnibus drivers raced each other as they needed to pick up and set down as many passengers as they could throughout the day, so passengers had to guard against being jostled into each other's laps or accidentally thrown into the street. Luckily, the newly invented tram arrived to offer a viable and cheaper alternative.[8]

Trams

Trams were large vehicles which ran on smooth iron rails set in the road. Because the smooth rails created less friction, they were easier for the horses to pull and so the animals could take more weight. Trams could carry up to fifty paying passengers at a time so many trams were double decked with the top deck open to the elements and originally reached by a ladder although later trams had small staircases fitted. Trams were easy to catch as they ran up residential streets. They were well lit with a conductor as well as a driver making them a safer option for women to use. Manchester, Leeds, Birmingham and Liverpool all established the popular tramway system after the 1870s Tramway Act allowed more tramways to be built around the outside of London and in other cities too. The instillation was cheap and easy because it just involved the laying of tracks; there was minimal digging required. The journey cost less than the omnibus for passengers as the tram could hold a bigger number of people and they moved quickly, setting down and picking up new fares, but without racing each other. Parliament ordered tram companies to provide cheap workman's fares so labourers could get the tram to work rather than walking at a time in the morning when the omnibuses did not run. Thus began the association of trams as the working classes mode of transport, helped along by the exclusion of tramways from central London and the West End.[9]

The First Railways

The Stockton and Darlington railway was the first railway to shift goods between two places by steam locomotive in 1825. It also took passengers but in carriages drawn by horses rather than steam locomotive. The first steam passenger railway line opened in 1830 between Liverpool and Manchester, mainly in order to send raw cotton imported from America into Liverpool across to inland Manchester to be spun and then woven into textiles which were then exported around the world. Because the railway was intended to carry people too in seated carriages and to timetabled journeys, a contest was held at Rainhill in 1829 in order to choose the best steam locomotive for the job. Rocket, designed and engineered by father and son team George and Robert Stephenson, won the contest and they won the contract to provide the locomotives. The popularity of the railway soon became clear, and so a fledgling railway network was already in place at the beginning of the era. As public confidence in Queen Victoria grew, so did confidence in the railway system. It rapidly expanded during the 1840s with a London to Birmingham line opening in 1838, London to Bristol in 1841 and London to Glasgow in 1848. By 1852, 7000 miles of track had been laid across England and Scotland and a basic network was in operation with steam trains transporting goods and people up and down the country.[10]

This new way of travelling was not for the faint hearted. Although cheaper and faster than horse drawn coaches, the first train carriages were little more than cattle trucks with seats in and a light covering overhead. Passengers were exposed to the wind and rain not to mention the soot and embers which blew out of the engine funnel in a steady stream behind it. They were also treated to the ear-piercing shrieks of the whistle and the clatter of the wheels against the tracks. There were many voiced concerns that the vibrations of the train would cause nerve damage over time, or the high speeds could cause insanity, asphyxiation or even a person to disintegrate. But despite this, railway companies continued to gain investment and build stations, railways and locomotives and passengers continued to brave this new mode of transport, pushing the companies into improving the overall experience.

The Victorian way of fitting everyone and everything into a class continued with rail travel. Passengers were strictly segregated depending upon their choice of ticket and had to wait for appropriate steam locomotive and set of carriages accordingly. Those travelling with a first-class ticket travelled in as much comfort as possible. The early first-class carriages were based upon the design of a stagecoach, with a step up to the door which was about waist height. Inside, the seats were padded and upholstered, and the small windows were hung with curtains for privacy. The guard had a seat at the back end of the row of carriages, and the passengers' luggage was stored atop the carriage, just like on a stagecoach.

Second-class passengers were shown to a set of carriages with open sides but some kind of roof covering to protect them from the worst of the elements. The plain wooden benches were very upright, unpadded and cramped. The third-class carriages were completely open from chest height upwards and usually without seats. Passengers just stood and clung on the best they could or sat on the floor. Third-class rail travel was very cheap and aimed at people who usually walked everywhere in all weathers, so it was actually no hardship to travel this way at first.[11] These trains were slower and sometimes had to be side shunted to let first class trains through. Gradually, steam locomotives began to pull a long line of different class carriages and platform signage instructed the different classes of passengers as to where they should stand ready to enter their carriage when the train arrived.

Railway Time

In 1839, George Bradshaw who was a cartographer, printer and publisher started producing little booklets of railway times. These were small enough for a male passenger to keep in his pocket or a female passenger to keep in her purse. The side Y-axis listed the towns, and the bottom X-axis listed the times, much the same as timetables today. Passengers relied upon these timetables to get them to where they needed to be.

As railway lines grew longer, following the timetables became more complicated as passengers travelled through different local time zones. Although the differences in time was only mere minutes, it was enough for passengers to miss their connection if they were unsure of the local time at the station. Passengers, guards and drivers all had to deal with this by constantly resetting their watches to the correct local time and carefully following the timetable.

It was when a group of businessmen from Bristol commissioned the great Victorian engineer Isambard Kingdom Brunel to build the fastest railway in the country from London to Bristol that the issue of local time zones became muddled. Greenwich, in London, established as the home of timekeeping and navigation by Charles II, provided the starting local time zone from London to Bristol. But the further across the west country passengers had to travel, the more they had to keep putting their watches backwards. Brunel decided to use Greenwich Mean Time for all of his stops on the Great Western Railway, but now local stations had to display clocks with two minutes hands, a red one for London time and the usual black one for local time. It was a good idea but just as chaotic. To help passengers, timetables showed both London time and local time as well as the prices for first-, second- and third-class services.

Greenwich Mean Time was disliked by many, especially churches which had always rung out the local time for residents to set their watch by. Others saw Greenwich Mean Time, or railway time, as another way form of control by the railway companies who were already buying and digging up land and demolishing houses whether local residents liked it or not. Working to a double timetable started to be phased out in the mid-1850s but still continued in some places until 1880 when the Definition of Time Act was passed by Parliament who declared Greenwich Mean Time as the standard time for the country.

London Underground

The railway companies who started to link London to many major towns and cities were not allowed to extend the tracks all the way into central London. Instead, they terminated their lines at Paddington, Euston and Kings Cross, which were all on the outskirts of London at the time, causing immense traffic and congestion by commuters as they used hansom cabs, omnibuses and trams to get to work in central London. The idea for an underground train system was inspired by MP for Lambeth Charles Pearson. The scale of the proposed plan was enormous and had never been attempted before. British railway engineers felt they had the knowledge and expertise to put it in place and so the Metropolitan Railway Company formed to build the world's first underground railway between Paddington and Farringdon. In 1863, the Metropolitan Railway opened to great acclaim.

Travelling by underground train was a smoky and steamy affair with passengers enduring clouds of smut and sulphur. But the alternative – slow horse-drawn buses and coaches - made it worthwhile for those who could stomach the ride and afford the fares for the privilege.[12] Despite the conditions below ground, underground railway travel was extremely popular, but it did have a rival in the way of the electric tram. Towards the end of the century, many cities had an established electric tram system which was cleaner and smoother and overall made for a far more pleasant journey. In order to compete, the London Underground needed to provide its passengers with an equal experience. It did this in 1890 by opening the City and South London line, a deep-level underground railway operated by electricity rather than steam. Passengers could travel between King William Street in the City of London to Stockwell in South London by passing under the Thames. This started the electrification of the whole of the London Underground railway system but whether steam or electric, trains in general became the main method of transport across the country.

Communication

In between journeys, the main way people communicated with each other across the miles was through handwritten letters instead.

The postal system really took off in the eighteenth century with new road building techniques and specially designed mail coaches for the post office enabling swift delivery of correspondence up and down the country. This incredibly organised system with its fixed schedule of postal runs through the day and night played its part in the growth of business and the industrial revolution as a whole.[13]

Unfortunately, for the ordinary person, sending and receiving letters could be expensive. The overall cost depended upon the number of pages in the letter, the distance the letter travelled the tax added and other charges. People worked their way around this by writing crossways on the letter. Once the page was filled with writing, it was turned ninety degrees and fresh text was written across it. This could be confusing to read but saved the recipient money as the recipient was the one who paid the postage. Many recipients declined to take the letter, with the sender writing a short message on the outside which could be quickly read by the recipient before handing it back to the post boy.[14]

Early Victorians wrote with quill pens dipped in bottled ink. The steel nibbed pen started to replace the quill, but it was slow to catch on and quills were still being used by some when Queen Victoria died. The paper was folded over itself with the address written on the outside and then sealed with sealing wax which was heated and dripped onto where the edges of the letter met and pressed with the family seal. Once cool, it held the ends of the letter together until the recipient broke the seal to open the letter. Envelopes were available but counted as another sheet of paper and so the letter cost more money to send.

Households with servants sent a servant to deliver the letter straight to the recipient if they were local, or to the post office to post the letter, where they picked up the household's mail at the same time.

Letter writing was very much a middle- and upper-class event for a number of reasons. Paper and ink were expensive. Also, in order to write a letter or read one, a person needed to be literate which meant they had to have attended school, an unlikely occurrence for the poorer working class at the beginning of the Victorian era. In the unlikely event an illiterate person did receive a letter, and could afford to pay the postage, they would take it to their nearest trusted literate neighbour to read it to them, which meant someone else knowing their business. Stories abounded of poor mothers who never received letters from their sons in the army or navy or even their death notices. Eventually, an overhaul of the postal system was planned at the end of the 1830s and the philanthropist and entrepreneur Rowland Hill was commissioned to take charge and shake it up.

The Penny Post

On the 10 January, 1840, the first ever pre-paid stamps were put on sale at one penny each for a letter weighing half an ounce or less. A penny was the only cost of sending a letter as Hill wanted all classes of people to be able to communicate with each other. He believed it would be good for trade and society in general. These 'penny black' stamps ensured that the postal service became the number one communication system across Britain for everyone. A person could receive a letter at breakfast and write an immediate answer to be sent by return of post, ensuring the original sender received their reply by evening if not before.

There was an explosion in letter writing and a plethora of stationery, writing implements and furniture flooded the shops. The family correspondence became the responsibility of the mistress of the house, who kept her writing materials in the parlour in a portable writing desk, a nifty piece of furniture which was a must for any middle-class lady. It was a large, lockable box with a sloped lid to write on and a pen holder and inkwell. Paper, blotting paper, spare pen nibs or quills, envelopes, sealing wax, stamps and ink bottles were stored away neatly inside.[15]

Men used writing desks too, and theirs were made out of a good quality wood such as walnut or mahogany and inlaid with leather. It was large and sturdy and could be taken on business trips. Ladies writing desks were smaller and daintier and decorated with fruit, flowers or birds with gold or silver accents. Inside would be lined with silk or velvet. Jane Austen was famously gifted a writing desk by her father to encourage her writing.

The penny post, as it became to be known, also encouraged the sale of decorated writing paper and envelopes, brass letter racks to hold correspondence neatly together, paperclips, stamp boxes to keep stamps safe. A wide variety of correspondence started to be exchanged via the penny post. People started to send condolence letters, congratulations letters, valentines' cards and later Christmas and birthday cards, birth announcements and engagements amongst other things. Letters were also a good way to impart advice, gossip and commiserate with each other. But in order to do this all properly, reference to a letter writing manual was a must.

The quality of a letter clearly demonstrated a person's level of education and hence the type of family they came from. Penmanship revealed an awful lot about the author, so manuals such as The Universal Letter Writer helped the author to apply for a job, accept or decline a position, to break off an engagement, to declare longstanding love or to offer condolences. These manuals positively encouraged letter writing. Anyone who was unsure of what to write or the best way to express themselves could consult a manual and copy the style. As a result, anyone who could hold a pen and write were able to conduct business, friendships and love affairs via the written letter.[16] Letter writing led to an increasingly literate society as people practiced with pride. In *Great Expectations*, Biddy teaches Joe the Blacksmith to write letters and Joe is inordinately proud of his achievement.

'When he did begin, he made every downstroke so slowly that it might have been six feet long, while at every up stroke I could hear his pen spluttering extensively. He had a curious idea that the ink stand was at the side of him where it was not, and constantly dipped his quill pen into space, and seemed quite satisfied with the results. Occasionally, he was tripped up by some orthographical stumbling block, but on the whole, he got on very well indeed, and when he had signed his name, and had removed a finishing blot from the paper to the crown of his head with his two forefingers, he got up and hovered about the table, trying the effect of his performance from various points of view as it lay there, with unbound satisfaction.'[17]

Clerks and Communication at Work

Clerks were recruited early on after school and served a five-year apprentice under the watchful eye of a senior clerk. Although not hugely exciting, the job of a clerk was a stable one with definite rules and income.

Clerks were needed by businesses to write out paperwork and then to make numerous copies as required. The stored documents were held together with string and hung on nails on the wall by the clerk. Invoices were impaled on spikes on the clerk's desk with the most recent one on top. Pins were used to hold bunches of paper together. When documents or messages were ready to be delivered, a small handbell summoned a messenger to take it to its destination. The messenger was usually a young boy or an elderly man whose sole job was to answer the bell promptly, deliver the goods and return quickly for the next job. Using a messenger boy in the early part of the Victorian era was the equivalent of picking up the telephone to speak to someone today.

The Spread of News

Newspapers were incredibly popular throughout the nineteenth century, especially amongst the educated men who they were mainly aimed at. The Times was the leading London newspaper, and The Manchester Guardian was the leading paper in the North of the country. The provincial papers gathered news stories from London and Manchester by gathering together copies of The Times and The Guardian and rewriting the stories. By the time the newspaper had been printed though, the news was often several days out of date. As the railways expanded, provincial journalists were able to travel to London and other major cities to gather fresh news. Equally, London journalists began to travel out to the provinces to gather first hand news too and London newspapers began to be sold further afield, rivalling the provincial papers as customers enjoyed the glamour of reading a newspaper fresh from London.

It was common practice to share newspapers with friends and neighbours as early newspapers were quite expensive to buy. News outlets had to pay a tax on the paper and a tax on the advertisements they carried. The printing process itself was laborious and slow, allowing for a limited print run. Once ready, the newspapers then had to go to a revenue office to be taxed and stamped. Once taxed and stamped, the newspaper was allowed to be carried by Royal Mail anywhere in the country and so avid readers sent on their newspapers to friends and family alongside a letter, especially if there was a particularly significant article to share.

In 1855, the Stamp Duty was removed followed by the tax on paper in 1861, causing the cost of newspapers to fall. As literacy rates improved alongside education, more newspapers opened to appeal to different readerships. The Daily Mail started up for lower middle-class readers and in particular, female readers with particular news articles aimed at them. Women's magazines already existed, with articles on cookery, fashion and romantic fiction and sporting papers emerged for wealthier men with news on fox hunting, horse racing meets, boxing matches and cricket leagues. Once football became popular at the end of the century, newspapers began to report footballing news aimed at the lower classes with a different tone and language.

Other newspapers sought working class readers with blunt accounts of crime. Costing one penny, they were printed weekly rather than daily due to the income of the readership and became known as penny-dreadfuls.

Magazines on all sorts of specialist subjects took off. These were perfect for railway travel as they could be perused at leisure and dipped in and out of. These were also good to read at home in between chores and servants in particular liked to read a newspaper or magazine where possible.[18]

By delivering newspapers and letters quicker than ever, the railways sped up communication. But conversely, new and faster ways of communication had to be discovered to enable the railways to run safely. This was where the telegraph came in useful.

Telegraph

As a way of text messaging, the telegraph had been around since the beginning of the century as scientists worked to improve its effectiveness. By the 1840s, the electrical telegraph had superseded the mechanical one, and electrical wires attached to pylons were built alongside the railway tracks in order to send and receive messages regarding signalling and other important railway issues. Britain adopted the needle telegraph developed by William Fothergill Cooke and Charles Wheatstone, where different strength electrical pulses moved needles towards different letters to spell out words. In America, Samuel Morse independently developed a similar system but where dots and dashes were embossed onto thin strips of paper and then attributed to letters, spelling out a message. Skilled operators soon began to learn the different sounds of the clicks and could transcribe the message from these rather than the paper. This became known as Morse Code.

In Britain, people were initially reluctant to adopt the use of the telegraph to send messages, but when the telegraph was used to announce the birth of Queen Victoria's second son, Alfred Ernest on 6 August 1844, at Windsor and the news was reported in The Times after only forty minutes of release, the telegraph began to be recognised as a world changing communication enterprise.[19]

By the 1850s, the sending and receiving of telegrams, as the messages became known, was widespread but only important news was sent, due to the cost. Only rich people could afford to send telegrams for trivial matters. The network of telegraph cables was run by telegraph companies. To send a message, the customer went to their local telegraph office and filled in a form with a brief message and the address of the recipient. Telegrams were costed per word and the distance it was to travel. Once compiled, the message was handed to a clerk who then transmitted the message using code down the line. When the message was received the other end at the nearest telegraph office, the message was written onto a piece of paper and then taken to the recipient by a messenger boy. If a reply was required, the messenger would take a slip of paper with the message written on it back to the office and give it to the clerk to be sent. Replies were usually prepaid by the sender.

The job of the telegraph boy was quite a good one. It was 'clean' work even though they had to deliver messages in all weather. They were expected to sweep and tidy the office as well and if it was quiet, they had the chance to see how the telegraph machine worked. This enabled them to move onto a better job within the company, especially if they were already literate with a good education as literate clerks were needed everywhere.

Global Communication

By the 1860s, Britain was connected to America and Europe via submarine telegraph cables and India by 1870.

The Victorians began to wonder how they had ever managed without the speedy telegraph. Although the penny post was still popular, it was the telegraph which sped up how business was carried out and how news was reported globally. Businesses were able to communicate quickly and directly with suppliers and sellers rather than relying upon mail. Head offices could control several branches of business easily by using the telegraph to send messages, updates and orders back and forth every day.[20] Businessmen also took a keen interest in global matters and how these could affect the importing and exporting of their wares and thirsted for the latest news. Newspapers obliged by stationing reporters abroad who could then telegraph their news across to Britain as it happened enabling several editions of newspapers to be published throughout the course of a day. The Daily Telegraph and Courier newspaper, established in 1855, was so named to showcase its rapid delivery of news.

In June 1875, Graham Alexander Bell was working on a harmonic telegraph when he had a breakthrough and recorded speech for the first time. He swiftly had his telephone, which he still regarded as a form of telegraph, patented and working and by May 1877 the newly formed Bell Telephone Company advertised its wares. The telephone quickly became the preferred form of communication in business, government and for the very wealthy, leaving the telegraph for the lesser well-off.[21]

As the century drew to a close, the Victorians continued to communicate through a vast network of letters, postcards and greetings cards, telegrams, the telephone, newspapers, magazines, manuals, pamphlets and advertisements, all delivered by trains, ships, horses, carts, messenger boy and electricity. Despite all the new technology and ways of moving around the country, the horse was still a dominant form of transport. In The War of the Worlds, the narrator secures a dogcart and horse from a pub landlord in order to escape the Martians and comes across the inhabitants of Weybridge who are packing up their belongings in the same way. 'Carts, carriages everywhere, the most astonishing miscellany of conveyances and horseflesh.'[22]

Experiments to replace the horse as a mode of power started at the end of the century but steam powered engines were too heavy and damaged the road and petrol and electric engines were too unreliable. Over 7000 horse drawn Hansom Cabs and horse buses operated in London and continued to do so right up until 1914 when there was a rapid switch to the motor bus.[23] It was to be another ten years before the scientists' experiments paid off and the humble horse could finally retire.

Chapter Thirteen

Science

'... by the glimmer of the half-extinguished light, I saw the dull, yellow eye of the creature open; it breathed hard, and a convulsive motion agitated its limbs.'

Frankenstein, Mary Shelley[1]

When *Frankenstein* was written, Georgian scientists had already discovered and experimented with electricity to reanimate dead frogs and then dead humans, discovered a vaccination against the dreaded smallpox and explored nitrous oxide (laughing gas) as an effective anaesthetic for surgery. In 1800, The Royal Humane Society, originally set up to help to save victims of drowning from inevitable death, published their annual report detailing not only their successes in this but also their tried and tested methods of resuscitation. This included stripping the body of wet clothes and drying it briskly with dry cloths and brushes to stimulate blood flow, wrapping it in blankets and pressing it with warming pans and hot water bottles. As the person started to come round, smelling salts were applied to the nose and a drink of fortified wine offered to warm the guts. One person to be 'bought back from the dead' this way was the feminist Mary Wollstonecraft, Mary Shelly's mother.

'The real events of the world have, in our day, too, been of so wondrous and gigantic a kind, - the shifting of the scenes in our stupendous drama have been so rapid and various, that Shakespeare himself, in his wildest flights, has been completely distanced by the eccentricities of actual existence,'[2] enthused an anonymous reviewer of the novel *Frankenstein* in 1818, Mary Shelly's cautionary tale of the pursuit of knowledge to all ends and purposes. At this time, the possibilities of science seemed endless and fantastical. In 1821, John Cuthbertson published a book called Practical Electricity and Galvanism, a series of experiments in using electricity to create shocks and make inanimate and dead objects move.[3] It was designed for other scientists to follow if they were interested in this science, and this dedicated interest in the preservation or extension of life continued well into the Victorian era.

Moving into the Victorian era, dedicated individuals who were curious, innovative and experimental speedily built upon each other's work to progress science in an unprecedented way. Alongside the technology of the previous chapter, and the inventions and medicine of the next chapters, the development of Victorian science was influenced by the rapid social and cultural changes over the century. It is far too large a topic to even begin to cover adequately here and so this chapter mainly concentrates on the Victorian's love of the natural world, something which all classes were interested in and had a stake in.

Science at the Beginning of the Era

Originally, Science was known as Natural Philosophy, and was more of a clerical study in that clergymen of the church were interested in finding out about more of God's great world and cataloguing it their way. They continually searched for proof of God's existence through evidence in the natural world. As natural philosophy developed, professional academics came to the fore with the word 'scientist' being coined in1840 when William Whewell wrote 'we need very much a name to describe cultivator of science in general. I should incline to call him a scientist.'[4]

The first Victorian scientists were pioneering amateurs who were not necessarily 'trained' in science but were extremely enthusiastic about it. Universities were still concentrating on teaching classics, theology, languages and mathematics and so there was very little formal science tuition in these institutions. As science was not government funded either, scientists needed to have some form of private income to fund their experiments, public lectures and to publish their books, with many scientists and doctors holding down part time jobs to pay for this. Irish born John Tyndall paid to study his PhD at the University of Marburg in Germany as he was unable to find an English one which supported science in the laboratory. Tyndall became an early experimenter of atmospheric physics and discovered that water vapour and carbon dioxide are far better at absorbing radiant heat compared to the gases in the Earth's atmosphere and discussed if this could affect the Earth's climate. He demonstrated how large molecules and dust diffuse light, known as the Tyndall effect, and also showed that the sun's rays are scattered by molecules, causing the sky to look blue.[5]

The rapid advancements in science led to the pressing need for scientists to receive public funding for their work. Science societies had already emerged in the late Georgian era to govern and regulate science as well as to help raise funds for scientists but more needed to be done, and quickly.

The Royal Society, founded in 1600 for the experimentation and communication of science, approached the government for financial backing for individual research projects its scientists wished to undertake. The society also garnered funds from private backers and public donations as well. Many scientists also funded their research themselves, especially if they had inherited a substantial amount of money, or they hunted themselves for their own private backer. It was rare for a scientist to be paid on a regular basis through public funds or an employer and so research and experiments took place on an ad-hoc basis, making it difficult to plan further research. In 1849, the Prime Minister Lord John Russell proposed that parliament made an annual grant to the Royal Society and in 1850 this went ahead with £1000 awarded to the society for scientists to apply for parts of it to fund their research.

The range of activities the grant initially supported was fairly narrow and focussed on astronomical and meteorological observation, the purchasing of new instruments and the publication of observations already accumulated by scientists, such as the differences between different fossils for example. But by the end of the century, it was offering a bigger grant to be shared and the government created its own Grants Board to distribute money directly to scientists based upon the subject they were studying.[6]

Public Lectures and Demonstrations

Working class and middle-class folk had a little more time on their hands due to a decrease of Saturday working hours and so men, women and children were all able to indulge their passions for sport, gardening, art and science. It was usual for Victorian middle-class adults to spend some time to attending lectures and demonstrations on the latest science, inventions and art. These open forums were crucial for explaining scientific and creative ideas and how these could develop in the future. Some were presented by formal societies such as The Geological Society, and others by lone entrepreneurs to demonstrate new technology or gadgets. Public lectures were explanations and demonstrations to convince the public of the importance of the scientific or technological idea. The public had an insatiable appetite for this information, especially those who had missed out on a decent schooling.

The Royal Institution gave public lectures in London and town halls all over England, showcasing local scientists' discoveries and endeavours. One such favourite was chemist and physicist Professor Michael Faraday who gave approximately 100 lectures on topics of general, popular science to the public before his death in 1867. John Tyndall, appointed to the Institution as Professor of Natural Philosophy in 1853, took over Faraday's positions at the Royal Institution, having co-lectured with Faraday on several occasions. Both men came from humble backgrounds and appreciated the public's appetite for scientific knowledge.

Scientists could be thought of and portrayed in both the press and literature as isolated individuals who beavered away on their own in laboratories, only emerging to share some wildly new fantastical idea with the public before going back inside to carry on. This could not be further from the truth as this portrayal does not consider the laboratory assistants who helped the scientist to organise and write up his work, the naval officers who allowed scientists to hitch a ride on their ships around the empire and the local people in British outposts who accompanied them around the land and introduced them to the traditional customs of the people.[7] Access to the ever-expanding British empire allowed the sciences of geology, zoology, botany and anthropology in particular to develop as new plants and lands were discovered and new plants and animals needed to be collected, examined, drawn and catalogued. Cartographers, geologists and naturalists made sense of these new discoveries. They collected, preserved, ordered and catalogued the exotic specimens of the empire and then displayed them for the public to see in the British Museum and at Kew Gardens.[8]

Scientific Leisure

Victorian were great collectors and cataloguers of science and many people collected and displayed dead insects, stuffed animals and pressed flowers. Nature rambles became a very popular past time as this was something adults and children could do together where they could build upon their reading and knowledge gained from books. They would visit a local common, forest, river, allotment or park where they could study plants, animals and insects in their natural habitat, recording what they saw through drawings and detailed notes, documenting the time of day to create a nature time trail on any given day. Steam trains meant that people could venture further afield to do this and trips to the seaside became popular, not only so people could relax and enjoy the sea air but so they could observe and draw nature in a completely different habitat.[9] Fossil and fern collecting became popular alongside the knowledge of the recent discoveries of dinosaurs.

They were mainly young men, although some women were just as interested but were not encouraged to pursue science. They carried out detailed observations and meticulous artistic drawings of creatures and plants. As there were no cameras at this point, this was the only way to record what they saw. Some beautiful artwork was produced as a result. Many women pressed flowers in special books, preserving all sorts of varieties over years at a time.[10]

Taxidermy was also a big trade as animals were preserved and sometimes presented against a diorama (big painted screen) of natural habitat. This meant that people could get up close and examine a bird's feathers, plumage, colours and textures and compare them to its neighbour. The Natural History Museum, set up in London in 1881, capitalised on the Victorians' love of natural history.[11]

Collecting and displaying curiosities from around the world had long been a gentleman's hobby as he needed the education and money to do so. Collections of butterflies, insects and so forth showed off his knowledge and provided a talking point for interested visitors to his home.[12] William Armstrong, the incredible engineer and inventor, went one better than this and used his home to pioneer the use of hydroelectric power.

Cragside, Armstrong's house near the town of Rothbury in Northumberland, was England's first home to make full use of electricity. By 1870, it had a domestic hydroelectric plant which powered some of the Estate buildings and Cragside itself. Gradually, each room became fully wired and lit by several lightbulbs, starting with the picture gallery lit by the first lightbulbs provided by Joseph Swann. Armstrong also added in an early dishwasher, a hydraulic lift and a central heating system. Outside, he and his wife Margaret transformed the barren, rocky heath into a landscape full of trees and shrubs and different garden rooms following the Arts and Crafts Movement. The Armstrongs embraced both physics and nature and enmeshed the two together at Cragside.[13]

Where Could a Victorian Learn about Science?

Even ordinary, working-class people were able to hear about the new discoveries of plants, animals, countries and cultures unknown before to the English people. The increase in education and literacy meant that teachers and governesses were able to increasingly teach science to their young pupils alongside geography and history. London University offered the first Science degree in 1860. But for those who had finished school and unable to go to university, newspapers, magazines and books were the next best thing.

Journalists would attend the lectures and demonstrations alongside the public and report their version of the scientific theory and their opinion. Much of the science reporting in the press in the early days was sensationalism but it soon became a vital resource for those who could not make the events.

The mass printing of books and pamphlets during the Industrial Revolution did not stop at fiction. By the 1840s, cheaper, shorter and easier to read science books were written and produced for the literate working classes. The Victorian era saw a development in literature which was populated with illustrations. The general public loved these and between 1830 and 1860 there was an upsurge in production of affordable magazines and newspapers which reported on all sorts of scientific news and were accompanied by beautiful, hand drawn illustrations.

New scientific journals appeared such as *Hardwicke's Science -Gossip* (1865), *Recreative Science* (1859) and *The Magazine of Natural History* (1828) and The Field Naturalist (1833). These journals were aimed at members of the public and students who were interested in science and all the latest discoveries. These upper working class and middle-class Victorians were happy to buy and read these periodicals which helped to both popularise science and encouraged discussion and opinions.[14]

Scientific journals or periodicals took on an increased importance as scientists, inventors and expeditioners published their work to communicate not only with other scientists but with the public too. They published articles detailing their results from experiments and their analysis. This meant they could build upon each other's work. Becoming published was crucial to scientists' careers and periodicals such as Nature, The Intellectual Observer and *The Lancet* provided space for this. A lot of the visual representation of science was also a way of selling science to both the general public and also the government so scientists could continue to obtain financial backing for their next exploration, experiment or hypothesis.[15]

Science as a Profession

For the poorer working-class person, science possibly did not impact their lives as much as the educated person unless it was through improvements to public health at work and at home, but changes were gradual; arguably not quick enough as the profession grew stronger and began to influence both technology and the medical world.

By the middle of the century, science had become an established profession in its own right. Clergy men were discouraged from studying science by both scientists and the Church and encouraged to concentrate on theology and pastoral care instead. By the end of the Victorian era, science and religion were two separate disciplines but that is not to say that scientists could not be Christian, and clergymen were unbelievers of modern science.[16]

Charles Darwin and Evolution

It is sufficient to say that generally at the beginning of Queen Victoria's reign, all sorts of upheavals were taking place in society. Social, economic, technological, geological and intellectual changes all challenged the Victorians' orthodox view of the world. For instance, middle class merchants became as rich as aristocrats and were able to build themselves country estates to rival those of the local duke and duchess. This upset the social order as people from a lower class were living the same lifestyle as the aristocracy, and the economic order because their money was earned through trade rather than inherited. By the 1830s, Victorians no longer searched for proof of God's existence, they took it as an act of faith that he existed. Alongside this, as the railways were built, geologists started to make discoveries about rock and fossil formations which threatened the orthodox view of Christianity and the timeline for the making of the world. English Victorians, along with their ancestors, believed that God made the world and that everyone had their own place in society, preordained by God. But now this idea itself was being challenged by Charles Darwin and his theory of evolution.

Charles Darwin's book, *On the Origin of Species*, questioned the accepted view that man was made in God's image, as laid out in the book of Genesis. Rather, he argued, man exists the way he does now because he has continually changed and developed in response to natural forces over which he had no control. He also argued against the Chain of Being where man is in the ultimate and superior position and therefore closest to God. He saw no end point to evolution; rather he saw the world of nature as a continuous struggle for survival. Darwin showed that the factors of chance and necessity were what caused creatures to evolve in their environment and therefore survive. All species of creatures and plants struggle against the odds to survive, and those who did were the ones who managed to reproduce the most.[17] The sociologist and philosopher Herbert Spencer called this idea 'the survival of the fittest' and Darwin's ideas were seized upon by some to justify a lack of state intervention in public health and the economy. Other scientists did not subscribe to this school of thought and towards the end of the nineteenth century, they were working extremely hard to disprove the miasma theory which had prevailed throughout the era and was stopping the progression of medicine and public health.

Germ Theory

Many scientists knew that microbes existed, and they were central to decomposition, fermentation and disease, but had yet to prove why they grew, how they multiplied and how they were passed on. In 1840, the German scientist Jacob Henle conjectured that organisms caused disease by attaching themselves to the host. Later, he proposed that germs were living organisms themselves.[18] Jacob's work was based upon insect expert Agostino Bassi, who after a long series of experiments on silk moth caterpillars concluded that the fungus which these insects tended to suffer from was spread via powdery spores when the moths were kept in close proximity to each other. Ten years later, Agostino Bassi theorised that this could happen in animals and plants too.

Meanwhile, in Vienna in 1847, obstetrician Ignaz Semmelweis conjectured that doctors were carrying decaying particles on their hands and clothes from mother to mother which entered the natural abrasions left from childbirth, causing puerperal fever to set in, leading to death. The idea of microbes entering the body via a wound, or the mouth was beginning to take hold. It was very difficult to prove the germ theory though, and more time for the development of the science industry in general was needed alongside more scientists to study the behaviour of microbes.

John Snow and Cholera

Scientists and doctors realised quite early on that cholera was most virulent in slum areas and other working-class areas where people lived in poor, crowded and dirty conditions. Many doctors tracked the demographics of cholera and noted who had it and where. They considered the environment and even the weather to work out how it moved so quickly from person to person. But the overall prevailing collective thought from the medicine community was that miasma passed on cholera. In a way, this makes sense because slum housing caused poor sanitation and ventilation so other diseases which were spread by droplets from the respiratory system such as such as TB, influenza and colds were also virulent amongst the poor. But when a particularly nasty outbreak in Soho in September 1854 killed 500 people in 10 days, Dr John Snow took drastic action.

He got to work plotting the deaths on a map of the area of Broad Street and Golden Square with the assistance of the Reverend Henry Whitehead. It became apparent that the deaths were clustered around the water pump on Broad Street, from which the residents of this area collected their water. After an engineer examined the well beneath the street and found it contaminated with faeces, the local board of Guardian agreed to remove the handle forcing people to draw water elsewhere. The epidemic quickly tailed off.[19] However, local public health experts refused to believe Dr Snow's theory that Cholera was waterborne and making its way into the body orally, and the infection had spread through the pump. Instead, they found other reasons for the end of the epidemic namely that people had moved away or were dead and so the area was less crowded, hence less miasma, hence no more cholera.

It took another 12 years and another cholera epidemic before the medical profession began to think that maybe there was some truth in Snow's theory when his ideas were built upon by Louis Pasteur.

Louis Pasteur

A French microbiologist and renowned chemist, like many scientists Louis worked in agriculture to stop animals getting sick and to stop food spoiling. In the mid-1850s he was asked to look at why beer spoiled so easily in the fermentation process. He identified that the fermentation process depended upon microbes and the wrong type turned the beer sour, effectively contaminating it. He found the same microbes spoiled milk and butter. He demonstrated how heating products in a specific way and to a specific temperature could kill the contaminants without spoiling the product, a practice which went on to become known as pasteurisation. Pasteur did not stop there though. He boldly stated that the microbes were already in the air and did not come into being as part of the fermentation process, but as this went against popular scientific theory at the time, it was not accepted. Pasteur went onto speculate that these microbes could cause putrefaction in wounds and the profession lost interest.[20]. Joseph Lister, however, found that Pasteur's theories fitted in with his own and decided to concentrate on how these microbes could be killed, thus preventing infection.

Joseph Lister

Born in 1827, at a young age, Joseph Lister decided he wanted to become a surgeon which was an interesting choice of career as socially, surgeons were looked down upon as they used their hands for a living. Luckily, this did not put Lister off, and he combined his love of surgery with his love of the microscope to study pus, tissue and blood from wounds infected with gangrene, drawing what he saw and questioning how the infection spread. It was whilst working as a surgeon at Glasgow Infirmary alongside Ignaz Semmelweis that Lister became convinced that the spread of infection was due to infective material entering the wound, causing inflammation, infection and death. He decided to try treating wounds with antiseptic, something similar to headlice lotion which had been discovered to kill the bugs in a child's hair without hurting the scalp. Lister decided such a potion was needed for wounds; a way of killing the microbes without harming the skin. He settled on carbolic acid to clean wounds and surgical instruments. He also soaked the bandages in it before applying them to the wound. It was not long before he saw an improvement in the healing of wounds.[21]

Lister applied his antiseptic methods for two years at Glasgow Infirmary and produced paper after paper of evidence, but he still struggled to get his theory accepted by the medical profession. Eventually, in 1876, Lister travelled to America to speak at the conference of the International Medical Congress and to sell America his antiseptic system. Whilst there, he performed several operations in front of an audience, showing off his methods of germ management. Massachusetts General Hospital endorsed Lister's practices and soon the rest of England followed. A year later, he was appointed Professor of Clinical Surgery at Kings College, London.[22]

Robert Koch

In the meantime, another scientist was working in agriculture. The German Robert Koch is most famous for discovering how the bacteria which caused the nasty disease Anthrax survived and multiplied. Attacking cattle, sheep, pigs and humans, Anthrax was a swift and deadly disease which first showed itself when the animal became agitated and excited with fever, staggering and confused before collapsing from cardiac arrest. Anthrax had always confounded scientists because they could not explain how or why the disease seemed to spontaneously erupt in animals and this constant re-emergence of the disease gave yet more weight to the miasma theory.

Through patient experimentation and observation, Koch discovered that each Anthrax bacterium could exist in the form a dormant spore. This tiny spore was unaffected by a lack of oxygen, water, food and warmth. It merely lay dormant until it came back into contact with these things, via its host of cattle or sheep and then the bacterium would germinate and spread, similarly, a plant seed can lay dormant all winter and then germinate in spring once the weather becomes warmer. Koch demonstrated how the Anthrax microbes lived in farm soil and so were easily transmitted back to the animals once the conditions became right.[23]

Koch's published theory and subsequent control measures greatly reduced Anthrax on farms and paved the way for Koch's work on Tuberculosis. He went on to discover the microbe which caused Tuberculosis, demonstrated its life cycle and how Tuberculosis was transmitted. He then developed a test for Tuberculosis in patients who could possibly have contracted the disease but were not yet showing the obvious symptoms and this allowed for infected patients to be isolated. Tuberculosis hospitals helped to prevent the spread of Tuberculosis and for some sufferers to live a longer life.

Robert Koch also used his special staining technique to isolate the cholera bacterium, definitively proving that cholera was a water borne disease and that the bacterium lived in faecal matter and could only enter the body orally through contaminated food, water, clothes and hands. The science and medical profession were still slow to accept this theory possibly because it meant that John Snow had been right, and thousands of deaths could have been avoided.

Because these bacteriologists were able to show how bacteria spread certain diseases, streets were cleaned up, rubbish was removed on a regular basis, bodies were buried properly, adequate housing was built, and hospitals became places of help rather than harm, a place where life was extended rather than shortened, a place that people could enter and then leave again possibly healthier than before.

The Heat Ray

Nearly a hundred years after Mary Shelley's Viktor Frankenstein used electricity to give life to the dead, William Kemmler was the first person to be executed by the use of electricity. The execution took place in New York City on 6 August 1890, and was as bungled as the public hangings which it was supposed to replace. It took 2000 volts to eventually kill William Kemmler with reports that after the first, timed dose of 1000 volts, Kemmler was still alive and starting to come round.[24]

The Victorian era closed with the great imagination of Herbert George Wells capturing a fictionalised future where science was used and abused in all sorts of ways. Born in 1866, Wells trained as a student teacher before undertaking a degree in biology at what is now Imperial College, University of London. He later became a biology teacher at a private school but was already experimenting with what would become known later as science fiction.[25]

He published The War of the Worlds in 1898 to great acclaim, inventing the concept of the Heat Ray, carried by the Martians' tripods and able to wipe out trees, houses and humans within the blink of an eye. The narrator attempts to explain the possible science behind the Heat Ray: 'Many think that in some way they are able to generate an intense heat in a chamber of practically absolute non-conductivity. This intense heat they project in a parallel beam against any object they choose, by means of a polished parabolic mirror of unknown composition, much as the parabolic mirror of a lighthouse projects a beam of light. But no one has absolutely proved these details. However, it is done, it is certain that a beam of heat is the essence of the matter. Heat, and invisible, instead of visible, light. Whatever is combustible flashes into flame at its touch, lead runs like water, it softens iron, cracks and melts glass, and when it falls upon water, incontinently that explodes into steam.'[26]

Science

H.G Wells uses his understanding of the popular sciences of the age to good use. Futuristic astronomy, physics and chemistry are all present and explained throughout the story. The Martians' machines which lead the characters to believe they have discovered the secret of flying, the deadly black smoke which gases people to death and the red weed which chokes the rivers and crops. But it is Wells' favourite subject which defeats these future warmongers in the end, lending hope to the readers that even if Martians really did land on earth, then our own bacteria and germs would soon wipe them out.

'Dead! – slain by the putrefactive and disease bacteria against which their systems were unprepared; slain as the red weed was being slain; slain, after all man's devices failed, by the humblest thing that God in his wisdom, has put upon this earth.'[27]

At the end of the book, an intact body of one of the Martians is preserved in a large jar and put on display in the Natural History Museum for scientific study and general curiosity. A typically Victorian reaction.

Chapter Fourteen

Inventions

> 'The true creator is necessity, who is the mother of our invention.'
>
> Plato[1]

As the era progressed, the self-confidence and ambition of British Victorians steadily grew. This was the era of the inventor, with British Victorians inventing many gadgets, household items and practices which they exhibited and demonstrated; some made fortunes from their inventions whilst others failed and died destitute. For most, it was somewhere in between but for all, inventing was a calling, a desire to pit their wits against nature, adversity and each other.

Towards the end of the 1840s, the idea for a national exhibition of nature, science, engineering and art started to form in the mind of civil servant Henry Cole. He had already assisted with the reform of the postal system and in 1843, he introduced the first ever Christmas card to the public by commissioning an artist to paint his design and then selling them in his art shop. Cole knew that he wanted to achieve an exhibition bigger and better than the Paris Exposition of 1849 as by now, Britain was known as 'the workshop of the world'[2].

The Great Exhibition of 1851

> 'It may be said, without presumption, that an event like this exhibition could not have taken place at any earlier period, and perhaps not among any other people than ourselves.'
>
> Henry Cole[3]

The Great Exhibition was a culmination of the manufacturing boom of the last thirty years which produced the plethora of successful engineers, inventors and designers alongside the writers, artists and radical thinkers of the time. There were three such men who all got on well together and had the same aims in the promotion of the arts and industry: Henry Cole, Prince Albert and Joseph Paxton.

Henry Cole was a leading member of the Society of Arts which Prince Albert joined in his role as patron of the arts, swiftly becoming president. In 1844, the Society of Arts began holding small exhibitions to showcase the latest useful inventions and the membership list steadily increased. In 1849, Henry Cole proposed a national exhibition to rival the ones held in Paris, except Henry and Albert agreed it should be a global exhibition to unite all the allies and countries of the British empire, as this had never been done before. Prince Albert hoped it would promote peace and goodwill whereas Henry Cole thought 'particular advantage to British Industry might be derived from placing it in fair competition with that of other nations.'[4]

Typically, this was an ingenious idea reflecting the industrious ambition of the time. The hungry forties were over, free trade was in full swing and the invention of products to improve people's lives were the focus of many traders, scientists, entrepreneurs and engineers. Britain had exhibited goods and objects of excellence at industry fairs for years. In 1756, the Society of Arts exhibited tapestries, carpets, porcelain and other goods with prizes awarded for the most excellent and finest skill and quality. The Royal Academy, with private patronage of the King exhibited paintings, engravings and sculptures from the artist of the day. In fact, since 1820, pretty much every city and important manufacturing town had held an exhibition of some kind of machines and goods manufactured.[5] But what made this project different was not only the sheer scale of it but the fact that it was for every man, woman and child regardless of class.

And so, the idea for the Great Exhibition was born, swiftly followed by a Royal Commission to plan and run the event. The members of the Society of Arts put up the original funds but there was no government grant to add to the treasury. Instead, the government sanctioned the project, provided the site of Hyde Park in London, helped with the correspondence with other countries and organised the new police force to help with security, all paid for out of Exhibition funds. Any profit, it was decided, would be used to fund future arts and science work.[6]

The building for the exhibition was designed by Joseph Paxton, a gardener for the Duke of Devonshire who had built the duke a giant greenhouse made of glass in which to store some of the duke's plants. Joseph based his design for the exhibition building upon his 'Chatsworth Stove'. The beauty of his design was in the amount of iron framed glass panels to be used which could be fabricated off site and then slotted together onsite. Once the exhibition was over, this building – dubbed the Crystal Palace – could be easily dismantled and moved to a new home. It took approximately 5000 navvies to build the Crystal Palace and it eventually stood at 564m long and 33m high[7]. It was the largest glass building in the world and a beautiful sight to behold. Its design had been adapted to be built around some large elm trees in Hyde Park, so they were incorporated inside as part of the exhibition alongside the centrepiece of a magnificent pink glass fountain.

The Great Exhibition opened on 1 May 1851, with a gun salute, a prayer led by the Archbishop of Canterbury, a choir singing the Hallelujah Chorus and the National Anthem all marking the momentous occasion. Queen Victoria gave a speech praising her husband's tireless work and declared the exhibition open.[8]

The first day was kept by for those who had bought a season ticket for the Exhibition, members of the government and the aristocracy and other worthy dignitaries. The next two days were also expensive at £1 per person and then the first three weeks of exhibition were aimed at the wealthy as tickets were 5 shillings each. The ticket price then dropped to 1 shilling per person except on Fridays when tickets were 2s 6d and Saturday when tickets were 5s each. Saturday tickets were eventually reduced to 2s 6d each by August, allowing for poorer people to attend.[9]

Exhibits of the Great Exhibition

The content of the exhibition fell into one of four categories: manufacturing, machinery, raw goods and fine art leading to an eclectic mix of 100,000 exhibits. There was something to interest everyone: a device for making cigarettes, luxurious gold embroidered shawls from India, the best watches from Switzerland, beautiful mosaics from Italy and sledges from Russia.

Wackier and perhaps more 'Victorian' products included an expanding hearse, an eighty-blade knife from Sheffield, a collapsible piano to take on a yacht and a galvanic bath which gave the bather mild electric shocks. [10]

Some exhibits showed a process such as Fry and Sons from Bristol whose display was made up of the objects required to make chocolate such as assorted cocoa leaves, a variety of cocoa nuts, the trunk of a cocoa tree, ground chocolate, chocolate paste, a drying house and a large, labelled illustration of a cocoa tree. Solid chocolate was a recent invention pioneered by Fry and Sons who had launched the first solid chocolate bar only four years previously.

Other inventions we can recognise today. Willoughby's invalid carriage which carried a person with fractures led down flat on a specially designed seat is a precursor to the ambulance. William Baddeley's portable fire engine for agriculture was not unlike a modern-day fire extinguisher. The multi-wheeled velocipedes, a contraption in modern eyes, were eagerly adapted later on to make the bicycle.[11]

There was one invention, its technology and processes exhibited by many at the Exhibition, but possibly underappreciated which then went onto undeniably capture the attention of every Victorian throughout the era: photography.

Photography

Emerging at the same time Queen Victoria ascended to the throne, photography captured and recorded practically the whole era. The first official photograph is attributed to Joseph Niepce, a French inventor and then Louis Daguerre and Henry Fox Talbot took this further but with two different ways of capturing an image. Louis Daguerre invented the Daguerreotype and Henry Fox Talbot invented the Calotype and both fought for photographic supremacy.

The Great Exhibition showcased a mixture of approximately 700 daguerreotypes, calotypes and stereo cards which were a particular favourite of Queen Victoria. Photographic equipment was also displayed and demonstrated.[12] The reports published after the exhibition included plates of photographs detailing a selection of exhibits.

At first, photography was appropriated by the wealthy which led to fast technical improvements as they had the time and the money to experiment with the new equipment and the taking of photographs. Early practitioners were a mixture of scientist and artist as they sought not only to capture images on paper for posterity but to fix them and make them permanent and also artistic and pleasant to look at. They sought to emulate the portrait, still life and landscape of the oil painting, concentrating on balancing the subject against the background and conveying an air of nobility and elegance which the middle classes soaked up. In 1851, there were 12 photographic studios in London; by 1866 there were 254.[13] Photography was rapidly becoming de rigeur as customers were happy to attend a studio in a fashionable part of town.

The most fashionable form of 19th century photograph was the carte-de-visite. Designed and patented by Andre Disderi, he discovered he could fit four smaller images onto a single plate, producing a strip of images which were cut up and glued onto card. Each not much bigger than a visiting card, hence their name, these photographs were sold in shops and swapped among friends and family. Collections were built and preserved in photo albums alongside illustrations and handwritten descriptions. Queen Victoria and Prince Albert had carte de visites made and sold as did other well-known people such as Charles Darwin.[14]

War Photography

Civilians and serving soldiers with photography training captured army life for the British people. Civilian photographers lived with the army in the same conditions. Roger Fenton, a renowned photographer and founder of the Royal Photographic Society, went out to Crimea to capture images of the army and the war for the newspapers back home. He used the wet plate, or wet collodion method, setting up a dark room in his caravan to develop the photographs which were sent back home. The London Illustrated News increased its readership from 100,000 a week to 200,000 as it reported the war in detail[15]

It was not just war which captured photographer's imagination. Photographers used the camera to research and capture real life in all its dirt and glory. As concern for the poor increased throughout the century, photographers started to record life on the streets and in the slums, capturing the effects of disease, poor housing and poverty and placing the images before the wealthier public who could no longer deny that an underclass of people really did exist, suffering indignities through no fault of their own.

The most well-known of all these is a series of photographs by photographer John Thomson and social journalist Adolphe Smith. Not unlike Henry Mayhew's earlier written accounts of London's poor, the duo teamed up in 1877 to photograph London's poor in their day-to-day conditions, producing a series of pamphlets called 'Street Life in London', the first photographically illustrated work to portray social life.

These pamphlets made it impossible for the authorities and the general public to ignore any longer the living conditions of the poor in Britain and added much needed weight to the cause for improved public health.

The Railway

The inventions, engineering and science on display in the exhibition were only part of the showcase of British ingenuity. People travelled to the exhibition from all over the country on the new steam railway put together by Brunel and the other great engineers, enjoying comfortable and speedy travel to the hottest event of the decade. But because no one anticipated that the wealthier working classes should like to attend too, the first 'en-masse' train excursions with overnight accommodation included were dreamt up by Thomas Cook and Joseph Paxton in a last-minute attempt to make sure that the Great Exhibition, which was marketed as 'for everyone' was attended by 'everyone'.

Thomas Cook is widely hailed as the inventor of the package holiday and the father of tourism. He was deeply religious, teetotal and committed to helping the working classes improve their lives. He also loved the new railways and saw them as a force for good for the midland and northern working classes who spent long days working inside factories and mills. Thomas believed that travel broadened the mind, educated people, fired their imagination, relaxed them and above all, gave them hope. He also believed deeply in the temperance movement and that day trips and excursions were a good alternative to drinking alcohol and gambling. With his skills in printing, travel writing and marketing, Thomas started running excursions across the midland's countryside for members of the temperance movement and the Baptist church. By 1850, he was running a thriving excursion business and happily rose to the challenge of getting the masses to the Great Exhibition.

Thomas hit upon the idea of providing accommodation as well as train journeys for all his excursionists, but the local hoteliers and lodging houses were reluctant to commit to a price so early on, hoping they would be able command a higher price nearer the time. So, Thomas found some suitable buildings, leased them and turned them into his own lodging houses. He leased the Ranelagh Club Mechanics Home in Vauxhall near Pimlico because it could sleep one thousand people every night. Thomas partitioned it into small units where each person had access to a clean bed, soap, a towel, hot water and a toilet, all for 1s and 3d a night. Boot cleaning was 1d extra. He even procured a policeman to be on hand should things get a bit drunken and disorderly.

Meanwhile, Thomas set up a travel club for the Great Exhibition where customers paid around sixpence into the club each week, ready to pay for their excursion. He also started up a new magazine called Cook's Exhibition Herald and Excursion Advertiser, to advertise the Great Exhibition and his travel plans. He included the fare prices, ideas for places to stay including his own lodging houses, and adverts from local businesses. Once the Exhibition was over, the magazine continued to be published under its shorter title of The Excursionist.

Thomas used The Excursionist to pose the question:' How are working men, their wives and children to get to the Exhibition?' He then spent many issues explaining the obvious answer: with Thomas Cook.

For three months, Thomas laboured to get people to the Exhibition and back for only 5 shillings. The word was spread throughout Leeds, Derby, Sheffield and Bradford, with advertising on factory gates, on street corners and even with a brass band. Once the Exhibition was open, Thomas spent the whole time travelling to London and back with his passengers to make sure everything went smoothly. In total, he transported 165,000 people to the Great Exhibition including 3,000 children from day schools and Sunday schools in Leicester, Derby and Nottingham. One fifth of the British population visited the Great Exhibition and Thomas Cook played a tremendous part in making sure the poorer people had their day out too.[16]

The Great Exhibition Legacy

Once the exhibition closed in October 1851, the Crystal Palace was deconstructed and carefully moved piece by piece to Sydenham Hill in South London. Here, it was rebuilt to become a museum of ancient and modern culture, hosting musical concerts, sporting competitions, dog shows, and exhibitions of photography, art, transport, animals and mining.

The surrounding grounds were landscaped into Italian style ornamental gardens with terraces, statues and fountains. The largest maze in the country added to the aristocratic feel of the place and the shores of the boating lake displayed life size replica dinosaurs representing three prehistoric eras. A topsy-turvey railway and a water chute added to the excitement and fireworks displays and balloon ascents heightened the theme park atmosphere. Here, visitors could access as many treats as they could afford or just enjoy the scenery and gardens with a stroll through the park or a picnic.[17]

The positive ramifications of the Great Exhibition were felt for the rest of Queen Victoria's reign, as the new technology and inventions continued to be embraced by both the monarchy and the general public. Having seen scientists and inventors in action and endorsed by the monarchy, the public no longer viewed them as lonesome mad men but as forward thinkers who only wanted to educate, entertain and improve the lives of the masses.

This ideal was helped by the profit made by the Great Exhibition. It was used to finance the Natural History Museum, the Science Museum, the Victoria and Albert Museum, the Imperial College of Science, the Royal Exchange of art, music and organists and the Royal Albert Hall, all based in South Kensington.

In 1905, the site at Sydenham also became home to Crystal Palace Football Club which is now the Great Exhibitions' only legacy as the Crystal Palace itself burned down in a fire in November 1936 and was never rebuilt.

Chapter Fifteen

Victorian Medicine

> 'She had a fever. He bled her, and told me to let her live on
> whey and water – gruel, and take care she did not throw
> herself downstairs or out of the window ...'
>
> *Wuthering Heights*[1]

The Victorians progressed medicine as much as industry. Thanks to the pioneering work of surgeons and scientists who also collaborated with those abroad, by the end of Queen Victoria's reign medical doctors had implemented the use of painkillers, anaesthetic and germ theory to cut death rates. But in 1837, there was still a long way to go on the arduous journey to prove the miasma theory a myth and the germ theory real.

Miasma Theory

The word miasma comes from the Greek language and means defilement or dirtied. As a noun, it means an unpleasant or unhealthy smell or vapour.

The ancient miasmatical theory of disease had been followed by the medical profession for centuries. The profession believed that foul smelling air carried disease and decomposing material, which was breathed in and made people sick. This theory was justified when cholera entered the country from Asia and wreaked havoc through the overcrowded, rubbish strewn and dirty slums of all the cities in England. This overshadowed John Snow's later work on germ theory and the spread of cholera through dirty water.

Florence Nightingale believed deeply in the miasma theory and so her reforms in nursing of open windows, fresh air, cleanliness, frequent changing of bandages and bedding were heavily based upon her desire to remove bad odour and decomposing material. However, this new approach led to a reduction in infection rate and so the miasmatical theory continued.

In order to guard against bad smells and thus infection, Victorians continued to use the age-old methods of their ancestors. Oranges studded with cloves and bunches of dried flowers and herbs decorated the houses of the wealthy to ward against bad smells. Ladies carried perfumed handkerchiefs or little metal pomanders filled with sponges soaked in vinegar when they went out and about on the streets, to sniff at regular intervals. Drinking tea was thought to strengthen the immune system against infection, which in a way it did because the boiling of the water to make the tea killed the germs. Later, smoking was feted as the best way to ward off miasma as it was thought it cleared the lungs.

Infectious Diseases of the Victorian Era

Cholera

Cholera is probably the one disease most associated with Victorian England. Introduced to this country in 1831, it had already been discovered in India and Asia and worked its way across Europe to enter England at the port of Sunderland. By 1832, it had spread throughout the British Isles.[2]

Cholera is caused by the bacterium Vibrio Cholerae which lodges in the intestines, causing cramping and burning in the guts. The body then tries to dispel the bacteria through copious amounts of vomiting and diarrhoea which leads to the body losing essential salts and dehydrating rapidly. In the latter stages of the disease, the skin wrinkles and turns grey with a blue tinge and the voice turns husky. At this time, cholera nearly always led to death as organ failure set in.

Tuberculosis (TB)

Throughout the nineteenth century, it is estimated that 25% of all deaths in Europe were due to TB.[3] The contemporary Victorian term for tuberculosis was consumption and someone could be described as consumptive or consumptive in appearance.

TB is caused by a bacterium which lodges itself in the lungs and causes legions which bleed so the sufferer then coughs up blood. Other symptoms include flu-like feelings such as a fever, achiness and a persistent cough. Sometimes, the lesions healed themselves, trapping the bacteria within a protective layer of scar tissue but mostly, the infection effectively consumed the lungs. The illness led to weight loss and anaemia and despite 'romantic' images of Victorian ladies and gents with pale skin, enhanced, rosy cheekbones and a slim fashionable appearance, there was clearly nothing romantic about the hacking cough and the feeling of suffocation the patient endured.[4]

Because human TB is spread through the droplets of sputum ejected through coughing, TB worked its way through families, especially those living or working in poor, cramped conditions. The Bronte sisters and their brother all succumbed to TB. Branwell, who was an alcoholic and opium user died first aged only 31; Emily died four months later aged 30. Anne died a year later, aged 29. Charlotte lived longer, managing to marry and become pregnant before succumbing to the illness aged 38. She died of TB but was also suffering from acute morning sickness which had weakened her. The family had already lost the two elder daughters to TB, caught at their boarding school some years earlier. It was unusual for middle class, comfortably housed families to all die this way and modern historians now conjecture if the drinking water supply had been weakening their immune systems over the years. The parsonage was next door to the graveyard and a nearby spring from which the family drew their water. It is possible that the rainwater which soaked through the graveyard contaminated the spring with a low-level constant supply of bacteria which weakened their constitutions.[5]

Typhoid (Bowel Fever)
Caused by the Salmonella Typhi bacterium, a relation to the bacterium which causes food poisoning, it is passed on orally through contaminated food and drink, so in the Victorian era it was commonly caught through contaminated wells and water pumps. It was virulent in the military, especially in war zones due to the lack of clean, running water.

The beginnings of the disease were similar to that of a cold or flu with a general feeling of weariness, aching and headache at which sufferers would typically take to their bed. Later followed a fever and a rash called 'rose spot' which was the tell-tale sign of Typhoid, and that the sufferer was in danger. Delirium would come next and then the stomach pain and diarrhoea caused by ulcers in the bowel. Typhoid typically lasted weeks rather than days and the sufferer could develop bronchitis or pneumonia which could then kill them. However, other patients recovered fine although recovery would take weeks even months.[6]

Typhus
Typhus was a group of illnesses which had been around for hundreds of years, but in the Victorian era there was a resurgence due to overcrowded living conditions. Transmitted to humans via bacteria from infected body lice, fleas, ticks or mites, the bacteria would work its way into the human bloodstream through the louse's infectious bite. The infected louse's faeces on the sufferer's body could be rubbed into the itchy insect bites through scratching, and faeces on the clothes could also spread this disease to others.

Symptoms of Typhus included a general achiness and weariness combined with the chills. A fever and delirium then followed, and sufferers often died from dehydration. In its early stages, Typhus was often muddled with Typhoid.

Typhus was definitely linked to slum housing and poor sanitation as many residents were unable to wash at all, let alone wash in hot water to remove the lice and their faeces. Bedding needed to be soaked in boiling water and floors and walls needed to be washed down with hot, soapy water too. Cases of

Typhus increased in cold weather because poorer people wore more layers of clothes and also wore them in bed, thus staying in the same clothes night and day. It was very difficult to get these clothes washed and dried in cold dwellings without adequate heating. Typhus also attacked common lodging houses, jails, ships and prisons. Anywhere there was famine, poverty or war, Typhus spread.[7]

Diphtheria
This nasty infection killed mainly children, but adults succumbed too. Queen Victoria's granddaughter caught diphtheria but survived; it was her mother Alice, Queen Victoria's second daughter who died from it.[8] Starting as a sore throat, the bacteria go onto attack the back of the throat and nose, making it difficult to breathe and coating the throat in a whitish grey poisonous membrane which is absorbed into the body.

The diphtheria bacillus thrived in damp conditions and so seemed to affect the poor who lived in foggy, damp urban areas with little drainage and ventilation.

Diphtheria was spread through infected people, clothing, milk, books, dust and even animals such as cats. It was difficult to distinguish at first from other childhood diseases such as scarlet fever, croup, measles, thrush and tonsillitis (quinsy) and so it could be some time before the patient was diagnosed and isolated from others, by which time the disease had already spread through the family and community.

Syphilis
Syphilis is a sexually transmitted disease and was another prevalent disease of the Victorian era. Starting with genital sores, the ulcers and lesions quickly spread across the body eventually attacking the eyes, mouth and nose causing horrific disfigurement and great pain all over the body. Sufferers were admitted to hospital once syphilis was fully blown, and there they usually died quite quickly. Unfortunately, it could take several years for syphilis to take hold and the sufferer was usually unaware they were carrying the disease at first, causing it to spread amongst prostitutes and their customers. Because so many prostitutes caught it, syphilis was thought to spontaneously erupt in immoral women, adding more weight to the miasma theory.[9]

Ailments
As well as the many diseases, Victorians suffered from many ailments for which there wasn't really adequate relief or a cure.

Chest complaints were the most common ailment especially amongst the working classes and the poor as they lived in the built up, urban areas. Upper respiratory infections were caused by fog, pollution and damp and the common cold but could easily develop into bronchitis and pneumonia, otherwise known as winter fever. Pleurisy, another lung condition where the membranous lining of the lungs becomes inflamed was also caused by the usual culprits of pollution, fog and damp. Emphysema, a chronic disease of the lungs marked by a shortness of breath, a hacking cough, a barrel shaped chest and a blue tinge to the skin, was also caused by pollution but also smoking.

Vitamin and mineral deficiencies caused a lot of damage, especially to working class and poor children. Iron deficiency caused tiredness and a shortness of breath, Vitamin D and calcium deficiency caused Ricketts bone disease and lack of Vitamin C caused scurvy leading to tooth loss. Wealthier adults who could afford a richer and varied diet didn't suffer from these deficiencies but instead were prey to nausea, stomach-ache, constipation and headaches, collective symptoms known as biliousness. A diet rich in red meat, salt and alcohol also led to gout, a build-up of crystals in the joints causing painful inflammation. This mixed with stress and being overweight could also lead to apoplexy, known today as a stroke.

Accidents

Every occupation in Victorian England had its danger. Labourers were at risk of being crushed, developing hernias, or falling. Sailors tended to fall from heights or drown. Firearms accidents were a frequent occurrence in the army.[10] Railway workers were open to steam scalds and burns and factory and mill workers were prone to eye injuries, mangled limbs and crushing injuries from machinery. In the home, occupants could easily burn themselves, accidentally poison themselves and fall down the stairs,

Dentistry

Toothache was another common complaint, mainly due to the increase in processed sugar in the diet but a lack of toothpaste, toothbrushes and a knowledge of oral hygiene in general. In the middle and upper classes, the increased consumption of champagne led to tooth decay also. But like doctors, dentists charged for their services and so the poor only ever went to the dentist to have a tooth extracted, and even then, they would try to see a volunteer dentist if they could. For wealthier people, dentists scaled and polished their teeth, treated gum disease, removed overcrowded teeth, filled teeth and made and fitted dentures. Sometimes they did more harm than good as whitening treatment included cleaning the teeth with powder made from ground chalk, salt, brick and charcoal. Overuse stripped the tooth enamel leading to sensitive teeth and decay. Dentists kept the good teeth they extracted and obtained teeth from dead people to make the early style dentures. These dentures were first known as 'Waterloo Teeth' because the teeth needed were extracted from the mouths of soldiers killed at the battle of Waterloo. Later in the century, dentures were made from porcelain.[11]

All dentists, or tooth operators as they were originally known, had to have hands on training and so completed apprenticeships first. However, dentistry itself was unlicensed and so although the wealthy could pick and choose their dentist, the working class and poor had to use who they could find and hope the dentist was sober and proficient enough in removing teeth. A trip to the dentist certainly was not fun for anyone, with most people preferring to take their chances with a sore tooth or try home extractions instead. The instruments used looked terrifying, there was no pain relief other than to get so drunk it would numb the pain, and the risk of infection setting in afterwards was extremely high. It wasn't until 1878 that the Dentists Act required all dentists to register as a Licentiate in Dental Surgery, but even then, the practice of dentistry itself was still unlicensed and unregulated. It was a pair of American dentists who wanted to make life easier for their patients and themselves who started to experiment with pain relief in the hope of advancing dentistry alongside surgery.

Pain Relief

There was very little effective pain relief in the Victorian era. Patients were given some alcohol to induce sleepiness, but most would vomit it back up before this happened. Instead, a wooden block was put between a patient's teeth so he could bite down on it and then usually a fainting fit helped the surgeon to finish the operation.

Opium, extracted from poppies and produced in the form of a resin, was widely available in Europe, but was highly addictive. It induced relaxation and then sleep and diminished pain but it could also lead to the physical and mental deterioration of users and eventually heart failure. It was obtained and smoked in establishments known as opium dens, or dissolved in alcohol to create Laudanum, a medicine used as a sleeping draught mainly by women. However, overdoses were common due to addiction and so laudanum was offered sparingly.

Nitrous oxide, or laughing gas is generally credited as the first general anaesthetic. Laughing gas was mainly used for entertainment at parties where it was noted that the participants could stumble around and hurt themselves and not seem to feel any pain. American dentist Horace Wells was inspired to try laughing gas on his patients, but enough to take them past the laughing and excitable stage to the unconscious stage. Wells had a wisdom tooth which needed extracting. He decided to use laughing gas to numb the pain whilst a colleague removed the tooth. Wells went under the anaesthetic; his colleague removed the tooth and Wells woke up fairly pain free and a lot happier having found something that worked.[12]

Meanwhile, Well's former partner in dentistry, William Morton went onto discover ether as an anaesthetic in 1846. He used ether to anaesthetise a patient for a tooth extraction. Two weeks later, he assisted in the successful use of ether on a patient who had a facial tumour removed at Massachusetts General Hospital.[13]

One of the biggest breakthroughs in pain relief was the discovery of chloroform by anaesthetist James Simpson in 1847. He thought it better than ether as it was non-flammable and quicker to work. John Snow, the same doctor who conjectured that cholera was waterborne, made a medical breakthrough in 1853 when he invented a device to give a measured dose of chloroform during surgery. Queen Victoria heard about it, and he was invited to administer chloroform to her during the birth of her last two children. Having given birth to seven children without any pain relief, she naturally loved it and so the use of chloroform as an anaesthetic was given the royal seal of approval and started to be administered to those mothers who wanted to try it and could afford a doctor to tend to her during childbirth.[14]

Childbirth

Childbirth nearly always happened at home in the mother's bed with the local midwife to help her. Men were removed from the room and sometimes the house, along with any other children lest they became upset hearing their mother's cries of pain. Neighbours, sisters and mothers would help the midwife by providing plenty of boiling water and towels where possible, holding the mother's hand and sponging her down with cool water.

Wealthier women had a lying-in period or confinement where they spent about 6 weeks resting and eating to prepare for the birth. No dancing, venturing outside for walks or visitors were permitted lest the mother became ill and was unable to birth her baby properly. For working class and poor mothers, a lying in meant no pay and no one to look after her other children and so these women were often on their feet working or doing chores right up until the first labour pains.

Childbirth itself was fraught with danger as the Victorian era saw natural vaginal delivery only; surgical caesarean sections were yet to be carried out.

There were very few instruments to assist with the delivery and midwives were not allowed to use them and had to wait on a doctor if forceps were needed.

Weak contractions often led to the birth not progressing properly leading to the death of both baby and mother. A lack of vitamin D contributed to deformed pelvic areas in some women causing the unborn baby to become fatally stuck. If a mother did manage to birth her baby successfully, she was then at risk of excessive bleeding, infection leading to puerperal fever and exhaustion. Her baby was immediately at risk of scarlet fever, measles, diphtheria and cholera amongst other infections. It was usual for the christening to take place immediately whilst the mother recuperated at home, especially if there was any uncertainty about the health of the infant.

After six weeks, the mother then went through a church ritual known as churching which cleansed the mother and allowed her to receive the sacrament. Churching also allowed her to commence sexual intercourse again and so the whole process possibly started again.

Apothecaries

Apothecaries, an ancient discipline reaching far back into Greek medicine, were a cross between a modern GP and a pharmacist. They dispensed physician's prescriptions, making up the medicine from the shop's book of recipes. From 1846, they followed the British Pharmacopeia guide to medicine. Before this updated version, they followed the one from 1618! Traditionally, apothecaries offered healthcare to everyone, not just the privileged.

Apothecaries could also make home visits to patients, provide medical advice during such a visit or within their shop and they could prescribe medicines but could not charge for these privileges. The Apothecaries Act of 1815 meant that apothecaries were seen as General Practitioners of Medicine which Physicians, with their degrees, disliked intensely because apothecaries were not required to attend medical school; instead, they undertook a seven year apprenticeship ending in exams.[15]

Chemists, Druggists and Pharmacists

In Victorian England, these three terms were interchangeable to mean a shop which sold medicine ready prepared or prepared as requested by a customer but without a prescription, otherwise known as over the counter medicine nowadays. The shops had their own recipe books of tried and tested formulas, so preparations of medicine varied from shop to shop.

Chemists, druggists and pharmacists were not required to have a dispensing qualification and the industry grew relatively unchecked until 1841 when the Pharmaceutical Society of Great Britain was set up as a regulating body and chemists and druggists were invited to join. The society then set up exams which chemists, druggists and pharmacists had to pass, and this allowed the society to regulate who could call themselves a chemist, druggist or pharmacist.[16]

People could read all about the latest developments in medicine in the newly launched *Pharmaceutical Journal* in 1841, whose aim was to educate the public on the science and pharmaceutical developments taking place. *The Chemist and Druggist* magazine launched in 1858 in order to report on the trade of medicine itself. It included reports of accidental poisonings, prices of ingredients, exchanges of recipes and business matters such as bankruptcy.

Chemists and druggists were tradesmen first and foremost whereas pharmacists went on to become fully trained and qualified dispensers of prescription medicines. Chemists and druggists became popular because they sold what people wanted and what was popular, enabling the everyday person to control their own medication. Early chemists and druggists started out trading in herbal remedies, as these were the main form of medicine at the turn of the century. Village dwellers in particular relied upon herbal remedies as apothecaries in towns were expensive and miles away. These herbal nostrums were made to old, very specific family recipes and passed down through the generations.

Everything was hand made by the chemist and his assistant. Twists of powders, pills, suppositories, lozenges, creams, toothpaste, soap and perfume were all made to specific recipes, with the ingredients weighed out by hand, crushed and mixed by hand and formed into the product by hand. The equipment then had to be washed, dried and laid back out for next time. It was very physical work and not for the faint-hearted!

Medicines Made and Sold by a Chemist or Druggist

Ointments, creams and liniments using a base of lanolin, lard or goose fat. Different herbs and spices were added such as arnica for bruises, decanted into a small pot. Tinctures were concentrated forms of medicine, and a few drops were added to water or wine to be drunk down by the patient, such as laudanum. Powers tasted bitter and so were either dissolved in water or wine or were wrapped in rice paper which dissolved on the tongue (a bit like the flying saucer sweets we have today). Pills were very difficult to swallow, hence the preferment of powders and tinctures. Elixirs were a sweet, syrupy solution made with sugar and honey which coated the throat and bought relief from dry tickly coughs and sore throats, as did the herbal and liquorice pastilles and lozenges also made for sore, dry throats.

Poultices were made to soothe and calm the inflammation of bruises and sprains. A relevant plat or herb was mashed up, mixed with boiling water, cooled a little and then applied directly to the skin. Mustard poultices were made from a paste of flour, mustard seeds and hot water, which was applied to a muslin cloth, folded over and placed on the chest to relieve congestion and chesty coughs.

As aspiring businessmen, chemists then began to supplement their herbal remedies with soap, creams, perfume, dusting powder, soap powder, boot polish, baby bottles and disinfectant, to name just a few things we are all familiar with in our chemists today. Anything related to health and beauty was sold in a chemist or druggist shop.

Cleaning and Disinfectant Products

Large, wealthy residences had their own still room where herbal medicines and cleaning products were mixed and stored but smaller, urban residents were not so lucky. Therefore, chemists and pharmacists manufactured these products for them.

Borax, a naturally occurring mineral was mixed with soap to make an effective laundry cleanser. Malt vinegar and lemon juice mixed with the thickener gum Arabic made a good antibacterial cleaner. Jeyes disinfectant was invented in 1877 and came in tablets or powder form to be dissolved in water and used as a cleaner. Carbolic soap and coal tar soap, made with by-products of the coal industry, were popular although not particularly nice smelling. Lavender water, made from dried lavender, vodka and water was used to spray clothes before ironing so they were left delicately scented. Chemists also made up and sold stain removers and pastes for polishing silver.

Poisons

At the beginning of the era, toxic substances were easily obtained from apothecaries and chemists, mainly to kill house pests such as flies, rats, lice, beetles and so forth. These substances were mostly herbal and had been used for centuries in products but mainly by the wealthier client. But as products became cheaper, toxic substances became easier to get. Arsenic, belladonna, opium, laudanum, oxalic acid, nux vomica, antimony and ergot were all botanical poisons used in medicines, household cleaners and beautifying products.

Calomel, made from mercurous chloride, was incredibly popular and mainly used to treat syphilis but was also found in soaps and teething powder for babies. Cox's Hive syrup which was used to soothe croup in babies and small children contained antimony, a toxic mineral. Fowler's Solution, which contained arsenic, was prescribed for morning sickness, malaria, skin issues and rheumatism. Arsenic was the murderer's weapon of choice as it was cheap, tasteless and odourless so could easily be slipped into food and drink, causing terrible stomach cramps similar to those induced by cholera and typhoid. Arsenic was easily obtainable as it was used in agriculture in sheep dipping to kill the lice and bugs in the sheep's wool, to kill rats and mice in both town and country and also to coat fly papers, sticky pieces of paper which flies would get stuck to and die, often used in homes and restaurants and food stores.[17]

Laudanum was highly addictive and cheaper than wine or gin. Originally used as a painkiller it was also useful as a sleeping draught and frequently prescribed to women described as highly strung or who needed to recover from an illness. Dr J. Collis Browne's Chlorodyne contained chloroform, laudanum and cannabis and was used to soothe asthma, bronchitis, coughs, croup and diphtheria. It was also administered to treat hysteria and epilepsy.[18] Belladonna, used in eye drop, brightened the high and dilated the pupils but could also lead to blindness.

After the 1868 Pharmacy Act, only people registered with the Pharmaceutical Society of Great Britain could trade in poisons or mix together medicines containing poisons.

Medicine Chests

Again, wealthier Victorians could afford to keep a medicine chest in the house, so they had everything they needed on hand in the case of an emergency. This was especially important in the great estates of the countryside where the local doctor could live miles away. Medicine chests usually contained a recipe book, weights and measures, a pestle and mortar, a lancet to lance boils and abscesses, blistering plasters, leech tubes, laudanum to help with pain relief and sleep and the cough expectorant ipecacuanha. Most houses grew their own herbs to make up restorative broths and tinctures to aid a patient's recovery.

In urban areas, most people had no need to keep a medicine chest as a chemist, druggist or pharmacy would be near enough to run to in an emergency. Poorer people couldn't afford to buy medicine to keep just in case of an emergency. If they needed it, they would buy it then, but more often than not they went without due to the cost.

Surgery

Victorian surgeons were known as 'mister' because they did not follow the same pattern of education as the gentlemen who became physicians. Surgeons were seen as tradesmen because they used their hands so in the hierarchy of the medical world, physicians were top followed by surgeons, then apothecaries and then nurses.

Student surgeons learnt their craft from demonstrations by top surgeons who taught crowds of students in operating theatres. Here, surgeons learnt anatomy and surgery from both the living and the dead. Student surgeons practised their knife skills upon the cadavers of executed criminals. But despite the easier access to cadavers and the advancement in medical education, both physicians and surgeons were limited in how they could alleviate suffering. Victorian surgeons were able to carry out only three main surgical procedures: trepanning to remove excess fluid from the brain, minor surgery to remove bladder stones and tumours, and amputations.[19] Of the three, amputations were the most common due to frequent crush injuries in factories, mines and agricultural work. A compound fracture, where the bone pierces the skin, was a death sentence to any person unfortunate enough to find themselves with this type of injury. As surgeons were unable to push the bone back together, the open wound could only lead to a long, lingering death from gangrene and sepsis, so the only chance of preserving life was to remove that part of the limb as quickly as possible. This was done by the surgeon working swiftly to tourniquet the limb, applying one sharp cut all the way around the limb through the skin and tissue and then a second swift saw through the bone. The wound was then cauterised, or the blood vessels were tied off with ligatures and a flap of skin sewn over the wound to close it. All of this took only two minutes as any longer and the patient bled to death.[20]

From the late 1840s, ether and chloroform were introduced as pain relief into surgery. Although this was better for the patient and they were less likely to die of shock, it gave a false sense of security for the surgeons who started to explore the body a little more, digging a little deeper and trying out new techniques. Unfortunately, this just spread germs and increasingly patients began to die from post operative fevers and infections. At the same time, this increase in surgical operations led to operating theatres becoming quite filthy and germ ridden places. Surgical instruments were not cleaned nearly enough, and surgeons rarely changed their clothes or aprons in between operations let alone washed their hands. The same water was used to wash the wounds of several patients, spreading bacteria amongst them like wildfire.[21]

Despite the advances in pain relief and anaesthesia, rampant infection made its way through hospitals and the patients. Pyaemia, a type of blood poisoning, and gangrene were extremely common, causing death when the surgeons had worked so hard to preserve life. Between 1840 and 1870 there was a 35% post-operation death rate due to infection, gangrene and shock.[22] Once Joseph Lister's use of antiseptics to kill microbes was accepted into the medical profession, this rate dropped dramatically, but it was common for many people to still hold a fear of hospitals as a place where patients went to die.

Getting Better

How did people get to a doctor?

In an emergency, a message would usually be sent to the named doctor via a family member or a local messenger boy, either on foot or on horse depending upon where the patient lived or where they had been taken ill. This itself took time, especially if the doctor was already out seeing another patient. A message would need to be sent to him at the other patient's residence or the messenger would leave a note with the doctor's wife or housekeeper and an address to attend to. Then, it was a case of sitting tight and hoping the doctor arrived in time to help.

At the beginning of Queen Victoria's reign, home visiting was the usual practice for all ailments, illnesses and accidents but as the century progressed, wealthy and middle-class patients could visit a physician at his doctor's practice and receive treatment in his consulting room. This treatment was paid for and ensured discretion and the best possible care although not always the most up to date medicine as many well to do doctors didn't always take on board new research and theories. Middle-class patients could also go to specialist hospitals as these began to become more available as the century progressed.

The working classes had to rely upon charitable hospitals or dispensaries to help them in their time of need. In an emergency, they would send for a doctor, but for many the cost was prohibitive, meaning they had to go without food or heat to pay him and in many situations, by the time the decision had been made it was too late for the patient any way. However, there were many doctors who served the working class and poor for free if the doctor had a private, inherited income and did not need to rely upon paying clients quite so much.

Outcome of Care

So much influenced the final outcome of the patient's treatment. If it was shameful illness such as syphilis, people were reluctant to seek help and died a protracted, painful death alone. Females were more likely to be misdiagnosed or mistreated thanks to a male profession which didn't really understand medical conditions constricted to females only, such as menstruation and hormonal issues, post childbirth ailments and cancers of the ovaries, uterus and breast. The education of the patient also had a bearing on the outcome of their care. Uneducated patients had less tendency to argue with the doctor, just accepting the diagnosis and recommended course of treatment whereas educated patients were more likely to question the doctor and possible even be well read in the latest medical theories and treatments open to them. The education and training of the doctor also had a bearing, and also if they were a good or bad doctor, drunk, drugged, up to date with the profession, open to ideas and so forth.

Doctors

Doctors in the Victorian era had the tough job of balancing saving lives alongside making enough money to live off and having enough time to research ailments and illness within their area of expertise. Attracting men to the profession was also a tough job because it was not seen as a gentleman's profession and so it was generally men whose fathers were lawyers, pharmacists, bankers or doctors themselves who were attracted into the profession. Unfortunately, a significant amount of money was needed to pay for a passage through a fee paying, private medical school and thus many were excluded from the profession this way. It makes sense then that those who did eventually qualify felt the need to earn substantial amounts of money by setting up a private practice in their own home. In most towns and cities, medical districts developed where doctors tended to buy houses, and doctors establishing themselves in these areas had more chance of success and thus financial income. Urban areas as opposed to country areas were preferred, as were more affluent customers who could pay. This meant that the poor often suffered as there were fewer doctors in these areas to attend to a bigger and more needy population. Also, it meant the doctor attending to the patient in their slum or lodging house, something some doctors did not want to do lest they caught a disease too.

Until the middle of the nineteenth century, the practice of medicine was disjointed and unregulated. Very few doctors actually held medical degrees as we know them today. Many doctors had part time jobs for another income, especially those who attended to poorer patients.

Doctors fell into two main categories: physicians and surgeons. Physicians diagnosed internal problems and prescribed and administered 'physic' or drugs. To do this they were required to become members of the Royal College of Physicians and hold a degree in a classical subject such as classics or maths.[23] Surgeons dealt with fractures and other minor surgery, namely the removal of kidney stones and tumours. Many surgeons worked in the army or navy, learning how to swiftly amputate parts of limbs in order to save lives. For non-life-threatening ailments, apothecaries sold drugs and herbal medicines to those who asked.

Hospitals

The enlightenment period in the eighteenth century saw the founding of many hospitals across England as attitudes towards sickness changed. Pre-enlightenment attitudes to sickness and death were judgmental and religious. Illness was seen as a punishment for sin and death happened because God wanted it that way. As these attitudes changed, so the population could start to be properly treated and cared for.

Eighteenth century hospitals were aimed at treating the working-class poor, otherwise known as the deserving poor. These were people who had jobs and a regular income and did not claim poor relief but if they got sick then everyone in the family would suffer due to the loss of wage. These people – mainly labouring men and mechanics – were unable to pay a doctor anyway. It was recognised that the unfit working class could quickly become paupers if their illnesses and aliments were left untreated and thus, they could quickly become a burden on the state, requiring a place in a workhouse. More importantly, these hospitals were secular and so had no religious attachment to a church.

Small hospitals gradually opened across the cities and bigger towns on England and so by 1837 there was one in every substantial town, serving the local population and adapting their care depending upon the town's trade.

The overall idea of early Victorian hospitals was to provide nursing and care to patients so they could rest and recuperate from seasonal complaints such as bronchitis or accidents at work or on the street. People with suspected highly infectious diseases as mentioned earlier were excluded and usually treated at home instead. Teaching hospitals liked to take in Accident and Emergency patients as it provided an opportunity to show off the skill of a doctor or surgeon in front of the student doctors and also provided interesting case studies for them too.

Funding the Hospitals

Nowadays, the NHS funds all our hospitals making them free on the point of entry. Private, paid for hospitals also exist and are usually paid for through health insurance.

In the Victorian era, hospitals were generally funded in two ways. Endowed hospitals were paid for through legacies or trusts funded by money left to them by deceased and usually local people. The contribution was held in a trust and the initial amount was invested to make more money which was then used to run the hospital.

Voluntary hospitals were funded by charity and relied upon regular donations from local families, church collections, will bequests, money raised through charitable events and donations from individual people and businesses. Voluntary hospitals were general hospitals, served by general physicians and nurses and they pretty much dealt with everything.

Other hospitals were directly paid for by the patient and their families, and the patient could only stay there if the fees were paid and so were usually frequented by the middle and upper classes. There were hospitals which specialised in diseases such as TB and other chest complaints, fever hospitals, ear nose and throat hospitals, eye hospitals, mental illness, skin disease and maternity hospitals.

Very few hospitals took in patients with an incurable disease. Instead, patients were sent home to live out their illness and die there, and a private nurse would be hired to attend them, if the family had the money. Paupers were sent to the local workhouse infirmary or home also, but usually with only family or a neighbour or a landlady to help nurse them towards their death.[24]

The Coroner's Office

In the case of an unexpected death at home, an inquest into the cause of death would sometimes be held by a coroner. During the inquest, a coroner and the jury would listen to evidence from witnesses, view the body and sometimes the place of death and decide whether the person died of natural causes, suicide, accident or unlawful intent. An inquest could not be held though until a member of the public reported their concerns.

Inquests were paid for by the parish, which needed to pay the coroner, a doctor to perform an autopsy or at least to examine the body and parish officers to do the paperwork and summon the witnesses and rent the premises for the inquest. By the 1840s, it had become usual for the newly formed police force to carry out these duties on behalf of the parish. After the 1856 County and Borough Police Act, arranging the evidence for an inquest became the responsibility of the new county police forces.[25] Police officers became Coroners Officers and had the power to decide if an inquest should even go ahead. This was the beginning of the entwining of the medical profession and the police forces of Britain.

Chapter Sixteen

Crime and Punishment and the Police Force

> 'How often have I said to you that when you have
> eliminated the impossible, whatever remains,
> however improbable, must be the truth?'
>
> Sherlock Holmes to Dr Watson:
> *The Sign of Four*[1]

As well as the economic leaders of the world, English Victorians viewed themselves as moral leaders too. The changing moral expectations of the Victorian people led to a vast change in the law throughout the era. Social justice in the early part of the Victorian era in England is often viewed as barbarous with its public floggings, hangings and dank and dangerous prisons. But there were very few prisons and no 'prison system' at all, neither was there a police force. The only deterrent against crime was the regular sight of gallows and a noose, and a dead criminal swinging from a gibbet in the breeze. As there were over 200 offences for which a person could be hung, the very real fear of death by hanging kept most of society under control.

From 1815, the Whig government gradually repealed the statutes for capital crime and in 1837 a Bill pushed through the House of Commons reducing the number of capital crimes to fifteen. Now that a sheep stealer was no longer hanged, juries were more likely to convict the accused leading to a rise in conviction rates and with them an increasing fear of crime. The burgeoning newspapers reported crimes and punishments with a sensationalism and an alarming bluntness, such as in the case of the murder of a Francis Crouch by her husband William Crouch, reported in the *London Illustrated News* on 6 April 1844.

'...and on hurrying up and entering the room she (Mrs Line, the neighbour) saw Mrs Crouch falling off her chair, with the floor covered in blood, and her husband standing by a chest of drawers, wiping a razor with a piece of rag.'

The surgeon called to attend to Mrs Crouch continues to paint the picture: 'the instrument with which the wound was inflicted having completely severed the windpipe, with the whole of the arteries and veins of the neck, leaving only the vertebrae.'

The newspaper then describes the inquest and the public baying for William Crouches blood: 'The crowd around the Court was very great, and it was with difficulty that the mob could be prevented from laying violent hands on the prisoner, both on his being taken to, and removed from, the Court.'[2]

What was a Crime?

Just like today, many crimes in Victorian England were a product of their time. Homosexuality was a capital crime until the punishment was reduced to two years hard labour in prison in 1861[3], a punishment endured by Oscar Wilde at the end of the century. Until the mid-century, debtors were imprisoned until they or someone they knew were able to pay off their debts and release them.

Industrialisation and the influx of workers to the towns and cities not only caused overcrowded conditions, disease and poverty, as we have seen, but also petty crime as a result of living in these conditions. The excessive consumption of alcohol led to assault both in the streets and in the home, where domestic abuse was rife. Employment laws were constantly broken, children still went up chimneys and parents could be prosecuted for not sending them to school. Hunger drove many people to steal food from street vendors, whilst in the countryside, men poached fish, rabbits and game from large landowners to feed their starving families. Many people stole from their employers, pocketing silver teaspoons and lace handkerchiefs to sell on at pawn shops. Others stole from the general public through pickpocketing and mugging. On the roads, highway men robbed rich people at gunpoint in their carriages, bagging money, jewels and horses. Later, on the rails, criminals robbed passengers, dodged fares and vandalised tracks. In ports, criminal gangs organised the import and export of stolen goods and reaped the benefits. On the coasts of England, smugglers traded in brandy, rum and tobacco to avoid paying expensive tax duties. In offices and shops, middle class fraudsters fiddled the accounts. In short, crime in the Victorian era was not a lot different to today. But the one crime Victorians really feared and despised was burglary.

Burglary

The Victorians loved their property and as the middle class became richer, and could buy more items for the home, burglaries increased. As the Victorians considered crime against property far worse than crimes against people, burglary was treated as seriously as murder and in 1837 it was a capital offence.

The new middle-class homes, stuffed with precious objects, provided temptation for house breakers. However, house breakers weren't usually lone men taking a chance in the middle of the night but more organised criminal gangs who worked in small groups to enter houses through windows to seize goods and hurry them away from the scene of the crime into the hands of handlers or fences who sold them on for cash, splitting the money between them. The best people to use for the actual entering of house through windows was small children, as in the case of Dickens' Oliver Twist, who is taken on a house breaking expedition by Bill Sykes and forced through a ground floor window to let in the other burglars.

Juvenile Crime

Juvenile crime in the first half of the century was indeed a problem. Many children lived on the streets, or as good as, if they were orphaned, or their parents were at work for twelve hours a day or one or both parents were chronically sick, disabled or an alcoholic. Many rarely went to school, Sunday school or church where they could be influenced by the honest and hardworking folk and instead would run idle in the streets, stealing to eat, or be sent to beg in the city, wearing an assortment of ragged clothes too big or too small for them, marking them out as neglected children and for others to be wary of them[4]

If an older sibling had fallen into criminality, then sometimes the younger ones followed. With little or no parental care or guidance, love and attention, these children were easily influenced into crime, tempted by new clothes, money and food. usually by older children, where they became part of a gang. They were fed, had somewhere to sleep and felt part of a family, something they weren't getting from home or the government. They were expected to be loyal to their new 'family' and not to anyone else. Unfortunately, as was the case in *Oliver Twist*, sometimes 'family' turned on them too and sold them on to the police for reward money.

In order to profit long term from theft, thieves needed a reliable network of friends or associates to help them procure the goods and swap them for money. These networks hummed with knowledge of empty homes, warehouses or offices which could be broken into and plundered. Other networks of thieves handled or fenced stolen goods. Many pawn shop owners happily took in pick pocket items, denying all knowledge of providence of goods and giving vague descriptions of the sellers to the police. Other criminal gangs imported and exported stolen goods from local docks, hidden amongst genuine goods.

Within this network, children were used as lookouts, housebreakers and pickpockets. In crowded markets, streets and fairs, pickpocketing was easy for small fingered children. They carefully lifted pocket watches, wallets and silk handkerchiefs, getting in and out quickly, without drawing attention to themselves. The stolen property was then taken back to the lodgings or a handler's house to be passed on for profit.

It was usual for young children to be trained in pick pocketing by teenage trainers or convicted thieves. A coat would be hung on a wall with a bell attached and a handkerchief in the pocket. The aim was for the would-be pickpocket to remove the handkerchief without causing the bell to jangle. A trainer would then walk up and down a room with the coat on and the would-be pickpocket would need to steal the handkerchief this way too.

Once deemed fit for purpose, a would-be pickpocket would be dressed in (usually stolen) clothing to fit in with the environment where they were to be sent to pick pockets. Many were happy to dress up in good quality clothes and go to the West End to pick the pockets of a wealthier clientele.[5]

Street Robbery

Pickpocketing was mainly carried out by children and women and was generally seen as a non-violent crime. It was the street robbers, or muggers as we say nowadays, who used violence to obtain what they needed. These ranged from gangs of 'cornermen' who hung around on street corners and harassed pedestrians for money, drink and cigarettes with a propensity to violence if refused, to footpads and garrotters.

Where ladies and gentlemen wore more jewellery and carried more money, street robberies increased. Common, low-level thieves known as footpads stalked the streets in search of gentlemen carrying money or expensive pocket watches. Ladies, with their expensive gloves, hats and jewellery were easy prey too.

Garrotting

This was a term used in the early part of the nineteenth century for a type of attack where robbers disabled their victim by attacking them from behind with an arm around the throat and the pressure caused unconsciousness, allowing the victim to be stripped of everything on him. Sometimes a noose was used, striking even more fear into the heart of the victim and not the heart of the public too. Garrotting was bought to the attention of the authorities by the attack on the MP for Blackburn whilst in London and soon a severe punishment of fifty lashes or up to 15 years transportation reduced the number of incidents.

Alcohol-fuelled Crime

Alcohol fuelled crime has been around as long as alcohol itself. The Beer Act of 1830 made beer tax free and readily available to wean the general population off gin. It cost only two guineas for any rate payer to obtain a license to sell beer and by 1838, 46,000 new pubs had sprung up across Britain[6]

Generally, most disorder on Victorian streets was down to alcohol and too much of it[7]. Excessive consumption caused brawling, common assault, sickness, vagrancy, and contributed to the use of prostitutes. Beer houses were regarded as immoral by the middle and upper classes, luring in sober men who would drink as much beer as feasibly possible thus causing addiction for them, poverty for their family, then leading to crime or members of the family to be exploited. Labourers – those much-needed men who built the houses, canals, factories, warehouses, roads and railways – all lodged together in lodging houses and went out on the town at night together for entertainment in the form of women and drink – as they were away from their families. Pubs sprang up everywhere and with them drunken, brawling and subsequently injured and hungover workers.

Physical abuse against women and children within a family wasn't a crime and was in fact, deeply ingrained in society but was mostly fuelled by alcohol. In 1876, it was thought alcohol was a factor in 40% of crimes committed in England and Wales[8]. Alcohol smuggling was a big crime, especially on the coasts of England as it meant goods entered the country without a customs tax paid at the port. The illegal distillation of alcohol was also a crime and extremely dangerous, leading to poisoning and death.

Not only did alcohol cause fights in the street and the resultant injuries to people and property, but it also fed domestic violence. It wasn't a crime for a man to beat his wife or children as they were his property to do with as he chose; it became a criminal act if they died as a result. In fact, the afore mentioned Mr William Crouch blamed his consumption of alcohol for the violent murder of his wife.

The propensity of violent crime such as the one committed by William Crouch was much debated in Parliament with many MPs believing that public hangings contributed to the incidence of violent crime. When debating the Bill for abolishing the punishment of death in certain cases, in May 1837, Dr Lushington was against the continuation of public hangings:

> 'The effect of public executions was to deprave the public mind. He believed that there never was an execution which did not produce a future candidate for the hands of the hangman.'[9]

Why?

Crime rates were higher in the cities rather than the rural areas possibly due to the sheer amount of people living in one place in relative poverty and all fighting or the same jobs and resources. There was also high unemployment after the Napoleonic wars. As is usually the case in times of war, taxes were raised so many people had less to spend on anything other than food rent and fuel. Unemployment increased due to the trade restrictions imposed on the channel and with France and food prices increased as a result. Once the war was over, returning men suffering life changing injuries and illness found they had no job to return to but very little in way of charity or pension. War widows were left to bring up the children on their own with little help from the government other than the workhouse.

In villages, the local employer, be it a farmer or local mill owner, knew everything about his employees' lives. He owned the cottage they lived in and saw them at church on Sundays. It was the same for landowners and their tenants.

In these villages, the employer knew about any misbehaviour and would reprimand or have a kindly word to keep the employee on the straight and narrow. In most cases, knowing their employer knew all about their lives was enough to keep most people on the straight and narrow. Neighbours also helped with this. Besides, continued bad behaviour such as drunken brawling at the local tavern was enough for a tenant to be evicted from their home or an employee from the mill. For servants, the same principles applied. Fear of dismissal from a good job in a large house was enough to keep servants' behaviour under control, although they increasingly didn't have much spare time and had to have permission from their employer to go to the local village for any form of socialising.

In cities though, factory owners didn't know the ins and outs of their workers lives mainly due to the high turnover of workers with people frequently leaving due to accident, illness, childbearing or death, but also because as the factories and shops got bigger, it was difficult to keep up. With children being way from parental influence, even apprentices and young people away from home for the first time, it was easy to fall into the wrong crowd and under the influence of salubrious people.

How Was Crime Dealt With at the Beginning of the Century?

Until the establishment of a formal police force, policing was dealt with locally and paid for by the parish. Night watchmen or constables patrolled towns at night, calling out the hours, keeping an eye out for fires and lighting the lamps at dusk. If they caught someone breaking the law, they had powers to detain the culprit in the local lock up until morning and call for the assistance of the local Justice of the Peace (JP).

As senior members of their communities but not necessarily with any legal expertise, JPs were able to arrest and detain culprits in a local jail until trial either at a quarterly session run by the JPs themselves, or, for more serious and capital crimes, at the assizes in the nearest big town.

JPs sat in pairs or small groups known as the bench, to pass judgement on minor crimes such as theft, brawling and drunkenness. These trials took place without a jury and became known as petty sessions. The JPs were expected to keep up to date and follow Parliament's regulations in applying and implementing the law. Courts of the Assizes, or assizes to use their common name, were held in every main county town across England and Wales twice a year and were presided over by visiting judges from London and a jury made up of twelve local residents. These assize courts dealt with the serious crimes such as murder, rape, burglars and forgers; in fact, anything regarded as a capital crime.

By 1837, a young Queen Victoria inherited a country where crime and antisocial behaviour was on the increase with drunk and disorderly conduct in the streets becoming normalised alongside petty theft and prostitution. Towns and cities became unsafe for women after dark, even for the prostitutes and costermongers who worked in the streets. At the same time, industrialists became concerned with unruly behaviour and agitation from their workers often leading to excessive drinking and fighting.

The New Police Force

The vast improvements to railways, hospitals and living and working conditions were overseen by arguably the most major change to English society of all: the establishment of a police force at the beginning of Queen Victoria's reign which grew and developed alongside England's industrial might and the empire was long overdue.

The London Metropolitan Police was established in 1829 after Home Secretary Robert Peel's Metropolitan Police Bill received approval from parliament. He wanted a full time, centrally governed and organised police force for a 7-mile radius of central London, separate to the City of London Police who already kept law and order within the square mile. Queen Victoria was the first monarch to have a police force at the coronation to help with crowd control.

From the beginning, the London Metropolitan Police worked on preventative policing to keep crime and disorder under control. Its headquarters were based in Scotland Yard, and 1000 men were recruited to supplement the 400 already acting as constables. It became a fulltime occupation with the first officers paid 16 shillings via a new parish rate and given a uniform. The new recruits were selected and trained by the commissioners, and although they took on some of the night watchmen jobs such as lighting lamps, watching for fires and calling out the time, their primary job was to be conspicuous on patrol, therefore, stopping crime before it even happened. By seeing more police on the streets, it was hoped that the general public would behave themselves if they knew they were being watched. This didn't go down well with the general public who resented being treated as if they were potential criminals. But the general public disliked the army keeping law and order even more as the army tended to use brute force and guns to enforce peace. The new police force wanted to approach law and order differently and defined themselves apart from the army by adopting a neutral blue uniform to contrast the red army uniform. By being civil, respectful and mindful of his language, a policeman hoped to be more approachable and therefore gain the public's help in catching criminals[10].

Although the new police force's authority came from the Crown and the law, securing the public's help was a lot more difficult but desperately wanted. Only by serving their local citizens and gaining their respect and consent rather than imposing their rule, could the police prevent crime or prosecute criminals. Public co-operation was very much sought after and required, but 'Bobbies' or 'peelers'(both nicknames for police officers based upon Robert Peel) weren't popular with everyone at first and were often jeered in the street as people saw their presence as an infringement of their civil liberties. They were also seen as enforcers of the unpopular poor law, by arresting people for vagrancy and begging who were then sent to the dreaded workhouse.

Keeping Law and Order on the Streets

A daytime constable was given a certain area of streets to patrol and check over. This enabled the constable to get to know the buildings and the residents and start to notice if anything was amiss. It was also his duty to keep the streets clean and hazard free by reporting to the local parish any footpaths, roads or pavements in poor order. Unlit lamps, unswept streets, obstruction and damage were all noted and dealt with. In heavy downpours of rain, constables were expected to lift out grating to the sewers to ensure the easy drainage of the rainfall and so prevent flooding.

Even firefighting could be included on an early constable's list of responsibilities. This was the overall responsibility of the chief constable of the police force, and he delegated certain constables and sergeants to attend fires and take control of the situation, paying them extra to do so. On discovering a fire, a constable was expected to alert everyone nearby by waving his rattle and shouting fire, going from house to house to make sure everyone was aware. Horse drawn fire engines resided in sheds next to the police station with horses stabled nearby so they were always at the ready and the constable would help the driver find his quickest way back to the fire, alerting other constables on the way. They needed to know the nearest point of water including the standpipes and where the water turners lived so he could direct the firefighters accordingly.

The new metropolitan police force was such a success that Lord John Russell swiftly allowed it to be replicated across the country with Manchester being the next city to set one up.

As the era moved on though, police work concentrated on upholding law and order by catching criminals, gathering evidence and helping justice to be done. The Town Police Clauses Act of 1847 allowed constables to act upon a number of nuisances or offences, especially ones classed as felonies.

Felony

A medieval word used to describe a serious crime such as murder, manslaughter, rape and arson, which could all be punishable by death, the list of felonies grew to include housebreaking, theft, serious assault, assault and robbery, plain robbery and receiving stolen goods. As this list grew, so did a constable's powers to arrest someone without a magistrate's warrant if he thought a felony had been or was about to be committed. This included arresting someone for threatening the life of someone else, for carrying house breaking equipment such as crowbars, picklocks, stolen keys or for carrying offensive weapons such as iron bars, cudgels and guns. A constable could also apprehend someone for lurking suspiciously in yards, stables, dark alleyways or outbuildings, whether seen by the constable or reported by someone else.

Stop and search rules meant that a constable could search any suspect's dwellings, places of work or anywhere they thought that stolen goods were being held. If a robbery had happened overnight, constables staked out local pawn shops and could arrest anyone looking suspicious there too. After the 1862 Poaching Prevention Act, stop and search rules also applied to anyone carrying a parcel, particularly at night and in the countryside in order to cut down on the amount of poaching taking place.

The constable was encouraged to watch and wait to gather evidence, taking notes in his notebook before apprehending the suspect whilst only armed with a truncheon and whistle. Once in custody, a constable had to make sure the felon knew what he was arrested for and could then question him in the presence of a superior officer. The identity and address of the suspect had to be established before he was locked in a cell overnight and then handed over to the magistrate in the morning.

Punishments

By 1815, over 200 offences could result in the death penalty of hanging from the neck until dead. Known as 'the bloody code', it wasn't just murder and manslaughter which resulted in capital punishment. Arson, destruction of property from riverbanks, fishponds, orchards, gardens, cattle, textile machinery to Westminster Bridge, forgery, sheep stealing, horse stealing, stealing rabbits from a warren, pickpocketing goods or money worth a shilling or more (around £30 today) and stealing from a shipwreck were all included in the bloody code.

By the time Queen Victoria ascended to the throne, many harsh Georgian punishments had been abolished or commuted to a lesser severity. The then Home Secretary, Robert Peel, was very keen on punishment and prison reform as well as cracking down on crime. The death penalty still existed but was only applicable for 15 crimes, not the 200 of the Georgian era. Instead, transportation of criminals to Australia was common but that itself was in decline too. A mixture of fines, short prison sentences, hard labour, flogging and the stocks helped authorities to deal with criminals, but public hanging was still used for capital offences and an overall deterrent.

Hanging

Once a trial for a capital crime had started, it was usually quick, and the death sentence promptly handed out to the guilty party. In London, the criminal was taken from The Old Bailey to Newgate Prison whilst the paperwork was prepared. The condemned did have the right to petition the monarch for a reprieve but weren't always successful. Meanwhile, the scaffolding was erected outside Newgate Prison ready for a very public execution within a matter of days.

Public executions were an example of state power: a way of the state reminding the ordinary person what happened if they broke the law. Despite Newgate Prison and its gallows casting a shadow across London, public hangings attracted thousands of spectators. Called by the Newgate bell, which started tolling at midnight, the public started to gather at the site where refreshments would be on sale, views from windows of nearby houses were booked and paid for and prostitutes plied their trade to drunken spectators and pickpockets took advantage of the crowds, the dark and the noise to relieve many of their pocket watches, purses and handkerchiefs.

Inside their dungeon like prison cell, the condemned person changed into their best clothes if they had any, and the prison chaplain took confession if their religion required it, or at least read to them from the bible and prayed for their soul. The arms and hands of the prisoner were constrained in a leather belt to stop them resisting the hangman, before they were led outside in front of the jeering crowd with the chaplain following as he continued to read sermons and pray. The 'short drop' method was used until 1868 where a trap door opened beneath the feet of the condemned, but they didn't fall far and so died by slow strangulation. The body was left hanging for an hour to ensure death had occurred.

Charles Dickens and William Thackeray were vociferous in their protests against these spectacles and the death penalty in general, stating it clearly didn't work as crime was still taking place. Dickens wanted executions to take place privately within prison walls, away from the callous, fighting crowds of vagabonds, thieves and prostitutes who catcalled and whistled all night and mocked the condemned prisoner.[11]. The *Times* disagreed with private executions, worrying that 'were it otherwise, the mass of the people would never be sure that great offenders were really executed, or that the humbler class of criminals were not executed in greater numbers than the state chose to confess.'[12] The Times also excused the crowd's behaviour: 'Men often hide the deepest of feelings with the wildest excesses of manner and of language.'

William Thackeray wrote extensively about the hanging of Courvoisier in 1840: 'On a Monday morning, at eight o'clock, this man is placed under a beam, with a rope connecting it and him; a plank disappears from under him, and those who have paid for good places may see the hands of the Government agent, Jack Ketch, coming up from his black hole, and seizing the prisoner's legs, and pulling them, until he is quite dead -- strangled.'[13]

Once the event was over, the condemned last speech was printed up and sold up and down the country. Execution broadsides describing the events leading up to the execution and the execution itself were also sold up and down the country the day after.

Reformers campaigned long and hard to end public executions although most of them wanted capital punishment abolished altogether. The last person to be publicly executed was Irish Republican Michael Barrett who had been found guilty of taking part in the explosion at the Clerkenwell House of

Detention. He protested his innocence but was sentenced to die on 26 May 1868. Thousands travelled on the new, modern underground tube network to Newgate to see the last ever old-world style execution. What was seen as a Georgian practice and therefore brutal and immoral was allowed to continue but behind closed doors away from prying eyes. This took away the public voice of protest from the prisoners and they now had no one to hear them. It became harder to campaign against capital punishment in general because it was now out of sight and out of mind. Capital punishment continued for another century before transmuting to whole life sentences instead.

Transportation

Transportation to America began in 1615 in the era of James I. This idea was originally conceived to banish beggars, vagabonds and mild criminals. In fact, men were needed to help run the galley ships as they travelled the trade routes and so these petty criminals were ideal for the job and eventually arrived in Maryland and Virginia where they were sold as labourers onto the new plantations. This was a profitable business for merchants with ships as the government paid them to take the convicts and deliver them to the new lands. The merchant was then able to stock up his ship with goods such as tea, spices, dried fruit, cloth and sugar for the return journey to England. The American War of Independence brought this lucrative trade to an abrupt halt in 1775.

In 1787, England started the transport of criminals to Australia, which Captain James Cook had claimed for Britain in 1770. There were two reasons for this: the civil unrest over people being hung for seemingly trivial crimes and bodies were needed in Australia to build the infrastructure required to support an influx of new inhabitants.

The crimes which resulted in transportation included murder and manslaughter but also arson, highway robbery, repeat offences of theft and burglary. Rioters and political protesters were also sent away and sometimes a trivial matter such as poaching was enough to send a man on a hulk ship to Australia, especially if more men were needed over there. Between 1787 and 1857, a course of 70 years, 158,702 men, women and children were transported to Australia, averaging 190 a month[14]. But transportation had to stop eventually and by the 1840s it had all but disappeared and hanging continued as a punishment for murder. Instead, the Victorians concentrated on prison as the ultimate deterrent. Their deep faith in progress meant they believed crime could be beaten and a spell in prison would soon deter anyone from reoffending.

Hulk Ships

When the transportation of criminals to the Americas ceased, it was decided that the new punishment would be between three- and ten-years hard labour in houses of correction with a basic diet of bread, cheap meat and small beer. In London, the hard labour proposed was the cleansing of the Thames which made it a foregone conclusion to house the convicts in shipboard prisons. Two old battleship hulks moored at Woolwich were already in use as a temporary solution and another was procured to house convicts at Woolwich Warren, the home of Naval shipbuilding where prisoners provided labour or dredged and cleaned the river Thames.

Life on the hulks themselves was dire. Not only was disease rife but the amount of food provided was completely inadequate, comprising of the cheapest cuts of meat available, usually ox cheeks, to make soup with barley or oats and bread, cheese and small beer, none of which was fresh. There were accusations of extra punishments dished out by the guards with the birch and cat o nine tails, rape, violence and gambling. The mentally disturbed were punished or chained to their beds and a lack of washing and toilet facilities spread encouraged vermin which spread disease.[15]

Although transportation to Australia then started, the hulk ships remained and served as a reminder to all Londoners of the fate that awaited them should they break the law. In Dickens' *Great Expectations*, Pip describes a hulk ship as 'a wicked Noah's ark. Cribbed and barred and moored by massive rusty chains, the prison-ship seemed in my young eyes to be ironed like the prisoners.'[16]

Prison Buildings

The late Georgian and early Victorian period was one of experimentation within the prison service. The question of what to do with prisoners was constantly debated in parliament with social reformers adding their opinions too.

Victorians loved their freedom and liberty and so saw imprisonment not only as a punishment but as a chance to reform the offender. Prison buildings ranged in size and style from small village lockups to cellars in castle keeps to large medieval structures such as Newgate Prison in London, where prisoners languished whilst they awaited trial, awaited execution or awaited transportation. Small, local prisons were modernised or rebuilt and although all were different base buildings, they all worked along the same provision: different classes of prisoners in separate cells with larger work rooms, exercise yards, laundry rooms, a chapel and an infirmary.

Prisons were seen as reformatories. Victorian deeply believed that people could see the error of their ways and change their attitudes if they were given enough time to think, and so the prison regime was deliberately made boring, repetitive and downright hard. Millbank prison, which opened in 1821, provided the template for all other prisons. First class inmates (those serving the first part of their sentence) both worked and slept in solitude in their individual cells. Second class prisoners (serving the second part of their sentence) carried out hard labour in groups, starting at 5.30am and finishing at 6pm when prisoners had their gruel in their cells. As a reformatory prison, Millbank failed. The solitary confinement, poor food and overwork led to illness, death and suicide. Despite this, the use of the 'separate system', adopted from America, was put into use all over England.

The 1839 Prisons Act required all new prison plans and rules to be submitted to the Home Secretary for approval. The separate system was approved time and time again and soon became the normal way of running a prison.

Pentonville Prison, which opened in December 1842, was a new 'model prison' based upon the separate system but without solitary confinement. However, the governors and the Home Secretary insisted on this in place and so each prisoner was given their own cell where they worked, ate and slept. When they were allowed outside for exercise or to go to the chapel, the prisoners wore masks to hide their identities from each other and to stop communication.

Pentonville Prison also aimed to train each inmate in a trade such as carpentry, tailoring, rug making, cotton weaving and so forth, as well as literacy, numeracy and scripture which they could use to make a better life for themselves once outside prison. In the earlier days, convicts awaiting transportation served the first part of their sentence in Pentonville learning a trade to take with them to Australia.

Following Pentonville, fifty-four new prisons were built[17] and as transportation declined, so did the use of the hulks and so even more buildings were needed. This was when Public Works prisons became the way forward with the first part of the sentence served in solitude, the second part working on public projects and the third part released on license as an early style of parole.

The hardship in prisons abated in the 1850s and at Pentonville the masks and general segregation was dropped. But a series of garrottings in London in the early 1860s spread fear that criminals were not being reformed enough during prison and were reoffending in a most violent manner. A House of Lords Select Committee, led by Lord Carnarvon, was created to see if there was any truth in the fear. They concluded that the prison system wasn't uniformed enough across the country and were missing the purpose of imprisonment in the first place which was to punish and deter future crime. This led to the 1865 Prisons

Act which laid down a uniform regime of hard labour, hard fare and hard bed to be adopted by all prisons across the country alongside the separate system of confinement.

The hard labour was to be clearly defined and measurable and so pointless tasks were put in place to give the inmate plenty of time to reflect on their misdemeanours. Popular hard labour included the treadmill, turning the crank, stone breaking and oakum picking.

The hard fare was part of the punishment too. There was no way the authorities wanted people committing crimes because they were better fed in prison, especially those inmates of workhouses.

The hard bed was exactly that: a hard plank on which to sleep with no mattress.

The Select Committee were convinced that this was the way forward to deter criminal behaviour and so began thirty years of harsh prison regimes.

Oscar Wilde's Prison Life

Literature's most famous inmate, Oscar Wilde, spent the first part of a two-year sentence of hard labour for indecent acts at Pentonville Prison in 1895. After a medical examination declaring him fit for work, he started the first month's regime in place for all new prisoners. He spent six hours a day on the treadmill, climbing 60 feet a day in twenty-minute spurts with a five-minute rest in between. He slept on a plank bed just above floor level, with sheets and blankets but no mattress. His food consisted of cocoa and bread for breakfast at 7.30, dinner at noon and tea at 5.30pm with nothing then to eat until breakfast the next morning. These two meals were made up of bacon and beans or suet pudding or soup or gruel or cold meat all served up with potatoes.

Inmates were also expected to take up industrial employment within their first month, and at Pentonville this consisted of oakum picking, sewing mail bags or tailoring.

Inmates were allowed one hour exercise a day walking in single file without talking and there was no communication with the outside world for three months. They visited the chapel at 9am every morning and twice on Sundays. A chaplain was allowed to visit the inmates as often as required.

The hunger and terrible food led to many inmates suffering from dysentery. The toilets at Pentonville had been removed so prisoners couldn't communicate with each other by tapping the drainpipes. Instead, each prisoner had a tin bucket in which to relieve themselves and they were able to empty it 3 times a day. The actual outside lavatories could only be used during the one-hour exercise time and after 5pm, no prisoner was allowed to leave his cell until 7.30am the next day for any reason, leading to overflowing slops buckets in the cells of prisoners with dysentery. The smell must have been indescribable, but also the dirt and the disease alongside it. Wilde himself lost nearly two stone in weight and fainted in the chapel, damaging his ear and his hearing.[18]

For health reasons, Oscar Wilde was moved to Reading Gaol, where the governor, Lieutenant-Colonel J Isaacson firmly believed in the 1865 Prison Act. He ran a tight separate system where talking at exercise time or in the chapel or at work was punished with solitary confinement and bread and water. The prisoners were known by their cell number – in Wilde's case this was C3.3 – which stripped them of their individuality. Wilde summed up his time there in the folk ballad poem *The Ballad of Reading Gaol*:

> 'With midnight always in one's heart,
> And twilight in one's cell,
> We turn the crank or tear the rope,
> Each in his separate Hell,
> And the silence is more awful far
> Than the sound of a brazen bell.
>
> And never a human voice comes near
> To speak a gentle word:
> And the eye that watches through the door
> Is pitiless and hard:
> And by all forgot, we rot and rot,
> With soul and body marred.'[19]

The Prisons Act of 1877 kept the control of prisons by the Home Secretary and so reform was slow, but just after Wilde left prison, the 1898 Prison Act abolished the two-years hard labour sentence which he had served.

Communication

Although the visibility of policemen in uniforms patrolling the streets definitely worked, with assaults and robberies on the main roads in Manchester reduced to virtually zero[20], hardened criminals watched the constables on the beat and learnt their routes and habits so they could commit their crime once the policeman had passed. It was quickly realised by the press and the police themselves that little thought had been put into the solving of crimes. The Metropolitan Police Force was also hampered by the lack of a decent communication system between divisions and the lack of coordination in information gathering and exchange. There was no telephone, and the Met didn't have a telegraph system yet. In 1837, 'route papers' were used instead. Details of a crime were written out and then delivered by messenger on foot or by horse to officers from the neighbouring division along the route. This information was then passed on to other officers further along the route and details were swapped back and forth this way in a type of relay. This was not the quickest method of information sharing though and was compounded in the case of Daniel Good who stole a pair of trousers from a shop on Wandsworth High Street in April 1842. He was working at the time as a coach driver for a Mr Shiell in Roehampton and so a PC William Gardner was dispatched to Mr Shiell's place to investigate. He searched the stables and instead of finding trousers, he found a dead body. He was about to raise the alarm when he was locked in the stables by Daniel Good. Also locked in with him was Good's 11-year-old son, the two shop boys who presumably were there to identify the missing trousers, and the estate factor. So Good made his escape and sparked a nationwide manhunt. With the route papers, they were not swapped and read out to officers quick enough and Good was able to leave London. He was caught and executed seven weeks later with the help of the public who wrote to Scotland Yard with information on his whereabouts.[21]

The Detective Branch

In August 1842, a plain clothes detective branch of the Metropolitan Police was put together specifically to gather and share information and to direct operations. Two inspectors and six sergeants were given some small offices at Scotland Yard, warrant cards to identify themselves and the freedom to solve crimes as they saw best.

However, by 1878 there was a certain amount of unrest within the detective branch with the detectives feeling they were being left behind the rest of the police force.

A Home Office Enquiry highlighted low pay, low allowances for food and drink when out and about, a lack of transport (they had to walk the first three miles of any enquiry), poor promotion prospects, a lack of legal assistance in preparing cases for trial, a lack of confidentiality within the paperwork and rivalry between the Scotland Yard detectives and the divisional detectives leading to a lack of cooperation. The Scotland Yard detectives felt that the divisional detectives lacked intelligence and were given the job to move them off the uniformed police force. To sum up, the detective branch was not taken as seriously as it should have been.[22]

CID

The Home Office recognised that all plain clothes officers needed to work together in one united but separated branch of the police force and so set up the Criminal Investigation Department in 1878. Centralised and headed by twenty Inspectors at Scotland Yard, each division of the Metropolitan Police was also given its own Detective Inspector – known as a local inspector – who was free to run operations within his station but was answerable to the CID at Scotland Yard.

CID itself was headed by Howard Vincent, the younger son of a Baronet who had studied continental police systems after becoming a barrister. Previously, he had been a Lieutenant in the Royal Welsh Fusiliers and he also had a special interest in Russia's military organisation. With his enormous experience in planning and strategy, Howard Vincent vigorously tackled the internal issues within the detective branch, using the French police system as a template. Although long recognised as a smart and efficient police force, the British had initially resisted a French-style CID due to concerns about French methods of investigation. The use of police spies, longer spells in custody, dubious methods to extract confessions and searching premises without warrants all seemed illiberal in the British public's eyes. But Vincent persuaded the Home Office that this was what Britain needed to tackle the new wave of crimes and gangs and he gradually increased detective numbers to 800 across CID and in 1884 Special Branch was set up to deal with terrorism. However, a bigger problem became apparent and that was the positive identification of suspects and bodies.

The Problems with Identification

With the cessation of the transportation of criminals, the police now needed to know where convicted criminals lived when they were released from prison, and what they were up to. The Criminal Records Bureau was set up in 1869 to keep ready information on criminals, suspects and crimes. But more needed to be done and so Howard Vincent took over the content and publishing of the Police Gazette newspaper which listed descriptions of known and wanted offenders. He also set up the Convict Supervision Office to help aid the identification of suspects. The viewing of suspects by witnesses in the custody suite was time consuming but essential. In 1882, Paris police started to use an identification system developed by Alphonse Bertillon. Known as the Anthropometric System, it involved taking the physical measurements of suspects and keeping them on record for evidence or future identification. Arm span, the height whilst sitting and standing, feet, hand and head size were all recorded alongside identifying marks such as eye colour, hair colour, scars and other bodily marks.

The British Association for the Advancement of Science were also interested in the Anthropometric system and persuaded the Home Office to take it seriously and try using it within the force. But the BAAS was also keenly interested in the very latest findings of Francis Galton and his fingerprint classification study.

Fingerprints and Other Forensics

Using data collected from William Herschel, Francis showed how every individual human being had finger-marks unique to them and that they never changed. He went onto publish a fingerprint classification study in 1882 and some enterprising detectives started to use them as means of identification of perpetrators at scenes of crime.

In Argentina, the police there set up their own methods based upon Galton's work. They managed to convict a woman of murdering her children by examining a bloody finger-mark left at the scene of the crime. Faced with this evidence, she confessed that she'd committed the atrocity because her new lover did not like them. Whilst this gave weight to Galton's work, there will still concerns about criminals trying to destroy their fingerprints to evade conviction or a person's fingerprints becoming ruined through manual labour. These concerns were subsequently proved unfounded, and it was shown that any attempts to destroy fingerprints actually made them more pronounced. The fingerprints of 100 prisoners at Pentonville prison who had taken part on Oakum picking, baking, tailoring or stoking were examined and found to remain intact too.

Taking the fingerprints of suspects was cheap and easy too. Each finger was rolled in black printers' ink and then rolled onto a piece of white card, much the same as today. Anyone could do it after some training. Matching the whorls and hoops was a lot more time consuming and so the identification of finger-marks was only accepted into the police force in July 1894 alongside a modified measurement system, other forensic tests such as the examination of blood stains and a record of other observations[23]

Sherlock Holmes

The advent of the new CID and newspaper reports helped to expand the public's appetite for detective stories. Although Charles Dickens had already introduced the first Scotland Yard detective in Bleak House, it was the private detective Sherlock Holmes who captured the imagination of the public with his cold, hard logic and scientific outpourings. The author, Arthur Conan Doyle, was a trained doctor from Edinburgh University who set up his own medical practice in Portsmouth. He had always written stories as a hobby and in 1887 he introduced the public to Sherlock Holmes and Dr Watson in their first case, *A Study in Scarlet*. Serialised in a 'shilling shocker' magazine at Christmas, it was well received and so Conan Doyle published *The Sign of Four* in 1890 and then six more Sherlock Holmes stories were serialised in Strand Magazine. These stories were perfect for the younger readers who, thanks to the Universal Education Act of 1870, could now read and enjoy such fiction.

Despite the new police force and the detective branch, private detectives were still very much in operation. A lot of their work was generated thanks to the 1857 Matrimonial Causes Act where evidence of infidelity was needed for the application of a divorce. Wealthy estate owners also engaged the services of private detectives to crack down on poaching and cattle theft. But Sherlock Holmes refrains from sullying his hands with unsavoury adultery cases; he is an English gentleman, a gallant and courteous sleuth who is always ahead of the Scotland Yard Detective Inspector Lestrade. Having dropped out of his medical degree because he knew more than his professors, Holmes employs all the tactics we as readers expect to see in a modern crime drama. A Study in Scarlet introduces the reader to Holmes' Baker Street laboratory where he is studying bloodstains. In *The Sign of Four*, the newly discovered finger-marks system is introduced. Holmes' staple detection items include a magnifying glass and a tape measure.

Towards the end of the nineteenth century, medical advancement enabled improved crime detection with police surgeons, doctors and detectives all helping each other to read the clues found whether they were at a crime scene, on a dead body or through the verbal information and body language of witnesses. This modern, scientific approach to solving crime went down a storm with the public who were looking forward to a new century of new inventions and a new approach to modern living.

Endnotes

Chapter One

1. Wells, H.G. https://www.brainyquote.com/authors/h-g-wells-quotes
2. Kitson Clarke, G. *The Making of Victorian England* (Routledge, London, 1991)
3. Kitson Clarke, G. *The Making of Victorian England* (Routledge, London, 1991)
4. Dickens, C. A Christmas Carol https://www.gutenberg.org/ebooks/24022/pg24022-images.html.utf8
5. The Museum of English Rural Life, Reading
6. https://www.nationalchurchestrust.org/explore/why/intriguing-insides
7. https://www.victorianvoices.net/ARTICLES/ILA/1879-Stats.pdf
8. https://victorianweb.org/religion/evangel2.html
9. Paterson, M. *A Brief History of Life in Victorian Britain* (Constable and Robinson Ltd, London, 2008)
10. ibid
11. https://www.studysmarter.co.uk/explanations/politics/political-ideology/classical-liberalism/
12. www.britannica.com/place/london
13. Inglis, L *Georgian London: Into the Streets* (Penguin Books, London, 2013)
14. *Ibid*
15. Dickens, C. Oliver Twist https://www.gutenberg.org/ebooks/730/pg730-images.html.utf8
16. http://archive.org/details/century-1883-v-3

Chapter Two

1. Wilde, O. The Importance of Bering Earnest, https://www.gutenberg.org/ebooks/844/pg844-images.html.utf8
2. Wilson, A.N *Victoria: A Life* (Atlantic Books, London, 2014)

3. https://www.britishnewspaperarchive.co.uk/viewer/bl/0001652/18500902/029/0002
4. Wilson, A.N *Victoria: A Life* (Atlantic Books, London, 2014)
5. https://www.gutenberg.org/ebooks/3760/pg3760-images.html.utf8
6. https://www.britannica.com/topic/aristocracy
7. https://www.bl.uk/romantics-and-victorians/videos/the-middle-classes
8. https://www.getreading.co.uk/news/reading-berkshire-news/every-single-uk-prime-minister-21474956
9. https://thehistoryofparliament.wordpress.com/2019/10/15/the-exclusion-parliaments/
10. https://mason.gmu.edu/~ayadav/historical%20outline/whig%20and%20tory.htm
11. https://www.victorianweb.org/history/Tory.html
12. https://victorianweb.org/history/Whig.html
13. https://mason.gmu.edu/~ayadav/historical%20outline/whig%20and%20tory.htm
14. https://www.parliament.uk/about/living-heritage/evolutionofparliament/parliamentaryauthority/revolution/overview/whigstories/
15. https://www.parliament.uk/about/living-heritage/evolutionofparliament/houseofcommons/reformacts/overview/reformact1832/
16. https://www.guideofengland.com/salisbury/Old-Sarum-Rotten-Boroughs-Salisbury.html
17. https://www.parliament.uk/about/living-heritage/evolutionofparliament/houseofcommons/reformacts/overview/reformact1832/
18. https://blog.nationalarchives.gov.uk/universal-manhood-suffrage/
19. https://www.parliament.uk/about/living-heritage/evolutionofparliament/houseofcommons/reformacts/overview/one-man-one-vote/
20. Wilson, A.N *Victoria: A Life* (Atlantic Books, London, 2014)
21. https://victorianweb.org/history/empire/Empire.html
22. https://www.futurelearn.com/courses/waterloo-to-the-rhine
23. Ferguson, N *Empire: How Britain made the Modern World* (Penguin Books, London, 2004)
24. Dickens, C. Great Expectations https://www.gutenberg.org/ebooks/1400/pg1400-images.html.utf8
25. Paterson, M. *A Brief History of Life in Victorian Britain* (Constable and Robinson Ltd, London, 2008)
26. Ferguson, N *Empire: How Britain made the Modern World* (Penguin Books, London, 2004)
27. Paterson, M. *A Brief History of Life in Victorian Britain* (Constable and Robinson Ltd, London, 2008)
28. https://victorianweb.org/history/empire/Empire.html

29. https://www.parliament.uk/about/living-heritage/transformingsociety/private-lives/yourcountry/overview/victorianarmies/
30. Manning, S. *Soldiers of the Queen: Victorian Colonial Conflict in the words of those who Fought* (The History Press, Stroud, 2009)
31. https://en.wikipedia.org/w/index.php?title=British_Army_during_the_Victorian_Era&oldid=1116867743
32. Manning, S. *Soldiers of the Queen: Victorian Colonial Conflict in the words of those who Fought* (The History Press, Stroud, 2009)
33. Paterson, M. *A Brief History of Life in Victorian Britain* (Constable and Robinson Ltd, London, 2008)
34. Manning, S. *Soldiers of the Queen: Victorian Colonial Conflict in the words of those who Fought* (The History Press, Stroud, 2009)
35. Manning, S. *Soldiers of the Queen: Victorian Colonial Conflict in the words of those who Fought* (The History Press, Stroud, 2009)
36. Manning, S. *Soldiers of the Queen: Victorian Colonial Conflict in the words of those who Fought* (The History Press, Stroud, 2009)

Chapter Three

1. Bronte, C. *Jane Eyre* https://www.gutenberg.org/files/1260/1260-h/1260-h.htm
2. Paterson, M. *A Brief History of Life in Victorian Britain* (Constable and Robinson Ltd, London, 2008)
3. Wilson, A.N *The Victorians* (Hutchinson, London, 2002)
4. Paterson, M. *A Brief History of Life in Victorian Britain* (Constable and Robinson Ltd, London, 2008)
5. Dickens, C *A Christmas Carol* https://www.gutenberg.org/ebooks/24022/pg24022-images.html.utf8
6. Dickens, C *Great Expectations* https://www.gutenberg.org/ebooks/1400/pg1400-images.html.utf8
7. https://www.victorianweb.org/history/gentleman.html
8. https://www.britannica.com/topic/gentleman
9. https://www.britannica.com/topic/gentleman
10. https://www.victorianweb.org/history/gentleman.html
11. https://www.bl.uk/romantics-and-victorians/articles/gender-roles-in-the-19th-century
12. Austen, J. *Pride and Prejudice* https://www.gutenberg.org/files/1342/1342-h/1342-h.htm
13. https://www.bl.uk/romantics-and-victorians/articles/gender-roles-in-the-19th-century

14. www.bbc.co.uk/history/trail/victorian_britain/women_home/ideals_womanhood
15. www.bbc.co.uk/history/trail/victorian_britain/women_home/ideals_womanhood
16. Horn, P. *Life as a Victorian Lady* (The History Press, Gloucestershire, 2011 e-book)
17. Horn, P. *Life as a Victorian Lady* (The History Press, Gloucestershire, 2011 e-book)
18. Horn, P. *Life as a Victorian Lady* (The History Press, Gloucestershire, 2011 e-book)
19. Horn, P. *Amusing the Victorians* (Amberley Publishing, Stroud, 2014)

Chapter Four

1. Dickens, C. Great Expectations https://www.gutenberg.org/ebooks/1400/pg1400-images.html.utf8
2. https://www.parliament.uk/about/living-heritage/transformingsociety/towncountry/landscape/overview/enclosingland/
3. Harrison, J. The Origin, Development and Decline of Back-to Back Housing in Leeds The Victorian Society Autumn Lecture series 2021
4. Dickens, C. Oliver Twist Penguin Group, London 2008
5. Dickens, C. Oliver Twist Penguin Group, London 2008
6. https://discovery.nationalarchives.gov.uk/details/r/55e5e921-cb40-4049-b786-3589d168c4d6
7. White, J. London in the Nineteenth Century Jonathan Cape London 2007
8. White, J. London in the Nineteenth Century Jonathan Cape London 2007
9. Mingay, G.E, Rural Life in Victorian England Alan Sutton Publishing Ltd 1990
10. Mingay, G.E, Rural Life in Victorian England Alan Sutton Publishing Ltd 1990
11. Wells, H.G, The War of The Worlds William Collins London 2018
12. Forshaw, A. The Origin and History of the Terraced House The Victorian Society Autumn Lecture Series 2021
13. Wedd, K. Design, Decoration and Construction of the Terraced House The Victorian Society Autumn Lecture Series 2021
14. Flanders, J. The Victorian House HarperCollins Perennial 2004
15. Holmes, S. The Sign of Four BBC Books London 2012
16. Paterson, M. A Brief History of Life in Victorian Britain Constable Robinson 2008
17. Flanders, J. The Victorian House HarperCollins Perennial London 2004

18. https://buildingconservation.com/articles/lighting/lighting.htm
19. Ibid
20. https://www.victorianweb.org/technology/domestic/1.html
21. Burton, Elizabeth *Early Victorians at Home 1837-1861* (Victorian and Modern History Book Club, Newton Abbot, 1973)
22. Flanders, J. *The Victorian House*, (Harper Perennial, London, 2004)
23. http://www.nationalgasmuseum.org.uk/cooking-with-gas/
24. Flanders, J. *The Victorian House*, (Harper Perennial, London, 2004)
25. Burton, Elizabeth *Early Victorians at Home 1837-1861* (Victorian and Modern History Book Club, Newton Abbot, 1973)
26. The Charles Dickens Museum Doughty Street London
27. Doyle, A.C. *The Sign of the Four* https://www.gutenberg.org/ebooks/2097/pg2097-images.html.utf8
28. Dickens, C. *A Christmas Carol* https://www.gutenberg.org/ebooks/24022/pg24022-images.html.utf8

Chapter Five

1. Wilde, O. *The Importance of Being Earnest* https://www.gutenberg.org/ebooks/844/pg844-images.html.utf8
2. Lewis, June R. *The Village School*. (Robert Hale Ltd., London, 1989)
3. Amusing Juvenile Answers by D. Lawson Johnstone in Cassell's Family Magazine,1889.
4. https://www.parliament.uk/about/living-heritage/transformingsociety/electionsvoting/chartists/overview/chartistmovement/
5. Horn, P. *The Victorian and Edwardian Schoolchild*. (Amberly Publishing, Gloucestershire, 2010)
6. Lewis, June R. *The Village School*. (Robert Hale Ltd., London, 1989)
7. Lewis, June R. *The Village School*. (Robert Hale Ltd., London, 1989)
8. https://www.bl.uk/collection-items/newspaper-report-on-a-visit-to-the-field-lane-ragged-school
9. https://www.britishnewspaperarchive.co.uk/viewer/BL/0000051/18460204/070/0004?browse=true Accessed 13/5/23
10. https://www.nationalarchives.gov.uk/education/resources/victorian-lives/industrial-school-timetable/
11. https://www.bl.uk/collection-items/a-letter-about-ragged-schools
12. Lewis, June R. *The Village School*. (Robert Hale Ltd., London, 1989)
13. Amusing Juvenile Answers by D. Lawson Johnstone in Cassell's Family Magazine,1889.
14. Horn, P. *The Victorian and Edwardian Schoolchild*. (Amberly Publishing, Gloucestershire, 2010)

15. Lewis, June R. *The Village School.* (Robert Hale Ltd., London, 1989)
16. Horn, P. *The Victorian and Edwardian Schoolchild.* (Amberly Publishing, Gloucestershire, 2010)
17. Lewis, June R. *The Village School.* (Robert Hale Ltd., London, 1989)
18. May, T. *The Victorian Schoolroom.* (Shire Publications Ltd., Buckinghamshire, 1999)
19. Horn, P. *The Victorian and Edwardian Schoolchild.* (Amberly Publishing, Gloucestershire, 2010)
20. ibid
21. ibid
22. Hughes, K. *The Victorian Governess.* (Hambledon and London, London, 2001)
23. Grieg, J. *The Young Ladies New Guide to Arithmetic* 1847 Retrieved from Google Books 13/5/23
24. Hughes, K. *The Victorian Governess.* (Hambledon and London, London, 2001)
25. Broughton, T. and Symes, R. *The Governess – an Anthology.* (Sutton Publishing Ltd., Gloucestershire, 1997)
26. ibid
27. ibid
28. Wilde, O. *The Importance of Being Earnest* https://www.gutenberg.org/ebooks/844/pg844-images.html.utf8
29. Bronte, C. *Jane Eyre* https://www.gutenberg.org/files/1260/1260-h/1260-h.htm

Chapter Six

1. Bronte, E. *Wuthering Heights* https://www.gutenberg.org/ebooks/768/pg768-images.html.utf8
2. https://www.victorianweb.org/victorian/history/work/burnett1.html
3. https://www.victorianweb.org/victorian/history/work/burnett6.html
4. https://www.ncbi.nlm.nih.gov/pmc/articles/PMC2672390/
5. https://www.populationspast.org/about
6. Dickens, C. *Great Expectations* https://www.gutenberg.org/ebooks/1400/pg1400-images.html.utf8
7. www.victorianprofessions.ox.ac.uk/about
8. https://www.gutenberg.org/files/14444/14444-h/14444-h.htm#INTRODUCTION retrieved 19.10.21
9. Paterson, M. *A Brief History of Life in Victorian Britain* (Constable and Robinson Ltd., London, 2008)
10. Paterson, M. *A Brief History of Life in Victorian Britain* (Constable and Robinson Ltd., London, 2008)
11. Horn, P. *Life as a Victorian Lady,* The History Press Gloucestershire 2011 e-book

12. https://www.striking-women.org/module/women-and-work/19th-and-early-20th-century
13. https://www.parliament.uk/about/living-heritage/transformingsociety/livinglearning/19thcentury/overview/factoryact/
14. https://www.parliament.uk/about/living-heritage/transformingsociety/livinglearning/19thcentury/overview/laterfactoryleg/
15. https://www.jstor.org/stable/2956111
16. Horn, P. *Children's Work and Welfare 1780-1890* (Cambridge University Press, Cambridge, 1994)
17. Goodman, R. *How to be a Victorian* (Penguin Books, London, 2014)
18. Goodman, R. *How to be a Victorian* (Penguin Books, London, 2014)
19. Horn, P. *Children's Work and Welfare 1780-1890* (Cambridge University Press, Cambridge, 1994)
20. https://www.parliament.uk/about/living-heritage/transformingsociety/livinglearning/19thcentury/overview/factoryact/
21. https://www.parliament.uk/about/living-heritage/transformingsociety/livinglearning/19thcentury/overview/laterfactoryleg/
22. https://www.parliament.uk/about/living-heritage/transformingsociety/livinglearning/19thcentury/overview/childrenchimneys/
23. Horn, P. *Children's Work and Welfare 1780-1890* (Cambridge University Press, Cambridge, 1994)
24. Horn, P. *Children's Work and Welfare 1780-1890* (Cambridge University Press, Cambridge, 1994)
25. Beeton, I. *Mrs Beeton's Book of Household Management* https://www.gutenberg.org/ebooks/10136/pg10136.html.utf8
26. Beeton, I. *Mrs Beeton's Book of Household Management* https://www.gutenberg.org/ebooks/10136/pg10136.html.utf8
27. Beeton, I. *Mrs Beeton's Book of Household Management* https://www.gutenberg.org/ebooks/10136/pg10136.html.utf8
28. Horn, P. *Life in a Victorian Household* (The History Press, Stroud, 2007)
29. Horn, P. *The Rise and Fall of the Victorian Servant* (The History Press, Stroud, 2004)
30. Horn, P. *Life in a Victorian Household* (The History Press, Stroud, 2007)

Chapter Seven

1. Austen, J. *Pride and Prejudice* https://www.gutenberg.org/files/1342/1342-h/1342-h.htm
2. https://www.royalmintmuseum.org.uk/journal/history/pounds-shillings-and-pence/
3. Wilson, A.N *The Victorians* (Hutchinson, London, 2002)

4. https://www.victorianweb.org/science/health/health9.html
5. White, J. *Mansions of Misery: A Biography of the Marshalsea Debtor's Prison*, (The Bodley Head, London 2016)
6. http://archive.org/details/povertyastudyto00rowngoog
7. http://archive.org/details/povertyastudyto00rowngoog
8. https://www.victorianweb.org/economics/wages3.html
9. Dickens, C. *A Christmas Carol* https://www.gutenberg.org/ebooks/24022/pg24022-images.html.utf8
10. https://www.victorianweb.org/economics/wages3.html
11. Dickens, C. *Great Expectations* https://www.gutenberg.org/ebooks/1400/pg1400-images.html.utf8
12. White, J. *Mansions of Misery: A Biography of the Marshalsea Debtor's Prison*, (The Bodley Head, London, 2016)
13. White, J. *Mansions of Misery: A Biography of the Marshalsea Debtor's Prison*, (The Bodley Head, London, 2016)
14. Becker, Jennifer Tate, 'Round the Corner: Pawnbroking in the Victorian Novel'(2014). All Theses and Dissertations (ETDs). 1286. https://openscholarship.wustl.edu/etd/1286
15. White, J. *Mansions of Misery: A Biography of the Marshalsea Debtor's Prison*, (The Bodley Head, London, 2016)
16. White, J. *Mansions of Misery: A Biography of the Marshalsea Debtor's Prison*, (The Bodley Head, London, 2016)
17. Tomalin, C. *Charles Dickens: A Life* (Penguin Group, London, 2011)
18. White, J. *Mansions of Misery: A Biography of the Marshalsea Debtor's Prison*, (The Bodley Head, London, 2016)
19. https://www.gutenberg.org/files/963/963-h/963-h.htm
20. https://www.gutenberg.org/files/963/963-h/963-h.htm
21. Tomalin, C. *Charles Dickens: A Life* (Penguin Group, London, 2011)

Chapter Eight

1. Dickens, C. *Oliver Twist* https://www.gutenberg.org/ebooks/730/pg730-images.html.utf8
2. Englander, D. *Poverty and Poor Law Reform in 19th Century Britain 1834 – 1914* (Routledge, Abingdon, 2013)
3. Longmate, N. *The Workhouse* (Temple Smith, London, 1974)
4. Longmate, N. *The Workhouse* (Temple Smith, London, 1974)
5. Crowther, M.A. *The Workhouse System 1834 – 1929 The History of An English Social Institution* (Methuen and Co. Ltd, London 1983)
6. Englander, D. *Poverty and Poor Law Reform in 19th Century Britain 1834 – 1914* (Routledge, Abingdon, 2013)

7. Englander, D. *Poverty and Poor Law Reform in 19th Century Britain 1834 – 1914* (Routledge, Abingdon, 2013)
8. Longmate, N. *The Workhouse* (Temple Smith, London, 1974)
9. https://www.workhouses.org.uk/Flegg/
10. Englander, D. *Poverty and Poor Law Reform in 19th Century Britain 1834 – 1914* (Routledge, Abingdon, 2013)
11. Englander, D. *Poverty and Poor Law Reform in 19th Century Britain 1834 – 1914* (Routledge, Abingdon, 2013)
12. Higginbotham, P. *Workhouses of London and the South East* (The History Press, Stroud, 2019)
13. Englander, D. *Poverty and Poor Law Reform in 19th Century Britain 1834 – 1914* (Routledge, Abingdon, 2013)
14. Higginbotham, P. *Workhouses of London and the South East* (The History Press, Stroud, 2019)
15. Longmate, N. *The Workhouse* (Temple Smith, London, 1974)
16. Dickens, C. Oliver Twist https://www.gutenberg.org/ebooks/730/pg730-images.html.utf8
17. Richardson, R. *Dickens and the Workhouse* (OUP Inc., New York, 2012)
18. Dickens, C. Oliver Twist https://www.gutenberg.org/ebooks/730/pg730-images.html.utf8
19. https://intheirownwriteblog.wordpress.com/category/letter-writing/
20. Crowther, M.A. *The Workhouse System 1834 – 1929 The History of An English Social Institution* (Methuen and Co. Ltd, London, 1983)
21. Higginbotham, P. *Workhouses of London and the South East* (The History Press, Stroud, 2019)

Chapter Nine

1. Dickens, C. Bleak House https://www.gutenberg.org/ebooks/1023/pg1023-images.html.utf8
2. Licence, T. *What the Victorians Threw Away* (Oxbow Books, Oxford, 2015)
3. *ibid*
4. Goodman, R. *How to be a Victorian* (Penguin Books, London, 2014)
5. Goodman, R. *How to be a Victorian* (Penguin Books, London, 2014)
6. Flanders, J. *The Victorian House*, (Harper Perennial, London, 2004)
7. Jackson, L. *Dirty Old London* (Yale University Press, London, 2015)
8. Flanders, J. *The Victorian City* (Atlantic Books Ltd, London, 2012)
9. Doyle, A.C. *The Sign of the Four* https://www.gutenberg.org/ebooks/2097/pg2097-images.html.utf8
10. https://discovery.nationalarchives.gov.uk/details/r/11747702-a2e8-4144-9a17-672772100e08

11. https://www.parliament.uk/about/living-heritage/transformingsociety/towncountry/towns/tyne-and-wear-case-study/about-the-group/nuisances/nuisances/
12. https://www.parliament.uk/about/living-heritage/transformingsociety/towncountry/towns/tyne-and-wear-case-study/about-the-group/public-administration/the-1848-public-health-act/
13. https://www.scienceandindustrymuseum.org.uk/objects-and-stories/water-and-sanitation
14. https://www.parliament.uk/about/living-heritage/transformingsociety/towncountry/towns/tyne-and-wear-case-study/about-the-group/nuisances/sewerage/
15. Halliday, S. *The Great Stink of London* (The History Press, Stroud, 1999)
16. https://www.museumoflondon.org.uk/discover/how-bazalgette-built-londons-first-super-sewer
17. Visit to the Museum of London 15/8/2021
18. https://www.npr.org/2015/03/12/392332431/dirty-old-london-a-history-of-the-victorians-infamous-filth

Chapter Ten

1. Wilde, O. *The Importance of Being Earnest* https://www.gutenberg.org/ebooks/844/pg844-images.html.utf8
2. Downing, Sarah Jane. *Beauty and Cosmetics 1550 – 1950* (Shire Publications, Oxford, 2012)
3. Course: *A History of Royal Fashion*, (University of Glasgow, Future Learn, 2022)
4. Bronte, E. *Wuthering Heights* https://www.gutenberg.org/ebooks/768/pg768-images.html.utf8
5. Matthews, M. *A Victorian Lady's Guide to Fashion and Beauty* (Pen and Sword Books Ltd, Barnsley, 2022)
6. Matthews, M. *A Victorian Lady's Guide to Fashion and Beauty* (Pen and Sword Books Ltd, Barnsley, 2022)
7. Matthews, M. *A Victorian Lady's Guide to Fashion and Beauty* (Pen and Sword Books Ltd, Barnsley, 2022)
8. Course: *A History of Royal Fashion*, (University of Glasgow, Future Learn, 2022)
9. Goodman, R. *How to be a Victorian* (Penguin Books, London, 2014)
10. Matthews, M. *A Victorian Lady's Guide to Fashion and Beauty* (Pen and Sword Books Ltd, Barnsley, 2022)
11. Paterson, M. *A Brief History of Life in Victorian Britain* Constable and Robinson Ltd, London, 2008

12. Course: *A History of Royal Fashion*, (University of Glasgow, Future Learn, 2022)
13. Course: *A History of Royal Fashion*, (University of Glasgow, Future Learn, 2022)
14. https://victorianweb.org/art/costume/nunn3.html
15. Goodman, R. *How to be a Victorian* (Penguin Books, London, 2014)
16. Goodman, R. *How to be a Victorian* (Penguin Books, London, 2014)
17. Course: *A History of Royal Fashion*, (University of Glasgow, Future Learn, 2022)
18. Goodman, R. *How to be a Victorian* (Penguin Books, London, 2014)
19. Goodman, R. *How to be a Victorian* (Penguin Books, London, 2014)
20. Goodman, R. *How to be a Victorian* (Penguin Books, London, 2014)

Chapter Eleven

1. Dickens, C. *Oliver Twist* https://www.gutenberg.org/ebooks/730/pg730-images.html.utf8
2. Dickens, C. *A Christmas Carol* https://www.gutenberg.org/ebooks/24022/pg24022-images.html.utf8
3. Kay, E. *Dining with the Victorians* (Amberly Publishing, Stroud, Gloucestershire 2015)
4. *ibid*
5. Vogler, P *Scoff* (Atlantic Books, London, 2021)
6. Clayton, P and Rowbotham, J. How the Mid-Victorians Worked, Ate and Died https://www.ncbi.nlm.nih.gov/pmc/articles/PMC2672390/
7. *ibid*
8. Colquhoun, K. *Taste* (Bloomsbury, London, 2007)
9. *ibid*
10. Vogler, P *Scoff* (Atlantic Books, London, 2021)
11. Vince, J *Bread and Butter* (Sorbus, 1992)
12. Dickens, C. *Great Expectations* https://www.gutenberg.org/ebooks/1400/pg1400-images.html.utf8
13. Vogler, P *Scoff* (Atlantic Books, London, 2021)
14. www.oxfordreference.com accessed 14/5/23
15. https://www.discoveringireland.com/the-great-famine/
16. Vogler, P *Scoff* (Atlantic Books, London, 2021)
17. Spencer, C. *British Food: An Extraordinary thousand years of history* (Grub Street, London, 2004)
18. *ibid*
19. Dickens, C. *Great Expectations* https://www.gutenberg.org/ebooks/1400/pg1400-images.html.utf8

20. Dickens, C. *A Christmas Carol* https://www.gutenberg.org/ebooks/24022/pg24022-images.html.utf8
21. Colquhoun, K. *Taste* (Bloomsbury, London, 2007)
22. Dickens, C. *Great Expectations* https://www.gutenberg.org/ebooks/1400/pg1400-images.html.utf8
23. Spencer, C. *British Food: An Extraordinary thousand years of history* (Grub Street, London, 2004)
24. *ibid*
25. Stevenson, R.L. *The Strange Case of Dr Jekyll and Mr Hyde* https://www.gutenberg.org/files/43/43-h/43-h.htm
26. Bronte, C. *Jane Eyre* https://www.gutenberg.org/files/1260/1260-h/1260-h.htm
27. https://www.victorianweb.org/science/health/hunger.html
28. Komlos, J. On English *Pygmies and Giants*: the Physical Stature of. English Youth in the late-18th and early-19th Centuries. Munich Discussion *Paper* No. 2005-6. https://epub.ub.uni-muenchen.de/cgi/export/573/Text/epub-eprint-573.txt
29. Clayton, P and Rowbotham, J. How the Mid-Victorians Worked, Ate and Died https://www.ncbi.nlm.nih.gov/pmc/articles/PMC2672390/
30. *ibid*
31. *ibid*
32. Spencer, C. *British Food: An Extraordinary thousand years of history* (Grub Street, London, 2004)
33. Clayton, P and Rowbotham, J. How the Mid-Victorians Worked, Ate and Died https://www.ncbi.nlm.nih.gov/pmc/articles/PMC2672390/

Chapter Twelve

1. Lockwood and Co. *The Railway Traveller's Handy Book of Hints, Suggestions and Advice Before the Journey, On the Journey and After the Journey* (Lockwood and Co., London, 1862)
2. Austen, J. *Pride and Prejudice* https://www.gutenberg.org/files/1342/1342-h/1342-h.htm
3. Hardy T. *Tess of the D'Urbervilles* https://www.gutenberg.org/files/110/110-h/110-h.htm
4. *ibid*
5. Visit to London Transport Museum January 14th 2023
6. Goodman, R. *How to be a Victorian* (Penguin Books, London, 2014)
7. Visit to London Transport Museum January 14th 2023
8. *ibid*

9. ibid
10. https://www.bl.uk/victorian-britain/articles/travel-transport-and-communications
11. https://victorianweb.org/technology/railways/p2.html
12. Emmerson, A. *The London Underground* (Shire Books, Oxford, 2013)
13. Visit to London Postal Museum October 29th 2022
14. www.victorianweb.org/technology/letters/intro.html
15. www.victorianweb.org/art/design/furniture/golden1.html
16. www.victorianweb.org/technology/letters/manuals.html
17. Dickens, C. *Great Expectations* https://www.gutenberg.org/ebooks/1400/pg1400-images.html.utf8
18. Ginn, P. and Goodman, R. *Full Steam Ahead* (William Collins Books, London, 2016)
19. Standage, T. *The Victorian Internet* (Orion Books Ltd, London, 1999)
20. ibid
21. ibid
22. Wells, H.G. *The War of the Worlds* https://www.gutenberg.org/ebooks/36/pg36-images.html.utf8
23. Bird, E. *Transport and the Development of London's Victorian and Edwardian Suburbs* The Victorian Society recording of online lecture accessed 20/10/2022 https://www.eventbrite.co.uk/e/transport-and-the-development-of-londons-victorian-suburbs-recording-tickets-220731512897

Chapter Thirteen

1. Shelly, M. *Frankenstein* https://www.gutenberg.org/files/84/84-h/84-h.htm
2. Anonymous, *Review of Frankenstein* from the Edinburgh Magazine March 1818 p249 https://www.bl.uk/collection-items/anonymous-review-of-frankenstein-from-the-edinburgh-magazine
3. https://www.bl.uk/romantics-and-victorians/articles/the-science-of-life-and-death-in-mary-shelleys-frankenstein
4. Whewell, W. *The philosophy of the inductive sciences: founded upon their history* 1840 p121 http://archive.org/details/philosofindu01whewrich /page/n3/mode/2up
5. https://www.britannica.com/biography/John-Tyndall
6. https://royalsociety.org/blog/2021/03/funding-victorian-science/
7. Lightman, B (Ed*) Victorian Science in Context* (The University of Chicago Press, Chicago and London, 1997)
8. *Ibid*
9. https://www.victorianweb.org/victorian/history/animals/studying.html

10. Lightman, B (Ed) *Victorian Science in Context* (The University of Chicago Press, Chicago and London, 1997)
11. https://www.victorianweb.org/victorian/history/animals/studying.html
12. *ibid*
13. https://www.nationaltrust.org.uk/visit/north-east/cragside/history-of-cragside
14. https://royalsocietypublishing.org/doi/10.1098/rsnr.2016.0026
15. Bernard Lightman (2012) *Victorian science and popular visual culture*, Early Popular Visual Culture, 10:1, 1-5, DOI: 10.1080/17460654.2012.637389
16. https://www.victorianweb.org/victorian/science/science&religion.html
17. https://www.victorianweb.org/victorian/science/darwin/diniejko.html
18. Parker, S. *A Short History of Medicine* (Dorling Kindersley, London, 2019)
19. Parker, S. *A Short History of Medicine* (Dorling Kindersley, London, 2019)
20. Fitzharris, L. *The Butchering Art* (Penguin Books, London, 2018)
21. *Ibid*
22. *Ibid*
23. Parker, S. *A Short History of Medicine* (Dorling Kindersley, London, 2019)
24. https://www.crimeandinvestigation.co.uk/article/the-strange-and-gruesome-history-of-the-electric-chair
25. Draper, M. *Modern Novelists – HG Wells* (Macmillan Publishers ltd, 1987, London)
26. Wells, H.G. *The War of the Worlds* https://www.gutenberg.org/ebooks/36/pg36-images.html.utf8
27. *Ibid*

Chapter Fourteen

1. Plato *The Republic* retrieved from Project Gutenburg https://www.gutenberg.org/files/55201/55201-h/55201-h.htm
2. https://www.encyclopedia.com/humanities/dictionaries-thesauruses-pictures-and-press-releases/workshop-world
3. The Great Exhibition Catalogue 1851 https://wellcomecollection.org/works/pdp6m5e3/items
4. https://victorianweb.org/history/1851/wenham.html
5. The Great Exhibition catalogue – Introduction https://wellcomecollection.org/works/pdp6m5e3/items
6. The Great exhibition catalogue – Introduction https://wellcomecollection.org/works/pdp6m5e3/items
7. The Great exhibition catalogue – Introduction https://wellcomecollection.org/works/pdp6m5e3/items

8. https://victorianweb.org/history/1851/wenham.html
9. https://victorianweb.org/history/1851/wenham.html
10. The Great Exhibition Catalogue https://wellcomecollection.org/works/pdp6m5e3/items
11. The Great Exhibition Catalogue https://wellcomecollection.org/works/pdp6m5e3/items
12. The Great Exhibition Catalogue https://wellcomecollection.org/works/pdp6m5e3/items
13. Morrison-Low, A.D, *Photography: A Victorian Sensation* (NMS Enterprises Publishing, Edinburgh, 2015)
14. Morrison-Low, A.D, *Photography: A Victorian Sensation* (NMS Enterprises Publishing, Edinburgh, 2015)
15. Course: *A History of Royal Fashion*, (University of Glasgow, Future Learn, 2022)
16. Hamilton, G. *Thomas Cook The Holiday Maker* (The History Press, Stroud, 2013 e-book edition)
17. Wade, J. *The Ingenious Victorians: Weird and Wonderful Ideas from the Age of Innovation* (Pen and Sword Books Ltd, Barnsley, 2017)

Chapter Fifteen

1. Bronte, E. *Wuthering Heights* https://www.gutenberg.org/ebooks/768/pg768-images.html.utf8
2. Parker, S. *A Short History of Medicine* (Dorling Kindersley, London, 2019)
3. *ibid*
4. https://www.victorianweb.org/science/health/health10.html
5. https://www.bl.uk/collection-items/sanitary-report-on-haworth-home-to-the-bronts
6. https://www.victorianweb.org/science/health/health10.html
7. https://www.nottingham.ac.uk/manuscriptsandspecialcollections/learning/healthhousing/theme3/diseases.aspx
8. Wilson, A.N *Victoria: A Life* (Atlantic Books Ltd, London, 2014)
9. The prostitute whose pox inspired feminists: https://wellcomecollection.org/articles/WsT4Ex8AAHruGfWl
10. Higgs, M. *The Victorian Hospital* (The History Press, Stroud, 2009)
11. https://www.bda.org/museum/the-story-of-dentistry/ancient-modern
12. https://pocketdentistry.com/3-how-two-young-dentists-changed-the-history-of-surgery-horace-wells-1815-1848-and-william-thomas-green-morton-1819-1868/
13. https://www.britannica.com/biography/Horace-Wells

14. Wilson, A.N *Victoria: A Life* (Atlantic Books Ltd, London, 2014)
15. Eastoe, J. *Victorian Pharmacy: Rediscovering Forgotten Remedies and Recipes* (Pavillion Books, Glasgow, 2010)
16. https://www.rpharms.com/about-us/museum/online-exhibitions/the-history-of-the-royal-pharmaceutical-society/the-founding-of-the-pharmaceutical-society-of-great-britain
17. Eastoe, J. *Victorian Pharmacy: Rediscovering Forgotten Remedies and Recipes* (Pavillion Books, Glasgow, 2010)
18. https://en.wikipedia.org/w/index.php?title=Chlorodyne&oldid=1124521777
19. Virtual talk on Victorian Surgery at The Old Operating Theatre, St Thomas' Hospital, London https://www.youtube.com/watch?v=wlzVLmr25sA
20. Virtual talk on Victorian Surgery at The Old Operating Theatre, St Thomas' Hospital, London https://www.youtube.com/watch?v=wlzVLmr25sA
21. Higgs, M. *The Victorian Hospital* (The History Press, Stroud, 2009)
22. Higgs, M. *The Victorian Hospital* (The History Press, Stroud, 2009)
23. https://www.rcplondon.ac.uk/about-us/who-we-are/history-royal-college-physicians
24. Higgs, M. *The Victorian Hospital* (The History Press, Stroud, 2009)
25. https://legalhistorymiscellany.com/2016/07/30/deaths-gatekeepers-the-victorian-coroners-officer/

Chapter Sixteen

1. Doyle, A.C. *The Sign of the Four* https://www.gutenberg.org/ebooks/2097/pg2097-images.html.utf8
2. https://www.britishnewspaperarchive.co.uk/viewer/bl/0001578/18440406/021/0007
3. Gray, A. *Crime and Criminals of Victorian England* (The History Press, Stroud, 2011) p173
4. Mayhew, H. and others *The London Underworld in the Victorian Period* (Dover Publications Inc., New York, 2005)
5. Ibid
6. https://runamarstonspub.co.uk/all-about-pubs-the-history-of-the-pub/
7. Haliday, G. *Victorian Policing* (Pen and Sword History, Barnsley, 2017)
8. Gray, A. *Crime and Criminals of Victorian England* (The History Press, Stroud, 2011) p10
9. https://api.parliament.uk/historic-hansard/commons/1837/may/19/capital-punishments
10. Haliday, G. *Victorian Policing* (Pen and Sword History, Barnsley, 2017)

Endnotes

11. https://www.britishnewspaperarchive.co.uk/viewer/bl/0000457/18491123/029/0004
12. Ibid
13. https://www.exclassics.com/newgate/courv.htm
14. Higginbotham, P. *The Prison Cookbook* (The History Press, Stroud, 2010)
15. Ibid
16. Dickens, C. *Great Expectations* (Penguin Classics, London, 1985)
17. Higginbotham, P. *The Prison Cookbook* (The History Press, Stroud, 2010)
18. Ellmann, R. *Oscar Wilde* (Penguin Books, London, 1998)
19. https://rpo.library.utoronto.ca
20. Haliday, G. *Victorian Policing* (Pen and Sword History, Barnsley, 2017)
21. Moss, A. and Skinner, K. *The Victorian Detective* (Shire Publications, Oxford, 2013)
22. Lock, J. *Scotland Yard Casebook* (Lume Books, London, 2018)
23. Ibid